Edward VI

Edward VI

Henry VIII's Overshadowed Son

Stephanie Kline

PEN & SWORD
HISTORY
AN IMPRINT OF PEN & SWORD BOOKS LTD.
YORKSHIRE - PHILADELPHIA

First published in Great Britain in 2023 by
PEN AND SWORD HISTORY
An imprint of
Pen & Sword Books Ltd
Yorkshire – Philadelphia

Copyright © Stephanie Kline, 2023

ISBN 978 1 39909 369 9

The right of Stephanie Kline to be identified as Author of this work has been asserted by him in accordance with the Copyright, Designs and Patents Act 1988.

A CIP catalogue record for this book is available from the British Library.

All rights reserved. No part of this book may be reproduced or transmitted in any form or by any means, electronic or mechanical including photocopying, recording or by any information storage and retrieval system, without permission from the Publisher in writing.

Typeset in Times New Roman 11.5/15 by
SJmagic DESIGN SERVICES, India.
Printed and bound in the UK by CPI Group (UK) Ltd.

Pen & Sword Books Limited incorporates the imprints of Atlas, Archaeology, Aviation, Discovery, Family History, Fiction, History, Maritime, Military, Military Classics, Politics, Select, Transport, True Crime, Air World, Frontline Publishing, Leo Cooper, Remember When, Seaforth Publishing, The Praetorian Press, Wharncliffe Local History, Wharncliffe Transport, Wharncliffe True Crime and White Owl.

For a complete list of Pen & Sword titles please contact
PEN & SWORD BOOKS LIMITED
47 Church Street, Barnsley, South Yorkshire, S70 2AS, England
E-mail: enquiries@pen-and-sword.co.uk
Website: www.pen-and-sword.co.uk

Or

PEN AND SWORD BOOKS
1950 Lawrence Rd, Havertown, PA 19083, USA
E-mail: Uspen-and-sword@casematepublishers.com
Website: www.penandswordbooks.com

Contents

Acknowledgements		vi
Introduction	A Footnote in Tudor History?	ix
Chapter 1	Long-Awaited Heir	1
Chapter 2	His Father's Son	13
Chapter 3	Royal Relations and Marriage Proposals	27
Chapter 4	The King is Dead	35
Chapter 5	King Edward VI and the Rise of Somerset	47
Chapter 6	England's Josiah	60
Chapter 7	Brotherly Rivalry	70
Chapter 8	How Far the Mighty Fall	83
Chapter 9	Changing Tides	98
Chapter 10	A King Rises; A Duke Falls	111
Chapter 11	The Second Prayer Book	126
Chapter 12	Devise for the Succession	137
Chapter 13	The Immediate Aftermath	150
Chapter 14	The Tudor Dynasty Continues	163
Conclusion	The Legacy of King Edward VI	176
Notes		180
Bibliography		206
Index		211

Acknowledgements

To say that writing this book has been a dream would be an understatement. In fact, it has been a dream in the making for over a decade, and I have pinched myself many times throughout the arduous process of its research and writing. But writing a biography of an English king while living in the United States is a challenge; and writing it during a pandemic that has prevented international travel for the past two years is even more so. I have worked hard to acquire and access as many primary sources as I have been able to get my hands on (or rather, my *eyes* on – as they have all been digital), and so I am first and foremost indebted to sources such as British History Online and Internet Archive, which have made so many invaluable resources accessible online. Truly, I could not have written this book without sources such as these.

I would not even have had this opportunity if not for my commissioning editor, Sarah-Beth Watkins, who so kindly reached out to me about writing a biography for Pen & Sword Books. She answered many of my initial questions about the process and made me feel confident and excited and able to say 'yes' to what felt like a once-in-a-lifetime opportunity. I must also thank Claire Hopkins, also of Pen & Sword, who has assisted me every step of the way as I've navigated this journey. She has tirelessly answered my questions and provided expert advice whenever it's been needed, and for that I am very grateful. Of course, I also need to acknowledge the talented editorial staff at Pen & Sword, who have taken this initial manuscript and transformed it into the beautiful book that it is today. It has been a pleasure to bring this project to life with their professional help and guidance.

I am indebted to the kind library staff at Loudoun County Public Library and Shenandoah University Library – both of which provided many resources for my research – and especially to the latter for having offered me a beautiful, quiet, and friendly space for me in which to work. Several fellow historians and researchers online were also very kind and sent me references, direct links, and even at times screenshots of helpful pages from sources that I couldn't quite attain. I am very grateful to every one of my online connections who helped me whenever I sent out a Twitter plea!

My graduate education at the University of Oxford taught me the fundamentals of thorough research and thoughtful writing. So, I must thank my supervisor, Dr Tracey Sowerby of Keble College, for instilling in me the principles, knowledge, and understanding of critical historical analysis, which was fundamental to the writing of this book. Many thanks also to Dr Steve Gunn of New College, who inspired me throughout my graduate year and provided expert help for my writing at that time. Little could he have known that his influence during that year has continued to motivate and inspire me in my historical research now.

Of course, I could not possibly write these acknowledgements without thanking the community that put me in the position that led Pen & Sword to approach me in the first place. Since 2011, my website and blog, *The Tudor Enthusiast*, has created an amazing community of fellow lovers of sixteenth-century England. My readers have continued to offer me unwavering support and enthusiasm since my very first blog post – and of course, since I first announced that I was starting work on this book. Truthfully, their interest in this project gave me much of the confidence necessary for me to begin – and continue! – my writing.

Finally, I have several personal thanks to give. To my best friend from my Oxford days, Dr Louise Campion – thank you for the encouragement and assistance whenever I needed it, and for giving me some idea of what I was getting myself into from the start. For the many friends (you know who you are) who have texted me regularly to ask about progress, and some who have been known to send more than a few, 'You'd better be writing,' messages to keep me on track. Thank you to my husband, Jason, for supporting me wholeheartedly over these past many months, and for reminding me on many occasions that I could, in fact, see it through to the end. Thank you to my children, Henry and Amelia, for being my constant source of inspiration to be the best version of myself that I can be. And lastly, I must thank my parents, who were the first to say enthusiastically, 'Of course you have to write that book,' and who truly believed that I could. You have known (more than anyone could) just how much of a dream opportunity this has been for me, and you've reminded me every step of the way that it was mine for the taking. It should go without saying that this book is dedicated to you both.

Introduction

A Footnote in Tudor History?

Henry VII as 'Father of the Dynasty'; 'Six-times-married' and 'larger-than-life' Henry VIII; 'Bloody' Mary I; the 'Virgin Queen', 'Good Queen Bess' and 'Gloriana' Elizabeth I; and even the ill-fated 'Nine Days Queen', Lady Jane Grey whose name is synonymous with the infamous moniker that keeps her place in history alive and relevant. We, as readers of England's sixteenth-century history, read these phrases and nicknames and know instantly to which monarch they refer, and why they are appropriate in the context of each reign's lasting legacy.

The 'father' of the dynasty is certainly a fair name for King Henry VII – the first Tudor monarch. He is known for having defeated the last Plantagenet King, Richard III, at the decisive Battle of Bosworth, and ending the thirty-two-year-long conflict known as the Wars of the Roses. But perhaps he is best remembered as being the father of Henry VIII – arguably the most familiar face of the dynasty. Nevertheless, his name tells us everything we need in order to bring to mind what he is best known for: being the first, the foremost – the original Tudor king.[1]

'Six-times-married' hardly warrants an explanation, as the marital history of King Henry VIII is one of the most recognizable stories in English royal history – with a well-known rhyme assisting us in remembering each wife's fate. 'Larger-than-life' speaks to the overall scale of Henry's impact on the country's history, for a number of reasons aside from his many wives, including his large (obese) physical presence and his impact on the Protestant Reformation – that infamous break from Rome that keeps his name significant to the Church of England's history today. No matter which nickname or phrase is used, Henry VIII is one of the most recognizable names in history, and at virtually the same level of familiarity sits his daughter, Elizabeth I. Remembered through the centuries for her unmarried status, her success in furthering the Protestant cause and unifying the country under one religion, as well as military triumphs like the defeat of the Spanish Armada, Elizabeth's significance has earned her some flattering monikers, as well as the association with one of the great 'golden ages' of England's history.

Less flattering is the name attributed to Elizabeth's older half-sister, Mary I – nicknamed 'Bloody' because of the more than 280 Protestant men and women burnt at the stake during her five-year reign, in a feeble attempt to revert the reformation process and return England to Catholicism.[2] Regardless of its malevolent undertone, the name is effective in reminding us of Mary's lasting legacy. Then there is Jane Grey, the ill-fated teenager who sat on the English throne for less than two weeks before her imprisonment and execution by Mary I's order. Again, dark as the name may be, the 'nine days queen' has been memorable through time for that very reason.

But there is another Tudor monarch that history all too often forgets; one who reigned from January 1547 to July 1553, and whose name is generally not synonymous with any lasting legacy or notable reputation. He is Edward VI, and at most he is given the name 'boy king' or 'child king', due to having ascended the throne at age nine and dying at age fifteen – never having reached the age of majority required to rule England in his own right. Many might argue that the moniker 'child king' gives us exactly the impression we ought to have of Edward's stamp on England's history, and that his age and inability to rule entirely on his own are precisely the things that should make him memorable – or, rather, not memorable.

In fact, a more apt argument would be that even this association – this lazily vague nickname that indicates to us nothing more than Edward's youth – is not even unique to him. Five other notable 'child kings' ruled England for some period of time before Edward came to the throne – one of whom (the ill-fated Edward V), also did not live beyond his teenage years, and is thus able to claim 'child king' in just the same way that Edward VI can. This is, of course, assuming that the name indicates the king in question never left the years of childhood; otherwise, it would suit any of the other four.[3]

Yet Edward VI has been saddled with the interchangeable 'child king' and 'boy king' throughout the last four centuries in unoriginal attempts to unite him with his fellow Tudor monarchs with a simple phrase linking him to memory. However, with only this association from which to draw Edward's kingship, it is little wonder why he is so often overlooked in comparison with his royal family members, or why the average reader of Tudor history might struggle to come up with any overall impression or lasting impact that resulted from his six years on the throne. Edward's is not the reign of seduction and scandal, burnings and beheadings (at least not all that many, when compared with his relatives' reigns). So, where does that leave him, and how does he stand out against his family members? In truth, Edward has been treated as little more than a footnote in Tudor history by many historians, garnering barely a fraction of the attention the rest of the dynasty's key players have received.

This fact is especially interesting when we recall that Edward VI was the only Tudor expected actually to rule at his birth.[4] Going back to 1457, Margaret Beaufort was probably one of only a few people to assume her newborn son, Henry Tudor, had any hope of sitting on the English throne, given his tenuous (at best) claim, via his great-grandfather, John of Beaufort – the illegitimate-turned-legitimate son of John of Gaunt.[5] When, in August 1485, he defeated Richard III's much-larger and highly skilled army at the Battle of Bosworth, he defied expectations and shocked much of England by crowning himself King Henry VII.[6]

Though the future Henry VIII was born to a true king in 1491, he was merely the spare to the heir, Arthur, and therefore was never expected to rule England, unless his brother provided no heirs of his own. It was certainly never assumed that he would one day take the throne, and he was in fact kept secluded, 'like a young girl', as a child; and while he was classically educated, he would have been more likely to assume the religious life following his elder brother's accession.[7] Henry VII may even have felt somewhat threatened by his younger son, and therefore prevented him from taking part in any official royal duties.[8] But fate – in the form of Arthur Tudor's fatal case of presumed sweating sickness – had other plans, and Henry did, in fact, succeed his father in 1509.[9]

Mary and Elizabeth, born in 1516 and 1533 respectively, were unquestionably not expected to reign over England – at least until

Henry VIII's final revisions of his last will and testament in 1547, and even that was more of a formality or worst-case scenario, rather than a true assumption.[10] The foremost reason for this was because they were mere females, and the thought of a woman sitting on the throne – albeit not unheard-of, given the example of the twelfth-century Empress Matilda – was decidedly undesirable nonetheless. We can be quite sure that Henry VIII resolutely did not intend for his daughters to succeed him when we recall his words to his first wife, Catherine of Aragon, following the birth of Princess Mary: 'We are both young; if it was a daughter this time, by the grace of God the sons will follow.'[11] These are the words of a king determined to beget a male heir – which, as history shows, was Henry's chief motivation. As well as this simple fact, however, both Mary and Elizabeth were, depending on the year and their father's pleasure, deemed illegitimate at several points in their lives – often being demoted from 'Princess' to 'Lady', due to the annulments of the marriages of each of their mothers to the king.[12] Even in his will, though he named them both as possible successors after Edward, he never re-legitimized them as true princesses. He even went so far as to strike through the words 'lawfully begotten' following their names on folio twelve of the legal document.[13] All of this is to say, rather decidedly, that the throne simply was not supposed to be in either of his daughters' futures.

Poor Lady Jane Grey, though able to trace her lineage to Henry VIII's younger sister, Mary (her grandmother), likely never conceived the idea that she would one day be proclaimed queen. She had been named one of Henry VIII's unlikely heirs – as the oldest of 'the heirs of the body of Lady Frances' (Frances Grey, Duchess of Suffolk).[14] This was an extremely unlikely scenario, however, as she was named after Edward's sisters in Henry's will, and the chances of none of them marrying and bearing heirs of their own was difficult to imagine.[15] The idea that she might one day be queen was certainly inconceivable when Jane was born in 1536 – at a time when Henry VIII was still relatively young and virile, and sure to produce enough heirs to keep the Greys away from the throne. So, when Edward VI abruptly changed his father's Order of Succession before his own death in 1553, Jane's ascendancy as queen shook England, as well as herself, which is evident by her crying out, 'The crown is not my right and pleases me not.'[16] The least likely monarch among any of the Tudor relation, this twist of fate for Jane was certainly a surprise.

Edward, however, was Henry VIII's heir apparent from the moment he took his first breath on 12 October 1537 – the 'goodly prince' his father had longed and hoped for his entire adult life.[17] Never was there any doubt that he would one day inherit the throne, and the whole of England expected it. As the rightful and true son of the legally-wed King Henry VIII and Queen Jane Seymour, Edward Tudor was destined to rule England from the moment of his birth – unlike every other Tudor who sat upon its throne. This fact is truly ironic, given how easily he has been pushed to the background, hidden behind larger and louder Tudor personalities. He was the only one of them meant for the Crown by his parentage, sex, and order of birth, and yet the majority of history books barely deign to give him a cursory mention – as if he was hardly a part of history at all. Though arguably unfair, there appear to be a few reasons for this.

As mentioned, Edward was a child when he became king, and still a child when he died – reigning from ages nine to fifteen. As such, he was never able to rule England on his own with full control, and was instead led by a regency council specifically crafted by Henry VIII to ensure the smooth running of government.[18] While this was commonplace for the time, and not at all unusual in the case of a child coming to the throne, it places Edward at a posthumous disadvantage.[19] Unfortunately, more attention has been paid to the noblemen who sat on this council – specifically, the two who took lead roles in heading Edward's government – than has been paid to Edward VI himself. Many historians' interpretations of Edward, as a result, paint the picture of a young boy who was nothing more than a marionette for the ruthlessly ambitious men who fought to wrest power and wealth from the Crown. He is seen as a boy who was manipulated and coerced into using his regal signature to validate virtually anything they wanted – all while being largely shut out of any real decision-making. Often, the impression is that Edward had no actual concept of his own kingship – that any religious changes that occurred during his reign (of which there were many) were not of his own doing, or perhaps even his knowledge. Even his momentous change to the order of succession upon his death has been too often dismissed as the work of John Dudley, Duke of Northumberland, and future father-in-law to Edward's named heir, Lady Jane Grey.[20] In short, Edward's age and minority status as king has deprived him throughout history of having any real legacy, or of earning any credit for the accomplishments of his reign.

In addition to his reputation as the child puppet king with no understanding or voice in his own government, one of Edward's chief impacts as monarch has also been falsely written-off as having little effect on England as a whole – namely, his decisive change to the order of the succession. In the early summer of 1553, just before his death, Edward cast aside his sisters (and Henry VIII's second- and third-in-line heirs), Mary and Elizabeth, in favour of his fervently Protestant cousin, Lady Jane Grey – naming her as his rightful heir.[21] This decision by Edward caused significant upheaval in the religious attitudes towards 'rightful' English monarchs of the latter sixteenth century, but it is given far less credit than it deserves, simply because this change was ultimately a temporary one. Queen Jane was deposed and imprisoned nearly as swiftly as she had succeeded to the throne, amidst cheers for the wronged and rightful Queen Mary.[22] Thus, within two weeks of Edward's death, 'the virtuous Lady Mary' was proclaimed queen, and his grand plan for a Protestant succession was thwarted.[23] The fact that Henry VIII's original intentions for the succession (provided that Edward did not have children) were ultimately fulfilled, means that this one enormous act of Edward's has been deemed by many to be inconsequential. In fact, the change to the order of the succession speaks loudly of Edward's personal religious feelings and aspirations for a Protestant England – regardless of whether or not the changes endured. Might not Edward's fervent Protestantism and actions against Catholic Mary have played a role in her violent attempt at an English counter-reformation between 1555 and 1558?[24] Might the imprisonment and ultimate execution of Edward VI's named heir, by Mary I, also have led to an increased number of Protestant sympathizers, and champions of Princess Elizabeth?[25] Such questions warrant greater scrutiny and thoughtfulness as we examine Edward's reign and the long-term effects they had on his successors. Edward's change to the succession, and the events that followed, had severe – and too often overlooked – consequences for the remainder of the Tudor Dynasty.

When one considers the Protestant Reformation in England, perhaps Henry VIII's is the first name to come to mind. He is, after all, the king who made the infamous decision to break with the Catholic Church and establish himself as Supreme Head of the Church in England.[26] Perhaps Elizabeth I's is also front and centre, for having been the queen to defeat the Spanish Armada, and largely unite England under one fairly clear Protestant religion by her death in 1603. But where Henry and Elizabeth enjoy the credit for Protestantism's foothold in England, precious little generally is said about Edward's own contributions – of which there are many. In fact, the reformation effort was furthered so significantly between 1547 and 1553 that some have pointed out that Henry VIII had never intended it to progress as far as it did. Though the dissolution of monasteries and stripping of Catholic churches had begun during the Henrician regime, the pace of work under Edward VI to remove icons, statuary, stained glass and prayer books of the Roman Church was vastly increased. While Henry VIII commissioned the original Ten Articles of 1536, which outlined the initial doctrine that would define his newly founded Church of England (as well as two subsequent revisions in 1539 and 1543), Edward and his government made substantially more Protestant alterations with the Forty-Two Articles of 1552. These articles raised Calvinist and anti-Catholic thought to unprecedented heights in England, and though they were never formally put into action, due to Edward's premature death, they did serve as significant building blocks for the ultimate Thirty-Nine Articles of 1571 under Elizabeth I. These articles remain the defining doctrine of the Church of England in the modern world. Would the Anglican Church look exactly the way it does today, without these substantial steps forward during Edward VI's reign, which influenced Elizabeth I's later administration? Most historians should be able to argue vehemently that it would not.[27]

Just as important as highlighting Edward's heavy involvement in the Protestant Reformation and his effect on the reigns that followed, however, is painting an accurate portrait of Edward as a boy, a child, a human – and arguing that his character, motivations, and relationships are just as important and influential to the Tudor dynasty as any of the other, more popular, figures. Edward was, in fact, remarkably similar to his illustrious father – boasting a maturity and precociousness that his tutors raved about. He also endured – and sometimes enjoyed – complicated relationships with other family members. His motivations and aspirations as a young king had him determined to rule as effectively and staunchly – perhaps even more so – than had Henry VIII before him. His was a colourful, vibrant, and fascinating personality that has for too long been overlooked and overshadowed. And even though champions of Edward VI's memory should rightly acknowledge that his government was indeed led and guided by the men of his regency council, such an acknowledgement should coincide with the understanding that he was, in fact, capable of – and well-practiced in – thinking for himself.

Is there enough evidence to present a convincing counterargument that Edward himself did, in fact, have more of an impact and influence on England's history than he has been credited with, or that the ripples of his reign continued to sway the direction of England's religious and political course throughout the five decades beyond his death? Ultimately, it is for the reader to decide. Is the moniker 'child king' an accurate portrayal of Edward VI's contribution – or lack thereof – to England's history? Or were the decisively Protestant actions taken during his administration perhaps worthy of granting him the title 'reformer king'? Given this brief introduction into the all-too-common view of Edward and the many ways in which his reign has been overlooked by historians and fans of the Tudor period alike, it is obvious that the mark given to Edward throughout history is simply the 'overshadowed son', and therefore sadly, the 'forgotten king'. It is the goal of this book to reopen the pages of Edward VI's story, to place him and his own motivations firmly at its centre, and to make the case for a king – albeit a child king – who is, in fact, worth remembering.

Chapter 1

The Long-Awaited Heir

Two thousand rounds of cannon fire shot from the grounds of the Tower of London on the morning of 12 October 1537 – the deafening booms mingling with the chorus of celebratory church bells tolling throughout the city of London.[1] Wine flowed freely and bonfires were lit as citizens took to the streets and threw parties to welcome the happy news they had awaited for twenty-eight long years. It had taken their king three marriages and one massive religious change – the severing of ties between England and the Catholic Church of Rome, which had been their guiding religion for over 900 years – but King Henry VIII had finally given the English people the thing they had yearned for the most. His third wife, the meek and mild Queen Jane Seymour, gave birth to 'the goodly prince' Edward Tudor in her rooms at Hampton Court Palace in the early hours of a Friday morning, following two arduous days of a very difficult labour.[2] Immediately, letters were sent across Europe to share the good news that the Tudor throne was secure at last – that generations of Tudor kings were now sure to continue. Despite the street parties, feasting, and drinking going on throughout the country, there was no one more pleased with this news than Henry VIII himself. Procuring a male heir for England had been his top priority throughout his reign thus far.

It had been a long journey to this happy event, ever since the day he had become King of England on 21 April 1509.[3] Two months after his father's death, Henry was married to his older brother's widow, Catherine of Aragon. This had been a feat in and of itself to accomplish, as she had been married to Prince Arthur Tudor eight years earlier, but had been widowed due to his untimely death just eight months later, when Arthur was sixteen years of age. Following the death of Henry VII's queen, Elizabeth of York, in 1503, rumours circulated that the king intended to take the young widow for his own bride – an idea that Catherine's mother, Isabella of Castile, considered 'a very evil thing'. But the young Prince Henry – now the unexpected heir to the throne, had his own ambitions regarding the beautiful young Catherine. This was a complicated situation, given the fact that Catherine had been married to Arthur, and one reasonably could have assumed that the two of them had consummated their short marriage in the five-month timeframe. But Catherine vehemently denied this, making it possible for the marriage to be dissolved in the eyes of the Catholic Church.[4] The young couple required a papal dispensation in order to wed, which they eventually received. In addition to this hurdle, it took seven long years of negotiations regarding Catherine's dowry between her father, King Ferdinand of Aragon, and Henry VII, but finally on 11 June 1509, the new King Henry VIII married his first queen, and they were crowned together twelve days later.[5] At ages seventeen (Henry) and twenty-three (Catherine), they were the very picture of a golden, vibrant young couple, ready to take to the marriage bed and produce princes and princesses for England. There was, of course, no reason to believe this would not happen.

Unfortunately, Queen Catherine had a difficult time providing her husband with the children – and most importantly, the male heir – that he needed. Her first pregnancy ended on 31 January 1510, when she delivered a stillborn daughter. This was a blow to both Henry and Catherine, and we can see the first glimmer of Henry's anxiety over his duty to procreate in the words of the Spanish ambassador in London, who wrote just a few months later in May, regarding Catherine's desire to keep news of her second pregnancy quiet until she had reached three of months gestation, in order to quell the king's 'annoyance'. In fact, this second pregnancy proved successful, and Catherine delivered a healthy prince, named Henry, on 1 January 1511. The joy that followed this momentous occasion, however, was short lived. The infant prince fell ill and died at just fifty-two days old. The Tudor throne had looked and felt secure with the promise of a prince who would one day inherit, but that security had lasted just less than two months.

In September 1513, the queen gave birth to another son, and it is unclear whether he was stillborn or died shortly after birth, but state papers and letters indicate that Catherine may have gone into labour prematurely, as the king was away in France at the time of the birth.

She conceived for the fourth time shortly afterwards, though, and it was confirmed around court by the following June that she was clearly with child. Once again, in November, the Venetian ambassador, as well as the chroniclers Raphael Holinshed and John Stow, all reported that the queen had delivered yet another prince who 'lived not long after'.[6] Catherine's fifth pregnancy was her only successful one, and it would have been an incredibly joyous occasion after years of loss, had it only been another boy. Instead, the birth of Princess Mary Tudor at Greenwich Palace on 18 February 1516 was a disappointment to both her parents – especially her father.[7] Daughters had their uses for kings, as they were marriageable and could be used to secure alliances with other countries, but there was no denying that a son was infinitely more valuable. In fact, it was not only valuable, but essential for proving to both one's own realm, as well as the rest of the world, that the country's Crown was secure – that the succession to a rightful prince would be undisputable, and citizens could sleep peacefully without fear of civil war or foreign threat infiltrating the government. Put simply, Henry needed a prince, and frustratingly, his queen was proving capable of providing him only with one healthy daughter.

Their chance came again in the summer of 1518, and Henry announced to Cardinal Wolsey in a private letter dated 1 July that he believed Catherine to be once again with child. But this, too, ended in disappointment with a stillborn daughter on 10 November. The Venetian ambassador reported at the time that Catherine had been in her eighth month of pregnancy.[8] In the ambassador's words, 'Never had the kingdom so anxiously desired anything as it did a prince.'[9] The pressure had mounted substantially on both Catherine and Henry, and perhaps as a result, the king's eye was beginning to wander. His mistress, Elizabeth 'Bessie' Blount, gave birth to his son on 15 June 1519, which indicates that she had conceived in the last few months of 1518 – perhaps overlapping the date on which the queen had given birth.[10] This was significant not only because the king acknowledged his son – named Henry Fitzroy (meaning 'son of the king'), but because it proved to the king that he was perfectly capable of producing male offspring. If Bessie could deliver a son for him, why couldn't Catherine? Though he was overjoyed at the birth, the child was nevertheless illegitimate.[11] Although he would later be raised to the peerage in 1525 and gifted the title Duke of Richmond and Somerset, there was no conceivable way that the boy could one day rule England, so his birth didn't actually solve Henry's problems.[12] It only made clear to him that the fault did not lie with him. Instead, there was clearly something wrong with his queen, and as she was already thirty-three years old by the time Bessie had given birth, it was becoming clearer and clearer to all that Catherine of Aragon could not give Henry the son he needed. In fact, the stillbirth in November 1518 had concluded Catherine's final pregnancy.

Throughout Catherine's struggle to birth another healthy son, the king grew restless and began to see their lack of legitimate male issue as a sign from God that something was amiss in their marriage. The warnings in the Book of Leviticus (18:16 and 20:21) nagged at him and made him question his queen's assertion that she had never consummated her marriage with his brother all those years prior. The penalty for failing to heed the warning, after all, was that such a union would bear no children – and in such a situation as this, where a son was essential, one healthy daughter simply did not count. In addition to Bessie, Henry had taken a few other mistresses – notably Anne Stafford in 1510, and Mary Boleyn from around 1520 until roughly 1525 (with whom he possibly fathered a daughter), but gone were the days when the king could be content seeking temporary comfort from a mistress before returning to the marriage bed with Catherine.[13] By the mid-1520s, Henry was quite convinced that his queen had failed him, and he had started seriously contemplating a new bride.[14]

Though the exact date of their first encounter is unknown, Henry crossed paths with his mistress's sister, Anne Boleyn, some time before 1523. By 1526, he was writing love letters to her in French, and doing all that he could to convince her to become his lover – which she soundly refused to do. As his doubts about Catherine and the true validity of their marriage continued to weigh on him, Henry decided before too long that Anne would become his second wife. In the spring of 1527, he made his first attempt at procuring an annulment from Pope Clement VII.[15] However, such a thing was not nearly so simple as the king had imagined, and thus began his troubles with the Catholic Church. While Cardinal Thomas Wolsey consulted colleagues in Rome on behalf of the king, Henry took matters into his own hands and employed scholars and researchers to help him make his case that the marriage could be annulled legally, on the grounds that Catherine's first marriage with his brother had included intimate marital relations. Sometime in 1527, it became known that he was no longer visiting his wife's bed, while debates in Rome continued on the matter of the annulment. While little progress was being made, preparations for Henry's marriage to Anne were underway by the end of 1528, which made Wolsey nervous. He wrote during this time that if Henry did not receive the annulment he so desired from Rome, he feared what this might mean for England's ties with the Catholic Church.[16] Wolsey probably could not have predicted the break with Rome that would soon occur, but he certainly seemed to understand that the king's need for a male heir had the potential to lead to unprecedented trouble. Indeed, as it would turn out, not even the pope could stand in the way of Henry in his pursuit of a legitimate son.

At the time that Henry married Anne, likely sometime in 1532, much was changing. Catherine had been banished from court in 1531 and was granted only the title of 'Dowager Princess of Wales', in reference to her first marriage. Catholicism was no longer the religion of England – having been replaced by the newly-founded Church of England, of which Henry had made himself 'Supreme Head'. New right-hand men to the king had risen during this massive change, including his first minister, Thomas Cromwell, and Thomas Cranmer, the new Archbishop of Canterbury.[17] The changes of the 1530s began the reshaping of England forever – the primary motivation behind it being the king's desire for a son. By most accounts, Henry and Anne did not consummate their relationship until after they were wed, but she had long been promising him the thing he most desired, sure that she could give him what Catherine had not. So, when on 7 September 1533 a princess was born, one can well imagine her parents' supreme disappointment. Princess Elizabeth, named after the king's mother, was bumped ahead of her older half-sister, Mary (now deemed 'Lady'), in the line of succession, but the king was still loath to imagine her one day inheriting his throne.

Eustace Chapuys, Ambassador to Spain, wrote in January 1534 to inform the Holy Roman Emperor, Charles V, that the queen was again pregnant, and this was confirmed in April in letters from court speaking of Anne's swollen belly.[18] However, references to this pregnancy tapered off as the year progressed, and it was assumed that she had miscarried – though pseudocyesis has also been suggested.[19] In any case, Anne had one more chance to make good on her promise to Henry, and that chance came sometime in 1535, when she became pregnant once more – only to miscarry on 27 January 1536. This was a great blow for the king, who had already been through the same situation with his first wife, time and time again. But to make matters worse, it was immediately reported that this miscarried child had been a boy – that unattainable heir.[20] Anne's subsequent downfall was swift, and she was beheaded on trumped-up charges of supposed adultery and treason on 19 May 1536.

Two queens. Nine pregnancies. Two daughters. Henry VIII still had only one illegitimate son and was no closer to being in the position coveted by any king – knowing that his realm would one day safely pass to a legitimate male of his own flesh. Similar fears to those he had experienced towards the end of his first marriage had cropped up by the end of his second, and he wondered how he had offended God by having married Anne Boleyn.[21] A third wife was essential now, and luckily, he already had an idea as to who that lucky lady might be. Henry had probably been acquainted with Jane Seymour by 1535, as she had served as a lady-in-waiting to both of his wives.[22] She was around twenty-seven years old at this time and was not seen as a great beauty of the court, with the Imperial ambassador once stating that she was 'of middle stature and no great beauty, so fair that one would call her rather pale than otherwise'[23] Still, she somehow managed to catch the king's eye, well before the execution of Anne Boleyn, and somehow convinced him that perhaps she would be the first of his wives to give him exactly what he wanted. Whether she served as his mistress prior to marrying him is cause for some speculation, but regardless, she encouraged his affections for her throughout the final year or so of his second marriage. The couple was betrothed on 20 May 1536 – the day after her predecessor's beheading, and three days after the nullification of that second marriage.[24] They married at Whitehall ten days later, and she appeared to be a refreshing change from Anne Boleyn, as one courtier asserted, 'She is as gentle a lady as ever I knew … The King hath come out of hell into heaven.'[25]

Henry's illegitimate son, Henry Fitzroy, succumbed to consumption and died on 23 July 1536 at only seventeen years old – adding yet another crushing disappointment to an already-long list. Of course, Fitzroy never would have succeeded his father (though this wild notion had been suggested only a month prior by the Earl of Sussex), and yet this was still a terrible tragedy for the king.[26] Now, even the unlikely and ill-advised scenario of an illegitimate son inheriting the throne was no longer an option, and Henry looked to his new bride with a renewed sense of determination. Would she succeed where two others had failed? Roughly eight months later – surely much longer than Henry was happy to wait – Jane was able to share the happy news with him. She was finally with child.

The news was announced to the Privy Council that April, and the *Te Deum* was sung in churches across England.[27] The country was on edge – excitedly awaiting the news they longed for, with one courtier writing, 'God send her good deliverance of a prince, to the joy of all faithful subjects.'[28] Their prayers were answered on 12 October when Edward Tudor was born and, as the Marchioness of Dorset wrote to the king, it was the greatest, most joyful news the country could have hoped to receive.[29] It was, indeed, a great victory for both England and Henry VIII, and Jane had given him the greatest gift a woman could give a king. But the process had been an ordeal, and one that Jane would pay for with her life. She had been confined to her chambers twenty-six days earlier and gone into the early stages of labour on 9 October. By nightfall of 11 October, the situation had become dire, and church members all over London were ordered to pray for the safe deliverance of the child, as well as for the life of the queen.[30] Afterwards, rumours would abound that Prince Edward had been delivered via caesarean section – specifically, that Henry himself had ordered 'that the mother had to be sacrificed for the child.'[31] Evidence for this, however, is unfounded, and it is highly unlikely that such a dangerous procedure occurred; at the time, caesareans were generally performed only once the mother had already died.[32]

Further rumours circulated within the following year – and even into the reign of Elizabeth I – claiming that Henry VIII had ordered

Jane's limbs to be stretched to make a passage for his son. A document in the Vatican even went so far as to claim that Henry had caused his wife's death with this order.[33] While there is no contemporary evidence to support any of these rumours, Jane's delivery was, reportedly, a long and difficult one. It lasted two days and three nights, but the wait was worth it when Jane held her son in her arms. Though she likely had no say in the name, the little prince was named Edward, as he was born on the eve of Edward the Confessor's feast day.[34] Chronicler Edward Hall recorded the royal birth as such:

> On St Edward's even was born at Hampton Court the noble imp Prince Edward ... at the birth of this noble prince was great fires made through the whole realm, and great joy made with thanksgiving to almighty God which hath sent so noble a prince to succeed to the crown of this realm.[35]

Jane was thought to have come out of the birth rather well, and while the king was not at Hampton Court for the happy event itself, he immediately rushed to Jane's side when the news was delivered.[36] He was forty-six years old, having sat on the English throne for nearly three decades – and he had finally accomplished his goal. The long-awaited birth of his son must have given some purpose to all that had come before: two failed marriages, numerous stillbirths and miscarriages, and the severing of ties between England and Rome. With his 'one true wife' and his heir beside him, Henry now had all that he needed.

Henry leapt into action – immediately the doting, overprotective father. The infant Prince Edward's rooms and brand-new nursery were scrubbed and swept to perfection. A wet nurse was placed in charge of feeding him, in place of his royal mother. A staff of nursemaids – including four cradle-rockers, of which two were named Jane Russell and Bridget Forster – were employed and sworn to the strictest and highest standards of infant care. A dry nurse, Sybil Penne, would be appointed to the prince's staff around one year later – indicating the approximate time at which he was weaned. The leader of this distinguished group of women was none other than Lady Margaret Bryan, who had also served as lady governess to the king's other three children, Mary, Elizabeth, and

Henry Fitzroy.[37] So guarded was the prince that no one could so much as approach his cradle without express consent from the monarch.[38] He had food testers (more so after he was weaned), designated launderers, and servants instructed to clean his nursery up to three times a day.[39] Every possible need of Edward's was met with haste, and the quality of his care was almost certainly unmatched – even by the care given to his siblings. The king would take absolutely no chances with his most valuable, sought-after child. In fact, as the plague had been ravaging London's surrounding areas for months, Henry hastily issued a proclamation forbidding anyone residing in the affected areas from coming to court. This may very well have had an impact on attendance at the prince's upcoming christening – though the audience still numbered around four hundred. Regardless, Henry was unapologetic in the steps he took to ensure his son's safety.[40]

As was customary, Edward was christened a few days after birth, on 15 October. This took place in the Chapel Royal at Hampton Court, and was not attended by his mother or father, as royal protocol instructed – according to the king's grandmother, Margaret Beaufort. Instead, Henry and Jane remained in the antechamber, dressed in regal velvet and fur, as guests proceeded past them on their route to the chapel. This procession reportedly took around six hours, with the christening not starting technically until midnight. At that time, all walking in pairs and carrying unlit torches, Gentlemen of the Privy Chamber led chaplains, bishops, councillors, and nobles, followed by officers of state and foreign ambassadors into the chapel. The prince's godparents were next – with godfathers Thomas Howard, Duke of Norfolk, Charles Brandon, Duke of Suffolk, and Thomas Cranmer, Archbishop of Canterbury. Edward's sister, Mary, age twenty-one, was his godmother. Though his other sister, Elizabeth, age four, was not granted such an honour, she did get to play a role in the ceremony by carrying the jewelled baptismal chrism, while she herself was carried by Edward Seymour – brother of Queen Jane, and the prince's uncle. Edward, carried by the Marchioness of Exeter, proceeded down the Chapel Royal aisle underneath a golden canopy, flanked by his wet nurse and midwife.[41]

Trumpeters heralded the magnificent occasion in the newly renovated chapel – the walls splendidly decked in cloth of gold, floors covered in rich carpets, with the silver baptismal font sparkling at the altar beneath a canopy.[42] The infant was proudly proclaimed 'Edward, sonne and heire to the King of Englande, Duke of Cornewall, and Earle of Chester'.[43] Following the ceremony, the procession made its way back towards the king and queen – this time with tapers lit. The prince was handed to his mother, where he was blessed by both parents before being handed back to a nursemaid and taken to bed. It is worth noting here the fact that Jane was well enough three days postpartum to take part in the christening ceremony. This further disproves the rumour of a caesarean – or otherwise terribly traumatic – birth, as no contemporary reports indicate that she appeared to be suffering on this occasion. On the contrary, Jane was likely just as joyous as her husband on this day. Seventeen months into marriage and her role as Queen of England, and she had already successfully performed her duty. There is little doubt that she felt anything but immense joy at the sight of her infant son being presented to God and proclaimed Henry VIII's heir.

On 16 October, Queen Jane was churched – a ceremony in which a Christian woman is blessed and spiritually 'cleansed' following childbirth. The fact that she went through this customary ritual shows how well she must have looked and felt in the days following Edward's birth; it was not expected that a sickly woman on her deathbed would be churched. However, within one more day, everything had changed. Jane was suddenly so obviously ill that it became clear to all around her that she may not survive.[44] On 19 October, there was a procession at St Paul's Cathedral for Jane's health, and courtiers prayed around the clock for her recovery. But on 23 October, her physicians reported Jane's heavy bleeding, or 'a natural laxe' (which may also indicate diarrhoea) – which rapidly worsened her condition. Henry rushed to be by her side, her confessor came to hear her last confession and administer the last rites, and the Duke of Norfolk wrote the following words to Thomas Cromwell from Hampton Court: 'I pray you to be here tomorrow early to comfort our good master, for as for our mistress there is no likelihood of her life, the more pity, and I fear she shall not be alive at the time ye shall read this.'[45] Jane died only hours later, around midnight.

Historians have speculated on the cause of Jane's death, citing puerperal fever ('childbed fever') – an infection leading to blood poisoning, and a postpartum haemorrhage caused by fragments of the placenta left in her uterus, as possible culprits. Much blame was cast around her chamber following her death – pointing fingers at poor hygiene practices, medical incompetence, and lack of experience in delivering babies. It has also wisely been noted that a woman of lesser status may well have received more thorough and advanced treatment. This is an ironic thought, given the fact that Jane was attended by the best physicians the king's money could buy, but they were also probably far less experienced at childbirth than were midwives. Such women were properly trained in coaching a woman through labour and childbirth, and also the practice of fully examining the placenta after birth to ensure that it was intact.[46] Queen Jane was not afforded such an expert in childbirth and postnatal care, despite her husband's efforts to give her (in his own opinion) the best medical care possible.

Henry, of course, was devastated. Leaving Jane's funeral arrangements in the hands of others, he fled immediately from Hampton Court and into a dark seclusion. His well-known words to the French king Francis I speak of his grief: 'Divine Providence … hath mingled my joy with the bitterness of the death of her who brought me this happiness.'[47] His words reinforce the feeling of gratitude he had for his third wife – the one at whose side he would one day choose to be buried – an honour given to the one who had gifted him with his heir. He was distraught by her untimely death, but that death had not been in vain. Even the Latin inscription on the plaque set above her vault in the chapel at Windsor Castle made that point clear:

> Here lieth a Phoenix, by whose death
> Another Phoenix life gave breath:
> It is to be lamented much
> The world at once never knew two such.[48]

The king was so distressed by his queen's death that he showed little enthusiasm when Cromwell began discussing options for another bride. In fact, he would not marry again for nearly three years, despite his ministers' warnings that, while having one male heir was good, having a spare to that heir would be preferable. Of this, of course, Henry was well aware, given his role as the spare heir of his own royal family. But at this time, immediately following Queen Jane's death and the birth of his long-awaited son, Henry had eyes only for Edward. The little prince, not even two weeks old when his mother died, was his primary and utmost concern. So too was he the greatest joy of the entire country, softening the blow of the loss of their beloved queen.

While the vast majority of English citizens held opinions of excitement and hope at the birth of Prince Edward – despite the loss of Jane – there were exceptions, which caused the king to worry for his son's safety. Just a few months after Jane's funeral, a voodoo doll of the prince was found in a London churchyard, complete with pins stuck through it. The news of this chilling find spread throughout the country, along with a prophecy about the type of king the prince may one day become. A man named John Ryan spoke of how the prince would be just as great a murderer as his father, if not more so, given that he had murdered his own mother while in the womb. This prophecy, according to Ryan, originated from the 'best' chronicler in England – Robert Fayery, a royal herald.[49] With threats and ugly words floating around about his beloved heir, Henry stepped up security precautions to further protect Edward. He made it abundantly clear through written regulations for his son's household, that Edward was a gift from God – not only for himself, but for the whole realm.

Once again, Edward's food, clothes, company, and cleanliness were seen to with the utmost attention to detail. No threat of disease or danger would reach the prince undetected by the army of servants who attended him, if Henry had anything to do with it. He simply could not afford anything happening to his only son. Now at nearly fifty years old and without a wife, all Henry's hopes for the future of his dynasty rested on the shoulders of the infant Edward. The realm his father had fought to control fifty-two years earlier could be secure only with the certainty that a male heir would inherit it someday. Citizens of England relied on this surety in order to rest easily in their beds, safe from outside threats against the throne, which would put the whole kingdom in jeopardy. Edward was England's saviour – the answer to nearly thirty years' worth of prayers. Indeed, from the very moment he was born, he was 'this whole realm's most precious jewel'.[50]

Chapter 2

His Father's Son

Roughly two years before his death, Henry VIII commissioned a special portrait which still hangs on display in the Haunted Gallery at Hampton Court Palace today. This painting, called *The Family of Henry VIII*, was created by an unknown artist, and sends a striking message about the family at the centre of Henry's monarchy. It shines a specifically bright light upon himself, Jane Seymour, and – most notably – Prince Edward. This is a long, horizontally oriented portrait, with Henry perched upon his throne front and centre beneath an ornate canopy – his coat of arms and the inscription 'HR-VIII' above him. Jane, his 'true' wife, sits to his left, her body positioned a few inches from where her husband's hand grips the throne's armrest. She appears demure and meek, as if knowing that she is not meant to be a focal point of the painting.

Edward, however (probably depicted around age eight) stands proudly at his father's right hand. Clothed in bold crimson and gold finery, he is not quite so opulent and eye-catching as Henry, but it is not his clothes that are meant to be on display here. Instead, the viewer's eye is drawn to the king's arm around his son, with his right hand set upon Edward's shoulder. This is a protective, affectionate embrace, the likes of which we do not see in any other portrait featuring Henry VIII. Even the king's right knee is inclined in Edward's direction, leaning ever-so-slightly towards his heir. Everything about Henry's presence in this portrait is, of course, drawing the eye towards himself first and foremost, but just as swiftly indicating where the eye should focus next. Prince Edward is, of course, deemed to be the second-most important person captured in the image.

We do not, in any other royal painting of Henry, see him direct the attention of the viewer to anyone other than himself. Here, the message is abundantly clear. His wife sits at a comfortably modest distance from his physical touch, and his two daughters stand several feet away to either side of the portrait (separated by columns beside the king to further indicate their distance from the throne). Edward is pressed right against his father, looking every inch a miniature version of Henry VIII. This is precisely the image that Henry meant to convey as he framed his 'true' family within the four columns surrounding him. At this time, Prince Edward was the most important of any of Henry's family members. He was the future of the Tudor dynasty – the only one Henry intended to rule after him. He was the entirely beloved prince, the much sought-after heir, and by many contemporary accounts, a near-perfect miniature of Henry VIII.

As Henry's finest jewel in the Tudor crown, Edward continued to have everything he needed as an infant and throughout the first six years of his life, as he was brought up 'among the women', mostly at a house called Havering, located in Essex.[1] Lady Bryan regularly relayed news of Edward to Thomas Cromwell, who then passed the information along to the king. One such update came towards the end of 1538, when Lady Bryan reported that the prince was 'in good health and merry', with four teeth – 'three full out, and the fourth appeareth'.[2] Lady Bryan worried that Edward did not have enough jewels for his capes and coats, and that his nursery was too bare, but she related to Cromwell that she would order the appropriate things for the prince, trusting that the king would be pleased with her diligence. Upon reading such a report, Cromwell promptly transferred £5,000 from the royal coffers into the baby prince's household funds – the equivalent of £1.5 million today.[3] Funds were used for the prince's necessities, of course, but also for toys and trinkets – including a comb in the shape of a horse and rider, puppets, spears, and javelins, and (a more appropriate toy for a baby) a rattle fashioned from coral and a wolf's tooth, ornamented with little bells.[4]

Far from history's misconception of Edward as a weak, sickly child, the young prince was a playful, happy, perfectly healthy baby who 'sucketh like a child of his puissance', in the words of Cromwell.[5] He was exceptionally well cared for, and apparently very well loved by the women who tended to him. All the while, the king remained a rather absent father – choosing to love his precious son from afar – not unlike many other kings. Henry kept Edward mostly at Hampton Court, while he himself travelled from palace to palace, paying only the odd visit here and there to spend time with his son. One such occasion was when Edward was around six months old and Henry spent the day 'dallying with him in his arms' in front of the window, 'to the sight and great comfort of all the people'.[6] Ambassadors and foreign dignitaries who were afforded the chance to meet the infant prince referred to him as 'the prettiest child we ever saw', and Chancellor Thomas Audley called him 'so goodly a child of his age, so merry, so pleasant, so good and loving [of] countenance.'[7] It is, of course, worth remembering that these compliments paid to the King of England's son were to be expected – and anything less would almost certainly have been met with royal wrath. However, we do have one piece of evidence that speaks to these men's truthfulness, and that is the portrait of the fourteen-month-old Edward, painted by Hans Holbein the Younger.

The painting, dated 1538, shows baby Edward clothed in crimson and gold, with a white feather protruding from his cap and a jewelled rattle in his left hand. Despite his regal attire, Edward looks exactly like any adorable infant one might drool over today – the image complete with wispy baby hairs and rounded chubby cheeks. His right hand, raised in the semblance of a wave, makes the viewer feel as if they could reach through the painting and invite his baby fingers to curl around their own. He is, undoubtedly in this portrait, a precious baby – but the symbolism and ultimate message of the artwork tells us much more. The rattle that Edward holds is reminiscent of a sceptre – foreshadowing the type of portrait he will one day pose for as King of England. His face – though that of a small child – holds a stern and knowing expression, with the unmistakable eyes of Henry VIII. Most telling of all is the inscription included below his likeness, written by Richard Morison, and transcribed from its original Latin:

> Little one, emulate thy father and be the heir of his virtue; the world contains nothing greater. Heaven and earth could scarcely produce a son whose glory would surpass that of such a father. Do thou but equal the deeds of thy parent and men can ask no more. Shouldst thou surpass him, thou hast outstrip all kings the world has revered in ages past.[8]

Given to Henry VIII as a New Year's gift in 1539 by Hans Holbein, the painting was instantly impactful, and conveyed the unmistakable message that Edward was Henry's miniature who would one day rule just as his father had done. This was, undoubtedly, also a message that was engrained in Edward from his earliest years – enforced by the words of a contemporary poet, by the name of John Leland, when he saw the Holbein portrait for himself: 'As often as I direct my gaze to look at your delightful face and appearance, so I seem to see the form of your magnanimous father shining forth in your face ...'[9]

Despite his 'good and loving countenance', as Audley had commented, Edward was still only a toddler in early 1539 when we see a glimpse of adorable (albeit embarrassing for the king) childhood behaviour, when German ambassadors paid a visit to Hampton Court. They came on behalf of the Duke of Cleves, with whom Thomas Cromwell had been negotiating a marriage agreement between the king and the duke's sister, Anne. While the ambassadors toured the palace they paid a visit to Prince Edward's nursery, where he was being held by his beloved dry nurse, Sybil. The Germans approached Edward and Sybil gently extracted the toddler's hand from herself, so that they might kiss it, but Edward shrank into his nurse's shoulder and reportedly buried his face there – unsure of the strangely-attired foreigners. When Lady Bryan attempted to intercede and salvage the diplomatic awkwardness, Edward burst into tears – inconsolable until the Earl of Essex finally was able to make him laugh.

By the early months of 1539, Edward was standing and walking on his own, losing his baby fat as he grew, and enjoying time at his country nursery in Hertfordshire. Once again, in 1540, Lady Bryan wrote to Cromwell that Edward was in good health, that he 'danced and played so wantonly that he could not stand still, and was as full of pretty toys as ever I saw child in my life'.[10] That 'goodly health' would, however, be tested the following year, when Edward would contract quartan fever, a type of malaria.[11] Suddenly, one of Henry's greatest fears presented itself – his only son and heir was in danger. Naturally, he summoned only the best physicians in the country to tend to Edward, and here we see a strange contradiction among the comments from doctors regarding Edward's health.

Following several reports from Lady Bryan, courtiers, and ambassadors, all of whom described the toddler prince as being of 'goodly health', in October 1541 a doctor described Edward to the French ambassador as being 'so gross and unhealthy that he could not believe, judging from what he could see now, that he would live long'.[12] Was he referring only to the young prince's illness, or something more? Was he insinuating that Edward was an overweight child? Later portraits do not support this theory, but the doctor's choice of words is certainly odd, given that all other contemporary reports point to a perfectly healthy Prince Edward – despite the short-lived bout with quartan fever. Indeed, it was apparently touch-and-go for about ten days, and doctors feared the four-year-old prince might not survive. Much to his father's relief, he made a full recovery – finally impatiently telling his doctor, William Butts, to go away, after referring to him as both a fool and a knave.[13]

By Christmas of 1543, Edward's older sisters had been restored to their previous places in Henry VIII's line of succession – behind their brother, of course. To mark this special occasion, Henry commissioned *The Family of Henry VIII* painting, described at the beginning of this chapter. As discussed, this painting sent a stark message about Edward's significant place in Henry's family. Both Henry and Edward stare straight into the eyes of the viewer from where they are perched at the throne, so it is easy to imagine that the young prince would have looked up to his father with a kind of wonder – emulating him, perhaps, and envisioning how he would one day fill those very large royal shoes. Indeed, the way that Edward was raised, educated, and influenced, as he passed from the care of women into the hands of men (around the age of six) makes this clear.

If there was one thing just as important to Henry VIII as the presence of his son and heir, it was the surety that the Tudor line would continue far beyond Edward. Thus, plans for the five-and-a-half-year-old prince's betrothal were well underway by the spring of 1543, when Henry sought to unite the realms of England and Scotland by wedding his son to the infant Mary, Queen of Scots. The Scottish King James V had died the previous December, leaving his six-day-old daughter as monarch of the northern country. Her ambassadors paid

Prince Edward a visit in March 1543, and it appeared at first as though the betrothal might go ahead. But Henry demanded that the infant queen be brought to England, as a toddler, to learn English customs, commenting, 'I look on her as my own daughter.' Her mother, Mary of Guise, was surprisingly in favour of this plan,[14] But many Scottish nobles, however, were not supportive of this arrangement. The Earl of Arran, in particular, was put off by Henry VIII's ultimatum and stated that 'every man, woman and child in Scotland would liever die in one day than accept [the terms]'.[15]

However, despite resistance against Henry's offer, the Treaty of Greenwich was signed on 1 July 1543 – establishing a peace deal between the two countries, and confirming the marriage agreement. According to the treaty, Mary would remain in Scotland until age ten, at which point she would marry Prince Edward and take up her rightful place in England. Once she was established as Queen Consort, her already sizeable dowry of £2,000 per annum – paid by Henry – would double. Some concessions were made in favour of the Scots' wishes – such as the young queen's education, which would be handled mostly by those appointed by her mother and other Scottish nobles. However, for her 'better care', Henry would send his own English nobles and governesses to ensure that the Scottish-born queen would one day pass for a well-raised English rose.[16]

It was Henry's grand plan to unite the two Crowns, as well as to weaken France's influence in Scotland. For some time, it appeared to be a success, but less than six months later, the treaty was rejected by the Scottish Parliament – which threw the English king into a rage and had him planning the largest military invasion since the thirteenth century. Arran knew to suspect violent action from the English by December 1543, when he wrote to Mary of Guise that Henry VIII was determined 'not only to destroy our liberty, than which nothing can be dearer to men, but also to overthrow our religion and the obedience paid for so many centuries to the Holy See'. She had previously acknowledged in a letter to him that, 'The realm is marvellously seduced and spoiled by the Lutheran sect, as well by the King of England.'[17]

Betrayed and incensed that the plans for his son's marriage had been voided, Henry sent a force of 15,000 men to Edinburgh in April 1544, led by his brother-in-law and the young prince's uncle, Edward Seymour, Earl of Hertford. This raid – instructed to begin at Edinburgh Castle and 'extend like extremities and destructions in all towns and villages', began what would be known for the next seven years as 'the Rough Wooing'.[18] The king's instructions were graphic and clear: 'Put all to fire and sword, burn Edinburgh town, so razed and defaced when you have sacked and gotten what ye can of it, as there may remain forever a perpetual memory of the vengeance of God lightened upon [them] for their falsehood and disloyalty.'[19]

This same year, little Prince Edward became more of a man in Henry VIII's eyes – a mature six-year-old, ready for his own official court. In fact, turning six years old (for boys) was known as 'breeching' – believed by the Tudors to indicate the beginning of adulthood, and thus a change in attire to include breeches.[20] Edward's household was moved to Hampton Court Palace, and the women who had long tended to him were discharged – many of whom were offered pensions. His apartments were redecorated to mirror his father's – featuring Flemish tapestries depicting popular biblical scenes, as well as rich fabrics and ornamentation. His wardrobe received an influx of furs, animal skins, and a plethora of new doublets and (of course) breeches. Every last inch of Edward's personal possessions glittered with jewels, precious stones, and gold – down to the covers of his books and his cutlery.[21] In fact, a love of material goods, ornate furnishings, and embellished clothing would remain with Edward throughout his life – probably due to the influence of Henry VIII and the special attention given to such details. Henry's own enthusiasm for excess would certainly be mirrored in his son.

Now that Edward was largely in the company of men, it was time for his formal education to begin. So too would begin the intensity of his father's influence over him. According to Edward's own chronicle (the diary he kept from around age twelve through most of the rest of his life), he was now surrounded by 'well-learned men', such as tutor Richard Cox, later Bishop of Ely, and deputy Dr John Cheke, a Fellow at St John's College, Cambridge. Other language instructors included John Belmayne and Master Randolph, who taught Edward French and German, respectively. William Thomas taught Edward about politics, and Roger Ascham instructed him in penmanship.[22] All in, his lessons from this time encompassed a wide range of subjects, including several languages (Cox reported that he was proficient in Latin), philosophy, liberal sciences, Roman and Greek classics, history, geography, scripture, etiquette, fencing, and horsemanship.[23]

Like any child, Edward benefitted from the ability to play with other children as he grew up. Aside from his sister, Elizabeth, who was only four years his senior, one of his earliest recorded companions was the granddaughter of courtier Sir William Sidney, a girl named Jane Dormer, who was a year younger than Edward. She would recall, later in life as the Duchess of Feria, how the prince frequently referred to her as 'my Jane', and according to her memoirs, the two of them spent much of their time conversing, reading, dancing, and playing cards.[24] He was reportedly surrounded by a group of fourteen schoolmates, including his cousins – Henry, born in 1535, and Charles, born in either 1537 or 1538, the son of Charles Brandon, first Duke of Suffolk.[25] The children of other nobles included Robert Dudley, born in 1532 (son of John Dudley), and possibly Edward's cousin, Lady Jane Grey, who was roughly a year older than the prince.[26] Many of these friends appear to have remained close with him for years to come, and when both Henry and Charles Brandon succumbed to the sweating sickness years later, in 1551, Edward was reportedly devastated.[27]

Edward's closest childhood friend, however, was a boy by the name of Barnaby Fitzpatrick – the son of the Irish first Baron Upper Ossory. According to many historians, Barnaby served a greater purpose beyond friendship, however, and acted as Edward's 'whipping boy'. This unenviable post would have meant that Barnaby received the punishments that tutors would have otherwise inflicted upon Edward himself, were he not the son of Henry VIII.[28] However, there is opposing evidence to support the theory that Prince Edward did not escape physical punishment for bratty behaviour at all – despite the fact that his tutor might risk the king's wrath. Chris Skidmore describes a scene in which Richard Cox, so fed up with the young prince's stubbornness, was led to giving Edward 'such a wound that he wist [knew] not what to do'. Edward's stubborn temperament earned him the nickname 'Captain Will' by Cox, but after this one incident, he was reportedly cured.[29] It is difficult to imagine that a tutor employed by such a famously turbulently tempered king would invent such a story if it were not true. On the contrary, it is not difficult to imagine that Edward might have had a bit of an attitude towards his tutor, believing that, as prince, he was untouchable. In fact, Reginald Pole, the future Archbishop of Canterbury, claimed that Edward once was in such a rage that he tore a living falcon apart in front of his tutors.[30] Whether or not this story holds any merit is impossible to know, but it might speak to Edward having inherited his father's vicious temper. Regardless, while Barnaby Fitzpatrick may not have served as the prince's whipping boy after all, he certainly did remain a close friend and servant of the future king until Edward's own death.

Richard Cox's assessment of Edward's temperament – at least on that one occasion – may have been indicative of the prince's developing character as he grew out of young childhood and into his more mature adolescent years. The incident with the falcon, if true, would certainly prove a rather savage disposition, but beyond that, there is plenty of evidence to show that Edward grew increasingly authoritative and pompous over time. By the time he was king, he was recognized by many, including his sister Elizabeth, as being quite spoiled, wilful, and difficult to please.[31] As he became more educated, he also became more devoutly religious and zealous when debating the new doctrine – which gave him an air of seriousness that bordered on severity. While the commanding and priggish attitude that Edward exuded points directly to his father's influence as a hotly tempered and at times cruel king, the prince may, in fact, have developed a sterner demeanour even than Henry VIII had demonstrated. Gone was the playful, jovial baby that Lady Bryan had described to Cromwell years prior. Now that Edward was reaching the ripe and mature age of Tudor manhood, he was shedding his interest in fun and games, and applying himself to more sober matters – finding little amusement in frivolity or light-hearted discourse.

When Edward was seven, he was starting to read Cato, Cicero, Herodotus, Aesop's Fables, and Solomon's Proverbs, and Cox reported that he 'learneth there to beware of strange and wanton women [and] to be thankful to him who telleth him of his faults'.[32] Edward was described by his tutors (save for that one incident) as intelligent, pleasant, and a fast-learner. He was given his own study for his lessons – including desks covered in black and green velvet, embroidered with his initials, writing tools (such as quills fashioned from goose, swan, or raven feathers), astronomical and mathematical instruments, and a collection of trinkets and learning materials gifted to the king and prince by ambassadors who travelled the world. No doubt, the prince received the greatest education, tools, and instructors that money could afford. One visitor to court noted that the prince suffered from poor eyesight, and two spectacle cases were counted among the belongings in his study.[33]

Another notable teacher was Philip van Wilder, one of Henry VIII's favourite musicians at court. In thanks for arranging for van Wilder to be his music teacher, the prince wrote to his father, 'that I may be more expert in striking the lute; herein your love appeareth to be very great'.[34] Through van Wilder, and possibly because of the minstrels who entertained at his father's court, Edward's love of music carried through his childhood and into his teenage years as king, when the number of court musicians increased. Tracy Borman notes that Edward's household accounts show payments for 'eighteen trumpeters, seven vial players, four sackbuts, a bagpiper, drummer, harpist, rebeck player and eight minstrels'.[35] In addition to music, Edward enjoyed theatrical productions, and was known to participate in them himself, even into his reign. Another pastime interest he shared with his father was gambling – reportedly losing upwards of £143 17d as a result of wagers on a number of games and sports.[36]

One of the most noteworthy aspects of Edward's education is, perhaps, the writing project that became his *Chronicle,* which he would not begin writing until 1550, around age twelve. This may have originated as a writing assignment by John Cheke, meant to sharpen Edward's writing skill and perhaps also practice his penmanship.[37] Its contents have, over the centuries, often been interpreted by historians as indicative of Edward's stoicism and aloofness regarding the events surrounding him – such as when he wrote the simple statement, 'The Duke of Somerset had his head cut off upon Tower Hill between eight and nine o'clock in the morning,' to commemorate the execution of his uncle, the Lord Protector of England, in 1552.[38] But the *Chronicle*'s structure should give one pause when considering how it was meant to be interpreted. Edward wrote his earliest entries in the third person – a curious way of writing, if it was indeed intended to be used as a diary. Instead, it is written much more like other chronicles of the time – which indicates that it probably began as a writing exercise.[39] Later entries began using the first person when referring to Edward's activities, and the grammatical structure of the writing became more fluid and verbose as Edward continued writing. However, one should use caution when attempting to link Edward's writings in the *Chronicle* with his own personal emotions and analyses. It is far more likely that the *Chronicle* acted, at first, as a school assignment for Edward to practice his writing, and later as a chronicle-style listing of events during his reign – not Edward's own personal diary or memoir. If it had been meant for such a purpose, we would almost certainly have more material at our disposal to tell us of Edward's personal motivations, emotions, and thoughts than we are left with today.

While it is well-documented that Edward was an avid and intellectual student, less emphasis has been placed on his participation as a sportsman – leading some to speculate that he was less inclined to physical activity than his father had been in his youth. However, an inventory of Edward's belongings reveals that he likely took part in hawking, fishing, tennis, and fencing, and that he kept greyhounds, horses, and even baiting bears. One Italian visitor at court also noted that Edward hunted regularly, so there appears to be plenty of reason to question the commonly-held view that he largely refrained from athletics, preferring instead to keep to his studies.[40] In fact, the Venetian ambassador would later comment on the fact that, during Edward's kingship, he had been 'taught to ride and handle his weapons, and to go through other similar exercises, so that His Majesty soon commenced arming and tilting, managing horses, and delighting in every sort of exercise, drawing the bow, playing rackets, hunting …'.[41] Though this quote is from later in Edward's life (when he was probably around fourteen), it is no less telling in its regard to Edward's interests. It is certainly without question that Edward was a good student, and may have favoured spending time in his study, but he grew up as any future king would have – becoming familiar with, and reportedly skilled at, a number of athletic pursuits – just like his father.

The curriculum of education that Edward and his classmates followed was largely influenced by Northern European Humanists, such as Erasmus. As such, he was expected to become proficient in Latin and Greek classics, which he reportedly enjoyed. This was, as Tracey Borman notes, a break from the more traditional royal educations afforded to heirs and their siblings – which tended to emphasize the importance of sports, horsemanship, dancing, and 'other gentlemanly pursuits'.[42] As is evident in the records left behind by Edward's tutors and his own writing, his education was a good mix of both the traditional and more progressive modes of teaching. It is unfortunate, given his role in the Protestant Reformation during his short reign, that we know so little about Edward's lessons in religion. Both Richard Cox and John Cheke were probably moderate in their religious leanings (similar to Henry VIII's 'Catholic-light' form of Protestantism). However, we do know that they, as well as Ascham, would later become exiles under Edward's severely Catholic half-sister, Mary – so it is evident that they became rather strongly reformed Protestants. Edward's band of religion tutors included John Pikington, Anthony Otway, Giles Eyre, and Roger Tong – all presumably chosen by Thomas Cranmer. So, while his instruction certainly would not have strayed so far away from Catholicism as, say, Lutheranism, it was understandably more Protestant in flavour.[43] John Cheke was reported to be 'always at his elbow ... and wherever else he went, to inform and teach him.'[44] His understanding of the reformation that his father had begun must have been relatively sharp, at least, as he was described in 1549 as being 'quite capable of following the theological controversies that were raging around him', and he managed to write a well-argued treatise on the Catholic pope as the antichrist.[45] Though we know relatively little about his religious instruction during these formative years, there is enough evidence to ascertain that Edward's later fervent Protestant convictions as king were influenced by these Protestant (if somewhat moderate) tutors, as well as the knowledge of his eminent father's self-made title of Supreme Head of the Church of England – which he knew he would one day inherit.

The admiration that Edward felt towards Henry VIII is evident in letters written by the prince during his childhood, when he was often parted from his father for long periods of time. While Edward was

Henry's favoured child – if for no reason beyond his sex – the king remained a distant parent, and there is evidence that the prince felt somewhat neglected as a result. While Henry campaigned in France, Edward worried about bothering him with his 'boyish letters', but finally wrote, among other sentiments, 'I hope I shall prove to you a most dutiful son.' Shortly after the sending of this letter, he wrote another expressing his desire for Henry to visit him soon. He wrote that he wanted 'to be assured that you are safe and well', and though Henry proved to be 'too busy', in his own words to his wife, to write back to Edward, he did ask that she 'send blessings to all my children'.[46] When Henry returned home to England, Edward was thrilled – writing yet again that both of his wishes had been granted: 'My first wish was, that you and your kingdom might have peace; and secondly that I might see you.'[47]

Henry's preferred method of parenting appears to have been lavishing expensive gifts upon his son – such as jewellery, buttons, garments, and adornments for his clothes – rather than spending time with him. Still, Edward was enormously grateful for anything and everything that he received from his father, and wrote to him saying, 'You have treated me so kindly, like a most loving father ... in which things and gifts is conspicuous your fatherly affection towards me; for, if you did not love me, you would not give me these fine gifts of jewellery.'[48] These heart-wrenching words, written by a child who desperately craved his father's affection, attention, and approval, speak of a prince who evidently idolized the man that Henry VIII was. Not only was Edward understandably told by the men around him just how powerful, magnanimous, and resplendent his father was – but he also clearly felt a need to please Henry, and we can imagine that this coloured his own understanding of the type of king he should one day be.

When Edward was around eight years old, he stood for a portrait in what is thought to be the Queen's Drawing Room at Windsor Castle. He appears standing at the window with a castle far in the distance, and it is unmistakable, when looking at his stance and expression (to say nothing of his attire) just who his father is. With his right hand gripping a dagger and his left resting at his hip, he poses for the artist in a distinctly Henrician posture, reminiscent of the Holbein portrait of Henry VIII from either 1536 or 1537 (arguably his most recognizable likeness). Edward's portrait was painted around 1546, when he was still Prince of Wales. Therefore, his clothing is different from his father's while still remaining sumptuous – the rich crimson robe trimmed with fur dwarfing his small frame. Equally eye-catching is Edward's stern, penetrating stare towards the viewer. His dark grey eyes are Henry's, as well as the strong bridge of his nose and his fiery red hair, which appears to have darkened from his baby blonde. Even the shape of his mouth bears a striking resemblance to his father. He is, in this image, every inch the son of Henry VIII – as he had been trained to be since birth. We can assume, based on the evidence we have regarding Edward's upbringing, that this stunning visual depiction of his eight-year-old likeness to the commanding father he so admired, mirrored the impression and expectation he held for himself, regarding his destiny as Henry VIII's heir.

Chapter 3

Royal Relationships and Marriage Proposals

From the time of his birth until his accession to the throne at age nine, there can be little doubt that the largest familial influence on Edward's life was that of Henry VIII – distant as that relationship may have been. Certainly, he lacked a mother's love and affection, due to Jane Seymour's untimely death when he was only twelve days old. But Edward enjoyed a number of other close family relationships during his formative years as a child, and these relationships had significant impacts on him both personally and as a future king. In addition to having two half-sisters by his father's first two wives, Edward also experienced three different stepmothers – though only one of them made a particularly notable impression on him. He enjoyed a close friendship with one like-minded cousin and shared a close bond with at least one of his maternal uncles. Each of these figures played a part in shaping the boy who would step into the large shoes of his father in 1547, and nearly all of them would be considerably affected by his reign in later years.

The first young woman to step into the role of Henry's queen and Edward's stepmother was Anne of Cleves, who entered the scene towards the end of 1539, when Edward was two years old. As Anne and Henry were married only briefly, from January until July 1540, there is no record of any bond between the toddler prince and his German stepmother.[1] It is very possible that he had no memory of her from childhood, and as queen, Anne surely had very little to do with the prince during her short time as Henry's wife. Katherine Howard, Edward's second stepmother, was no different. The teenage queen was married to Henry VIII from July 1540 until her beheading on 13 February 1542, when Edward was around four-and-a-half. While he may have known who she was, there remains no record of Katherine's involvement in her stepson's life, so it is likely that she made little to no impression on him. However, when Katherine Parr entered the king's life and became Edward's third stepmother in 1543, he gained his true mother-figure – a woman who would influence his upbringing and identity, and who would prove to hold a special place of affection in his heart.

Edward's closeness with Katherine may have been due, in part, to the fact that he turned six years old in the same year that she married the king – marking the transition of his household to Hampton Court Palace, where the newlywedded couple also resided.[2] This was a big change for the not quite six-year-old, who had spent his early years in the care of his female attendants at the houses of Hunsdon, Havering, Hertford, and Ashridge.[3] Now at Hampton Court, this close proximity would naturally have afforded them the opportunity to spend time together, which Edward would not so easily have had with Anne of Cleves or Katherine Howard. In addition to this, his entering Tudor manhood at age six invited his new stepmother to play a role in establishing the prince's education, and perhaps helping to appoint some of his primary tutors – including John Cheke.[4] At thirty-one years old at the time of her marriage, Katherine was also more mature than her predecessor, having already been married once before, and was longing for children of her own. She was also a highly educated woman for the time, who both enjoyed and excelled at debating philosophy and religion and favoured a Reformist view of scripture. According to Edward's own words, she became his 'most dear mother', and evidence from their many letters suggests that they shared a warm and loving relationship.[5] In fact, in September 1546, Edward wrote to her saying, 'I received so many benefits from you that my mind can hardly grasp them.'[6] The primary method of their bonding seems to have been through education, which was a commonality that they both shared, as Katherine continued her own studies – particularly in Latin – into her time as Henry's queen. On this subject, she and Edward corresponded and exchanged notes regarding their progress.

While Edward desperately craved favour and attention from his father, it was much easier for him to access his stepmother, and the two exchanged frequent letters. Even John Cheke took note of Edward's closeness with her. According to Katherine's biographer, Dr Linda Porter, 'It was Katherine's love that helped to shape him and provided the maternal constant that was lacking in his life.'[7] In another letter written to her, Edward mentions that he prays to God that he 'may be able in part to satisfy the good expectation of the king's majesty, my father, and of your grace, whom God have ever in his most blessed keeping'. He even closes the letter referring to himself as 'your loving son'.[8] She evidently considered herself his mother, too, judging by her words in a letter replying to him, in which she recognizes the need for him to balance his correspondence with her, alongside his studies: '… toward your mother on the one hand and desire of learning on the other;.[9] Though she enjoyed visiting him whenever she was able, Katherine most likely communicated with Edward more by letter than in person. She did ensure that Edward was with her during Henry's campaign in France (along with his sisters), and she would also have spent time with him at holidays and on special state occasions.[10] Katherine frequently complimented Edward's skill at writing, and we can only imagine the thrill this gave the young prince – who wanted nothing more than to please his father, and by now, his stepmother as well. Until her death, Edward would remain close to his dear stepmother, praising her 'godliness and knowledge, and learning in the Scriptures' – which would echo his own Protestant leanings as he matured.[11] These religious similarities certainly kept them close and affectionate into his reign, while conversely, religion would strain certain of Edward's other relationships.

Edward was two decades younger than his eldest half-sister, Mary, and from the time he began his lessons in religion and gained an understanding of the Protestant Reformation, it was evident that their relationship would come under fairly regular strain due to their religious differences. Staunchly and unapologetically Catholic, Mary was frequently warned by her younger brother – who, despite his youth, was keen to act as Mary's protector, influence, and perhaps guardian of her soul – to abandon her ties to the Roman Church and 'the wiles and enchantments of the evil one".[12] In letters written to Katherine Parr when Edward was around eight years old, he beseeched her to remind Mary that 'the only real love is the love of God', and begged his stepmother to help him convince his stubborn sister 'to attend no longer to foreign dances and merriments which do not become a most Christian princess,' which speaks to another of the differences between the siblings – that being their outlook on and involvement in gaieties.[13] Mary appears to have been decidedly more outgoing and anxious to take part in activities that Edward clearly considered frivolous.[14]

But Edward's relationship with Mary had not always been strained. According to his sister's maid-of-honour, Jane Dormer, the young prince had enjoyed the much-older Mary's company quite a lot in his youngest years and had even promised her that she could confide in him regarding any of her secrets, and he would never tell.[15] In fact, he included quite loving words in a letter written to her in 1546, after hearing that she was ill:

> Although I do not frequently write to you, my dearest sister, yet I would not have you suppose me to be ungrateful and forgetful of you. For I love you quite as well as if I had sent letters to you more frequently, and I like you even as a brother ought to like a very dear sister, who hath within herself all the embellishments of virtue and honourable station ... even so I write to you very rarely, yet I love you most.[16]

Mary had been an attentive and affectionate older sister to Edward since his birth and appears to have taken her role of godmother seriously. While Edward was a newborn living at Richmond Palace, Mary frequently travelled from her own residence at Hampton Court to pay him regular visits – notably in November 1537 when Edward was a month old, and throughout the following spring. For the New Year of 1539, Mary gifted him with a custom crimson coat embroidered with gold and pearls, and many of her gifts were more personal than any he ever received from Henry VIII. As an example, Henry's New Year's gift to Edward that same year was a gilt cup.[17] Whenever she visited him, they were entertained by minstrels, and Mary was known to leave gifts and money for their entertainment, as well as for Edward's nursemaids.[18] They shared a close bond when he was an infant and toddler, and as he grew to hold a quill and master languages, he and Mary shared frequent letters in Latin. It is likely that Mary's interest in Edward differed from the strained relationship she shared with their half-sister, Elizabeth, because of

Edward's parentage. While Mary had always denied the validity of her father's marriage to Anne Boleyn (and boldly detested her), she had been fond of Jane Seymour, and grateful to her for her influence in regaining Mary's place in Henry VIII's family life – not to mention the succession. With her own mother, Catherine of Aragon, dead since before Jane's marriage to the king, this second stepmother almost certainly played a role in Mary's motherly affection for her baby brother. The adoration and tenderness that she felt for him was well-reciprocated throughout his childhood – at least until their religious differences came between them enough to cause irreparable damage.

A very different sibling relationship existed between Edward and Elizabeth, who was only four years older than the prince. As a result of their closeness in age, they probably had much more in common as children – possibly being educated together for a time at Ashridge when Edward was quite young.[19] Later in his childhood, when he had been established in his formal household, the two siblings would see each other less frequently. Instead, they, too, would exchange letters – sharing words of regret regarding their distance from one another, as this example from 1546 shows:

> Change of place did not vex me so much, dearest sister, as your going from me. Now there can be nothing pleasanter than a letter from you. It is some comfort in my grief that my chamberlain tells me I may hope to visit you soon if nothing happens to either of us in the meantime. Farewell, dearest sister.[20]

Elizabeth also gifted Edward with personal presents – such as the white linen shirt 'of her own working' that she gave him for the 1539 New Year.[21] When they were not together, they exchanged letters – generally written in Latin, but occasionally in French – and, both being precocious and fascinated by their studies – they encouraged and pushed each other academically, perhaps forming a sort of healthy sibling rivalry.[22] Later, when Edward would succeed to the throne, Elizabeth would be careful to maintain his favour and affection by continuing their regular correspondence. Edward had far less to criticize about Elizabeth than he did Mary, given that they were more aligned in their Protestant way of thinking. Having been educated by some of the same tutors in their youth – not to mention having been born during their father's initial reformation efforts – they shared their interest in religious change and both opposed their older sister's Catholic sympathies. This bond would serve Elizabeth well in her continued relationship with Edward, and as king he would continue to express his favour for her with letters and occasional gifts.

Perhaps the most notable of Edward's family relationships – and the one which would result in one massive succession-altering decision – was that of his cousin, Lady Jane Grey. Though there is some speculation that Jane may have been educated alongside the prince (at least temporarily), more evidence points to Jane having been educated primarily at her family home of Bradgate Park.[23] In fact, it is possible that she did not even formally meet Edward until after he became king, when he paid her family a visit in 1549.[24] Unlike the relationship Edward shared with his half-sisters, there are no personal letters from which we can glean any knowledge of his personal feelings towards Jane, but we know that the two were very similar in a number of ways. Just as Edward had proven in his educational years, Jane was an apt and eager student – excelling in reading and writing several languages.[25] They were apparently quite similar in intellect, though the martyrologist John Foxe would later indicate that she may have had the upper hand – particularly as it related to languages. In addition, she learned The Lord's Prayer in English, and was raised in an evangelical, pro-Reformation household, encouraged by the religious views of her parents (particularly those of her father).[26] Jane, like Edward, would grow to hold those Protestant beliefs with the utmost zeal – consequently making her his perfect successor later on.

Lady Jane Grey was actually considered at one time to be a potential bride for Prince Edward – the idea having been suggested by the prince's uncle, Sir Thomas Seymour, Lord Admiral, sometime early in 1547. Carrying this message to Jane's father, Henry, was a man named John Harington, who was employed by the Lord Admiral.[27] As Jane's mother was King Henry VIII's niece (her parents had been the king's sister, Princess Mary, and Charles Brandon, Duke of Suffolk), Jane and her sisters already held their own places in the line of succession, but this tantalising offer for Jane to become the guaranteed Queen Consort of Prince Edward must surely have brought about excitement in her parents, Lord Henry and Lady Frances Grey, if not a healthy dose of scepticism. After all, the marriage negotiations between Prince Edward and the infant Mary, Queen of Scots – as well as the resulting 'Rough Wooing' – had been going on since 1543. As of at least 1546, it was not yet clear which direction those negotiations would take, though it seemed unlikely that Mary of Guise would agree to the proposed match with the English heir, as she appeared determined to ally Scotland with France.[28] Still, sceptical as they may have been, Lord Henry and Lady Frances did indeed send the ten-year-old Jane to the Lord Admiral's home of Seymour Place, placing her under his wardship in February 1547 – where she remained off and on for the next few years.[29] While there, Jane's education was heavily influenced by the Lord Admiral's new wife and Prince Edward's stepmother – Katherine Parr – following the death of Henry VIII. The curriculum followed by Jane, the encouragement and support she received from Katherine, and the reformist theology she absorbed, all very closely resembled the prince's.[30]

While Jane's parents may have been cautiously hopeful that a match between their daughter and the young heir would indeed come to pass – especially with Jane residing in the household of Prince Edward's uncle and stepmother – the 'Rough Wooing' of Mary, Queen of Scots, continued until June 1548. Though the Earl of Hertford, Edward's other uncle, had led a series of attacks throughout Scotland since 1544 – setting fire to houses, abbeys, and destroying entire towns – a brief eighteen-month period of peace was established between England and Scotland in 1546, following the signing of the Treaty of Camp.[31] This may have given the ageing King Henry VIII some reason to hope that his efforts to unite Scotland and England under one crown through the marriage of Edward and Mary might truly come to pass. Little could anyone have known at the time that Henry himself was only months from death, and that peace with Scotland would come to an abrupt end shortly following his son's accession, with the decisive English victory at the Battle of Pinkie Cleugh in 1547, followed by the betrothal of Mary, Queen of Scots to the Dauphin of France in August 1548.

By the time it became evident that Henry VIII's health was failing (and for a period afterwards), both of Edward's Seymour uncles were fighting for two different potential royal brides. While Hertford laid siege to Scotland and pursued the king's hoped-for treaty and the Scottish Queen's hand for his son, the Lord Admiral sweet-talked Henry and Frances Grey into handing over their daughter, Jane, so that he might arrange her royal nuptials with his nephew. Meanwhile, the nine-year-old Prince Edward – likely blissfully unaware of much of the scheming and concocting of plans surrounding his future marriage – continued to spend his time devoted to his studies, 'reading, playing, or dancing' with his companions, and visiting (or at least corresponding frequently) with his half-sisters and stepmother.[32] For a young boy who spent his childhood unlike most boys his age, family appears to have been quite important to Edward, and the relationships he shared with specific family members from these young, formative years certainly made lasting impressions.

As a child he shared warm relationships with both his sisters – viewing Mary, for a time, as a maternal figure, and Elizabeth as an affectionate rival and playmate. Though he possibly saw them infrequently as he grew, both sibling relationships clearly made an impact on the young Edward, though the bonds with each of his sisters would change in the years to come – one relationship much more negatively than the other.[33] Though he had never known his mother, he came to view to Katherine Parr as his *Mater Carissima,* who, as he professed, held 'the chieftest place in my heart'.[34] While Katherine certainly filled the role of the loving and encouraging mother figure Edward had never had, she was arguably even more important to him as the link that bound him more closely to his father – the family member who had – and would always have – the greatest influence over Edward's life. As January 1547 approached, however, Edward had no idea just how that precious relationship with his magnificent father – as well as those with all his family members – was about to change.

Chapter 4

The King is Dead

Henry VIII's final few months, as 1546 drew to a close, were miserable for the ailing king, then aged fifty-five. In near-constant pain from an ulcerated leg that had never quite healed, he had also grown increasingly obese and unhealthy over the last decade. Unable to move about as he had previously done, he now depended upon a 'tram' – an early form of wheelchair – to transport him around Whitehall Palace.[1] Two of these trams were counted among his household inventory in 1547, and they were described as chairs 'for the king's majesty to sit in to be carried to and fro in his galleries and chambers … covered with tawny velvet all over [and] quilted with a cordaunte of tawny silk'.[2] He could not move up or down the stairs 'unless he was raised up or let down by an engine' (probably a pulley of some sort), and his eyesight suffered to the point of needing spectacles, which were called 'gazings' at the time.[3] Everything now exhausted him – including the act of being bathed, and his wardrobe accounts indicate that in the last months of his life, the king's preference was for warm, comfortable garments – rather than the sumptuous items of clothing he had long chosen for public displays of his glamour.[4] Henry's body was failing him, and it has recently been suggested that he may have been suffering from Type 2 diabetes – which might explain a number of symptoms in his later life, including his gluttonous appetite, unquenchable thirst, and the stubborn ulcer that had refused to heal since his jousting injury of 1536.[5]

As he physically withered, he also became increasingly tempestuous and severe with those around him, lashing out even at his queen. But when conservatives Stephen Gardiner and Thomas Wriothesley failed in their attempt to turn the king fully against his wife – whom they considered to be a radical and dangerous Protestant – Henry angrily banished them both from his presence, bellowing the words 'arrant knave, beast and fool'.⁶ He may have felt somewhat insecure in his final months as he was unable to take a large part in the business of his government – and indeed, his wardrobe accounts of 1546 reveal a newfound desire to wear shades of purple (the colour of royalty) – which might support the notion that he felt, in his weakening position, the need to reassert his kingship.⁷ As a result of Henry spending more and more of his time secluded in his chambers, the factions of court grew in intensity. They knew they were near the end of Henry VIII's reign, and that a child king would soon be succeeding him, in need of grown men to take the helm of government. A number of powerful conservatives and evangelicals were part of Henry's inner circle, and both factions wanted to take the young Edward under their guidance when the time came.

Knowing by the end of the year that he was nearing death, Henry revised his will on 26 December 1546, altering certain names from a list of regency councillors that he needed to establish before his nine-year-old son took the throne. A notable name which he struck off the list at this time was that of Stephen Gardiner.⁸ Many historians have pointed to Gardiner's loss of royal favour as one of several examples that the evangelicals were plotting to take over the government and manipulate Henry in his final months. The same argument has been made for the downfalls of Thomas Howard, Duke of Norfolk, and his son, the Earl of Surrey – both of whom had been arrested for treason by the time the king revised his will. The belief that the reformist camp of Henry's coterie – including figures like Sir William Paget, the Earl of Hertford, and Viscount Lisle – had plotted against the conservatives and determined to take them down, was exacerbated by Imperial Ambassador Francois Van der Delft, who claimed in December that, 'Nothing is now done at court without their [Hertford's and Lisle's] intervention, and the meetings of the Council are mostly held in the Earl of Hertford's house.'⁹

Yet, historian Dr Suzannah Lipscomb has poked holes in this claim by Van der Delft – pointing out that between 8 December 1546 and 2 January 1547, the councillors did not, in fact, meet at Hertford's residence, but instead at Ely Place – the town house of conservative Thomas Wriothesley.¹⁰ Fact-checking in this way is crucial when considering this critical point in Tudor history, as it has been much debated by historians over the centuries. While it is known that the two religious factions at court were battling for power of the government as the old king's health faded, we should not be too quick to assume that, because of this, the reformist camp took great immoral leaps to ensure its success. Specifically, the theory that Henry VIII's last will and testament was doctored by certain evangelical power-players, such as the three men mentioned above, requires closer inspection.

Henry's reasoning for editing his will in December – which had first been drafted sometime in 1544 – was to ensure that he was appointing the right men for the job of running his young son's government – revising names 'he meant to have in and some he meant to have out'.[11] As already mentioned, he had struck Gardiner from the list, as well as a man named Thomas Thirlby, Bishop of Westminster, who had apparently been 'schooled' by Gardiner and thus found himself at odds with Henry VIII. The resulting list of names after the 26 December revision does look remarkably Protestant in nature – but it would be a stretch to make the assertion that it included only men well-liked by reformist leaders like Hertford and Paget. The names of the men who Henry appointed as executors of his will and Edward VI's councillors are listed below (with asterisks (*) to denote the few known conservatives):

> Thomas Cranmer – Archbishop of Canterbury
> * Thomas Wriothesley – Lord Chancellor of England
> William Paulet, Lord St John – Great Master of the King's Household and Lord President of the Privy Council
> John, Lord Russell – Lord Privy Seal
> Edward Seymour, Earl of Hertford – Great Chamberlain of England
> John Dudley, Viscount Lisle – High Admiral of England
> * Cuthbert Tunstall – Bishop of Durham
> * Sir Anthony Browne – Master of the King's Horse
> Sir William Paget – Chief Secretary
> Dr Nicholas Wotton – Dean of Canterbury and York
> Sir Anthony Denny – Gentleman of the King's Privy Chamber
> Sir William Herbert – Gentleman of the King's Privy Chamber

Sir Edward North – Chancellor of the Court of Augmentations
Sir Edward Montagu – Lord Chief Justice of the Commons Pleas
Sir Thomas Bromley – Justice of the King's Bench
Sir Edward Wotton – Treasurer at Calais[12]

In addition to these sixteen, the king named twelve men as assistant executors and advisors to the regency council 'when they or any of them shall be called'.[13] These names included:

Sir Richard Rich
Henry FitzAlan, Earl of Arundel – Lord Chamberlain of the Household
Sir Thomas Cheney – Treasurer of the Household
William Parr, Earl of Essex
Sir William Petre
Sir Thomas Seymour
Sir Richard Southwell[14]

The Act of Succession of 1536 stated that in the case of the king's death and his heir's minority, the young king's mother should govern along with 'such other your councillors and nobles of your realm as Your Highness shall limit and appoint by your last will made in writing signed with your most gracious hand.'[15] Henry saw to the second part of that declaration, but his soon-to-be-widowed queen, Katherine Parr, was evidently not to be made regent upon his death. Some historians have questioned whether this might have been down to the foul play of the reformist faction, who took control of the king's will and ousted Katherine from her rightful position of power. However, it is more likely that this was due to her not being Prince Edward's natural mother – thus, the clause did not have the same legal technicality it would have had if Jane Seymour had still been alive. In such a case, we may have seen a very different hierarchy of authority, as dictated by the king.

Admittedly, it is difficult to know where several of the councillors' religious sympathies lay, as it was all too common throughout the shifting religious climate of the Tudor period for courtiers and politicians swiftly to change their allegiances and adapt their moral compasses accordingly. Sir William Petre is one such example – he appears to have been of a reformist mindset at the time of Henry VIII's death, but a proud Catholic in his later years (as well as a staunch and well-loved supporter of Mary I). Other ambiguous examples from these lists include Sir Edward North, Sir Richard Southwell, Sir Richard Rich, and Sir Thomas Cheney – all of whom later served on Mary I's privy council, though Rich's appearances were rare, and Cheney was at times mistrusted by Mary as a fickle courtier.[16] Henry FitzAlan would proclaim Mary as queen in 1553 over Edward's chosen Lady Jane Grey, soon after being appointed Lord Steward of the royal household. He was a passionate Roman Catholic – even going so far as to advocate for Mary, Queen of Scots and the deposition of Queen Elizabeth several years later.[17]

It is not only the Protestant leanings of the majority of these executors, councillors, and assistants that has caused historians to question the validity of Henry's will. Several have noted the eyebrow-raising 'unfulfilled gifts' clause, which states that any gifts, grants, or promises made by Henry VIII and unfulfilled prior to his death, should be fulfilled thereafter. The exact words (transcribed with modernized spelling) are as follows:

> Furthermore, we will that all such grants and gifts as we have made, given, and promised to any, which be not yet perfected under our sign or any [of] our seals as they ought to be... and be not yet accomplished, shall be perfected in every point towards all manner of men for discharge of our conscience, charging our executors and all the rest of our councillors to see the same done, performed and accomplished in every point.[18]

This was, in effect, a blank cheque left by Henry for any nobleman who might claim an unfulfilled promise from the king. Although Henry could be known for bouts of extreme generosity extended to those who enjoyed his favour, this invitation for his executors, essentially, to reward themselves for whatever they pleased, seems rather out of character. Thus, this clause has been the source of much debate. Some have even claimed that Henry had no knowledge of the clause at all, and that Hertford (perhaps with the support of Paget, Lisle, and Denny) added it during – or even after – Henry's final moments.[19] Yet, the layout of the will and its twenty-eight folios makes it unlikely that this particular portion of folio eighteen would have been added at a later date. As Dr Lipscomb argues in her analysis of Henry VIII's will, the lines of its contents 'are spaced out on the page with the great precision and care of an expert calligrapher… there are no squeezed characters or cramped lines.'[20] Where edits have been made and words struck-through, the changes are obvious, as well are the gaps left for later additions, 'in the case of forgotten names' and the document 'flows from one folio to the next without breaks.'[21] Given these facts, we are left wondering if Henry VIII – suddenly confronted with his impending mortality – chose to offer a much more generous gift to the men closest to him at the time of his death, than most would consider representative of his character. Though certainly cause for dispute, it appears most likely that these were his own words.

Another head-scratching detail of the will is the much-debated method of its signing – namely, that of dry stamping, rather than pen-signing by Henry's own hand. Much has been made over the centuries of this method, and the questionable validity that this could potentially reveal. This stamp, carved with the impression of Henry VIII's signature, could have been dipped into ink and pressed to the parchment of this document of utmost political significance at any point, from the time the king took to his deathbed to the announcement of his death to Parliament on 31 January. In the latter half of the sixteenth century Sir William Maitland, Lord of Lethington and secretary of state for Mary, Queen of Scots was one of the first recorded individuals to question the date of the will's stamping, calling into question its legitimacy. Many historians since have wondered the same.[22] A later stamping date would certainly reinforce the conspiracy theory of Hertford's addition of the 'unfulfilled gifts' clause, but such a thought ignores crucial details about the nature and use of the dry stamp.

In fact, this stamp had been used for the signing of many official government documents since at least 1545, when the king's deputy groom of the stool, Anthony Denny, was given the authority to use it on necessary papers.[23] Certainly, as Henry's health declined, he signed fewer and fewer of these important documents by his own hand – and so, while his dry stamp had already been in frequent use for some years, it was even more so in those final months. While Chris Skidmore believes that the evidence for forgery is compelling, pointing out the fact that the will's signing by dry stamp is listed at a later date than the official witnessing and signing of 30 December – in fact, 27 January, both Dr Lipscomb and Eric Ives have reasoned that this fact actually proves its legitimacy.[24] The argument that the dry stamp's use is proof of forgery by power-hungry noblemen is a 'mischievous and fallacious claim' according to Lipscomb, and 'undermines the legality of all the documents produced in the last eighteen months of Henry VIII's reign'. Though the nature of the dry stamp does allow for misuse, evidence and understanding of its purpose during the final years of Henry's reign paint an unlikely picture for blatant falsification to have occurred. Once again, there appears to be plenty of reason to believe that Henry's will was written and authorized by him, in the presence of his chosen witnesses, and that the nature of its contents was exactly as he had intended.

The most integral element of Henry VIII's last will and testament was the formation of the regency council for his son, and by 1547 England had every reason to believe that such a council was essential in the event of a boy king's succession – both for the sake of the boy and for England. After all, 'Woe to thee, O land, when thy king is a child,' declared Ecclesiastes 10:16, and the country's history had proved thus far to echo the sentiment. It was well-known by now that the reign of a child king was unstable – 'an invitation to civil war, an incitement to noble tussles over position and precedence, and an opportunity for the unprincipled to seize power'.[25] Edward would become the sixth child king of England since the year 1216, and the lives of his predecessors told ugly stories of over-ambitious, manipulative courtiers, political unrest regarding the country's security, and, at times, the very death of the young monarch himself.

Henry III, crowned at nine years old upon his father's untimely death in 1216, was appointed a regent to guide him through the remaining precarious years of his minority – and his crown was threatened by a rival prince of France.[26] The fourteen-year-old Edward III was crowned only in 1326 at the deposition of his father, and was controlled entirely by his mother, Queen Isabella, and Roger Mortimer for the first couple of years – much to the division and unrest in the country.[27] Richard II, crowned in 1377 at ten years of age, was technically able to be considered an adult, though his minority reign lasted until he turned twenty-one. Nevertheless, he proved himself 'not yet mature enough to govern with the wisdom and good judgment expected of an adult'.[28] This immaturity posed a risk to England, in the eyes of his opponents – leaving him and his country open to multiple threats and the pushing of various other political agendas, due to the 'apparent deficiencies in Richard's rule caused by his youth'.[29] At about nine months old in 1422, Henry VI was the youngest king by a wide margin to take England's throne, and his minority saw struggles for ultimate power among the men closest to him.[30] Finally – the saddest of all stories told of kings in their minority – Edward V was twelve when he succeeded his father in 1483, only to be deposed by his uncle Richard III a mere ten weeks later.[31] As his body (as well as that of his little brother, Richard) was never found, it was deemed likely that he had been murdered in the process of his uncle's usurpation. This last example, in particular, was 'the most terrible warning against political ambition' to date, while Edward VI waited in the wings of kinghood.[32]

With this as the most recent example of the fate that might befall a child king, Henry VIII was right to be meticulous in setting up a council of men he trusted to guide his son. After all, the entire goal was to ensure that Edward was taught the ways of ruling while his government was steadily maintained by well-meaning and loyal advisors – until he reached the age of majority when he would rule on his own.[33] Clearly, of the utmost importance to Henry was the assurance that young Edward would not be 'ruled' by one man alone – as poor unfortunate Edward V had been ruled by his usurping uncle. Handing ultimate power to a single 'Protector' was dangerous, and history told Henry that it could come at a damning cost. Indeed, this attitude had prevailed by the time Machiavelli published *The Prince* in 1532, in which he specifically warned against depending on one single councillor who might harbour ambition and greed.[34] Therefore, the conciliar option for Edward's government was the safest solution by mid-sixteenth-century standards. This model shared influence and authority among the sixteen men whom Henry valued and respected the most. He certainly wouldn't have believed at the time of his death that he had any reason to question their loyalty to the young Tudor heir. By his will and the appointment of these vital men, he surely believed that he was solidifying a stable minority rule for his son; upon reaching his majority, he would be fully able to reign in his own right and ensure the longevity of the Tudor dynasty for generations to come. Nothing had ever been more important to Henry VIII.

King Henry was struck with fever on 1 January, and after weeks of being kept away from Whitehall, finally Queen Katherine was admitted to his bedside. There is no record of Prince Edward or Elizabeth paying a final visit to their ailing father, but the much older Mary at least attempted access to him, alongside her stepmother. The king received Holy Communion on 27 January, and Sir Anthony Denny was evidently the only courtier brave enough to utter the words Henry most feared, when he told the king that 'in man's judgement, he was not like to live'.[35] His purpose was to urge the king to make his final confession, and he reportedly asked who should hear it. Henry replied, 'It should be Dr Cranmer, but I will first take a little sleep, and then as I feel myself, I will advise upon the matter.'[36] These are Henry VIII's last recorded words, and when Cranmer arrived shortly after midnight on 28 January, the king was already beyond the ability to speak – instead squeezing the archbishop's hand when asked if he would die in the faith of Jesus Christ.[37] He died around two o'clock in the morning.

Though the larger-than-life Tudor king had breathed his last, life carried on as normal in the days following. Food was carried to Henry's chambers as it always had been, accompanied by trumpeting fanfare and ushered inside the quickly closing doors. Parliament remained in session, when it was customarily dissolved immediately following the death of the monarch.[38] These things were done in order to conceal the king's death from the rest of the court, and this was not necessarily unprecedented. Henry's own father's death had been concealed for a full two days, with court life proceeding as usual, and the highest-ranking courtiers acting as if nothing at all was amiss.[39] This practice was meant to buy the government time to secure a smooth succession for the heir, and to avoid affording any enemies time to mount an attack on the empty throne. As true as this might be, these crucial days following Henry VIII's death also served as ample time for Hertford to wrest for himself as much power as he could, with the assistance of Paget. A substantial piece of evidence to support this is a letter from Paget to Hertford, dated July 1549. In this letter, Paget urges Hertford (by then the Duke of Somerset) to remember promises made to him two years prior. The reason for his writing related to a rebellion in the West Country that threatened to undo Edward VI's reign and Somerset's career, and though the context in 1549 had nothing to do with Henry VIII's death, Paget's words regarding 1547 certainly paint a picture of two men who may very well have plotted and planned for the future together:

> Remember what you promised me in the gallery at Westminster, before the breath was out of the body of the King, that dead is. Remember what you promised immediately after, devising with me concerning the place which you now occupy, I trust, in the end to good purpose, however things thwart now. And that was, to follow mine advice in all your proceedings, more than any other man's.[40]

That 'place you now occupy' that Paget referenced in 1549, was none other than the title Lord Protector of England (the very position that Henry VIII had fought to prevent anyone from claiming, by appointing the sixteen-man regency council). Hertford would indeed gain the position on 4 February – a mere week after the king's death. It appears likely, with this letter serving as evidence, that Hertford's manoeuvre into the protectorship came with the agreement that he would be advised and assisted by Paget, his right-hand man.[41] This partnership would not have come as much of a surprise to anyone at court, as proven by the Imperial ambassador, Eustace Chapuys, who ironically speculated on 29 January that if the king were to die, 'It is probable that these two men will have the management of affairs, because, apart from the king's affection for them, and other reasons, there are no other nobles of a fit age and ability for the task.'[42] If this is true, then it is little wonder why things proceeded as they did. Within just a few days, Hertford (with Paget's help) would have the other fourteen members of the young king's council convinced that he was fit to lead them – and in so doing, he would breach one of the most critical elements of the late king's will.

While this ambitious political manoeuvre was taking place, where was Edward? The young prince was situated in Hertfordshire, and while he probably knew of his father's failing health, he had not been summoned to court to be at his side. He was clearly caught by surprise when his uncle, Hertford, along with Sir Anthony Browne, came urgently to collect him on 28 January. They hastened him to Enfield, where he was met by his sister, Elizabeth, and there told the devastating news of their father's death. It was said that Edward and Elizabeth, both so overcome by grief at the unexpected loss of the king, gripped each other and wept together 'for several hours'.[43]

Hertford had not ceased his power-grab even as he informed his new young monarch of his role. In departing London, he had conveniently taken the key to the box containing Henry VIII's will – causing Paget to write anxiously to him, asking if it should be opened. In answer, Hertford suggested that, 'For divers respects, I think it not convenient to satisfy the world [about the contents of the will] … In the meantime, we should meet and agree so there may be no controversy hereafter.'[44] He also wasted no time in getting his travel companion and fellow council member, Sir Anthony Browne, on his side in his efforts to secure the title of Lord Protector. Another letter from two years later, written by a William Wightman, Browne's former servant, stated the following:

> communing with my Lord's Grace [Browne] in the garden at Enfield, at the King's Majesty's coming from Hertford, gave his frank consent [in] communication in discourse of the State, that his Grace [Hertford] should be Protector, thinking it (as indeed it was) both the surest kind of government and most fit for that Commonwealth.[45]

Thus, by the time Hertford, Browne, and the new King Edward VI returned to London on 30 January, he was already gaining the authority he coveted – unbeknownst to the young king, who had no idea of the wording of his late father's will or his determination to forge a council that would share equal power among its members. In fact, Edward most likely felt comforted by his uncle's presence in this vulnerable and unsure time. New king or not, he was, after all, a nine-year-old boy who had just lost his father. As he now travelled to London and prepared to settle into the role he had been born to inherit, it is probably safe to assume that he already looked to his one close blood relation for reassurance and guidance. It should come as little surprise then, just how swiftly Hertford's dominance asserted itself upon arriving back at court. The events of Henry VIII's death and Edward VI's accession would soon prove nearly as impactful for the ambitious earl as they would for the new boy king himself.

Chapter 5

King Edward VI and the Rise of Somerset

It was not until 31 January that the news of Henry VIII's death was announced to the House of Commons, via a tearful speech by Wriothesley. According to Edward's *Chronicle,* '[there] was great lamentation and weeping' among members of Parliament, and that same day '[Edward] was proclaimed king.'[1] By design and agreement of the regency council, only the details of the succession were publicly shared. Certain other clauses of Henry's will – such as the much-debated 'unfulfilled gifts' clause – were kept quiet. That same day, the executors of the will met to discuss the most esteemed man among them – Hertford, whom they unanimously agreed to 'be preferred in name and place before others, to whom as to the state and head of the rest all strangers and others might have access.' Due to his 'proximity of blood... being [the king's] uncle', it simply made the most sense to the sixteen men of the council that Hertford should take the helm of leadership. Though it betrayed the late king's intentions, Hertford was determined to have 'first and chief place among us, and also the name and title of the Protector'.[2] They likely determined that this was an acceptable decision to make, because Henry's will had also stipulated that the council could do virtually anything it wanted, so long as it benefited his son's rule and realm, and they agreed on it through a written majority vote. The decision was made official on 4 February.

Edward went on to write that, the day following the announcement of his father's death, 'he was brought to the Tower of London, where he tarried the space of three weeks'.[3] Though his description is brief and nondescript, in reality he was greeted by cheering crowds and gun salutes, and his entire regency council awaited there to pay him homage as their new sovereign. When he was escorted to his lodgings, the walls were hung with cloth of gold and elaborate decoration. One of his first acts as king was to sign the commission authorizing his uncle's appointment as Lord Protector of the Realm, which he did that very same day.[4] In addition to this, he wrote to his beloved stepmother, who had recently sent him a miniature portrait of herself and Henry VIII as a New Year's gift. While Edward had already written to thank her for this gift that he professed 'delighteth me much', he now wrote with a very different purpose.[5]

> It hath seemed good to God that my father and your husband, our most illustrious sovereign, should end this life, it is a common grief to both. This, however, consoles us, that he is now in heaven, and that he hath gone out of this miserable world into happy and everlasting blessedness. For whoever here leads a virtuous life, and governs the state aright, as my noble father has done, who ever promoted piety and banished all ignorance, hath a most certain journey into heaven. Although nature prompts us to grieve and shed tears for the departure of him now gone from our eyes, yet Scripture and wisdom prompt us to moderate those feelings.[6]

It can be easy to forget, when reading these words, that they came from a nine-year-old boy. Though one can easily imagine that he felt a great sadness at the loss of his father (evidenced by the hours of weeping that he had shared with Elizabeth just days earlier), it is clear by his words of consolation that he took great comfort in scripture when dealing with these emotions, and that he viewed the late king's death pragmatically. He wrote similarly to his sister, Mary:

> We ought not to mourn our father's death, since it is his will, who works all things for good ... So far as lies in me, I will be to you a dearest brother, and overflowing with all kindness.[7]

Of the two, it was likely Katherine Parr who required more consoling. As well as mourning her late husband, she was a 'deeply frustrated woman' – finding that, far from being named Regent upon Henry VIII's death, her name had been omitted from the regency council altogether.[8] The late king had referred to her in his will as his 'entirely beloved wife', though he left her only £3,000 'in plate, jewels and stuff, beside what she shall please to take of what she has already, and further receive in money £1,000 besides the enjoyment of her jointure'.[9] While this inheritance would ensure that she lived a comfortable life, and would 'always be served and waited on as befitted a queen', it was not quite the generous offering she had expected.[10] Fully anticipating the elevated title that should follow her husband's death, there is evidence of two documents from 1547 being signed 'Kateryn the Quene Regente KP' – possibly from soon after the king's death, before she was informed of the regency council members and her exclusion from it.[11] No doubt she was now left wondering what her future would hold, what influence she might have (if any), and how a relationship with her stepson, the new king, might look.

The first task at hand was to plan and execute the late king's funeral. Now that the death had been made public, council members and noblemen had the opportunity to look upon the royal corpse before it was embalmed. Through that process, it was noted by a surgeon that Henry's arteries were so clogged that 'there was hardly half a pint of pure blood in his whole body'.[12] A coffin was then built around Henry's body where it lay on his bed. He was, apparently, far too massive and heavy to be moved.[13] For five days, his coffin lay in state in the Privy Chamber at Whitehall, draped in gold and surrounded by candles. It was attended continuously by various gentlemen of the chamber. It was a sombre scene, with the walls draped in black cloth. In the palace chapel, a requiem mass was said and continual masses were held for the king's soul.[14]

On 16 February, the coffin was solemnly taken from Westminster to Windsor, along with 'more than 1,000 horsemen and hundreds of mourners on foot'.[15] Seven horses pulled a gilded chariot, holding the dead king's coffin and elaborate funeral effigy – in which the king's likeness 'looked exactly like that of the king himself ... just as if he were alive,' according to an onlooker.[16] The funeral ceremony was officiated by Bishop Gardiner and the bishops of Ely and

London, and the widowed Katherine Parr watched from above in the chapel gallery. As was customary, none of Henry's children were in attendance.[17] As Henry had intended, his body was interred beside that of his favourite queen – Edward's mother, Jane Seymour – within the vault in the chapel quire. It reportedly 'took sixteen yeomen of the guard using five linen towels to lower the coffin into the vault'.[18] Next, as Edward recorded, 'the officers broke their staves, hurling them into the grave', as was custom.[19] This humble resting place – covered only by a simply-inscribed black slab on the floor – was, of course, meant only to be a temporary arrangement. In typical fashion, Henry VIII had planned a grand and sumptuous tomb and monument to be erected after his death, but none of his children would bring those plans to fruition.

The day following the funeral, the most important men of the court – namely, the king's councillors – met with Hertford in London. Edward recorded in his chronicle that, 'at length [they] thought it best that the Earl of Hertford should be made Duke of Somerset'.[20] Not only was Seymour now Lord Protector and the highest-ranking man at court, save for the king – he was now raised from the earldom of Hertford to the dukedom of Somerset. Along with this came a new income of £7,400 per annum.[21] This was, again, evidently agreed upon by a majority of council members. In addition, his brother, Thomas Seymour, was named Lord High Admiral and Baron Seymour of Sudeley, as well as a Knight of the Garter. A number of other knights also benefitted, according to Edward – including John Dudley being made Earl of Warwick and Great Chamberlain of England, and Wriothesley being named Earl of Northampton.[22] Here we see clearly the council taking full advantage of Henry's 'unfulfilled gifts.' It is likely that these titles and lands were gifted by the Lord Protector himself, as rewards for the support of various council members.

However, despite the majority of the council favouring Somerset's rise to power, all was not entirely peaceful among the twenty-three men in charge. Though Thomas Seymour had also enjoyed favours and new titles, he was already resentful of his older brother's place at the centre of government. He was frustrated that he himself had not been named one of the core sixteen council members, but merely an advisor. Dudley, (now

Warwick), also harboured bitterness towards Somerset, and reservations about his new role of Protector. So early into the boy king's reign, it was already evident that tensions would rise in the months to come, and that a power-struggle among the former king's prized men would soon come to a head.

For now, with the old king buried, it was time to set plans in motion for young Edward's coronation. It was a swift turnaround, with the procession from the Tower to Westminster on 19 February. Edward was on full display for his people to see as he travelled the streets on horseback, dressed in vivid white with a gold cape – his clothes embellished with lavish jewels. Even his horse was covered in crimson satin and pearls.[23] Not to be (too) outdone by the new king, Somerset ensured that he too was decked out in the finest attire he could get his hands on. In the days leading up to the coronation, he had arranged for several furs, gowns, and robes of the late king's to be transferred to his own wardrobe, so that he might look his best.[24]

Ahead of Edward on horseback was a lengthy train led by messengers, gentlemen, foreign ambassadors' servants, and trumpeters – all of whom were 'clothed in redde damaske'. Following them were chaplains, esquires of the body, knights, and then the sons of certain lower-ranking nobles. Next came the barons, the bishops, sons of earls, marquesses, and dukes. The comptroller of the household followed next, alongside the Venetian ambassador, and flanked by treasurers, almoners, the lord privy seal, the lord great master of the household, and various other ambassadors. Then came the Archbishop of Canterbury, the knight harbinger (who carried the king's cloak and hat), two gentlemen ushers, the garter king of arms, the mayor of London, and the sergeants at arms. Finally, and just ahead of Edward, were the most powerful nobles in the land – the Marquess of Dorset, Viscount Lisle, and the Earl of Arundel. Riding only slightly ahead of the new king was Somerset, whom, it was noted by Imperial Ambassador Van der Delft, 'kept always nearest to the person of the king'.[25] Behind Edward, the enormous retinue continued with Sir Anthony Browne, nine henchmen, and their master, Sir Francis Bryan. They were followed by gentlemen and grooms of the privy chamber, guards, and servants of various noblemen, walking in order of the ranks of their masters.[26]

The ceremonial route to Westminster contained a number of celebratory and allegorical pageants and entertainments. One of these, which particularly appealed to Edward, was an Aragonese tight-rope walker at St Paul's Churchyard, who made the king pause and 'laugh right heartily'.[27] Despite delights such as these, the pageants organized by the city were reportedly disorganized and not well-rehearsed. Many of them, however, were taken directly from the coronation celebrations of Henry VI – the last (fairly successful, for a time) boy king – thus holding a special meaning for this momentous day.[28]

One of the most fantastic pageants along the route was a scene depicting heaven, from which a phoenix descended. A crowned lion emerged from the far side of the stage, meeting the phoenix at the centre, 'making a semblance of amity' – after which, a young lion cub emerged from behind them. Following this, two angels flew down from heaven and placed a crown on the cub's head, with the lion and phoenix disappearing off-stage. This allegory must have touched Edward – as it clearly depicted his birth to Jane Seymour (whose royal emblem was the phoenix) and the late Henry VIII. This pageant impressed upon all observers the divinely ordained birth of the rightful Tudor heir, and the lawful and holy union of his parents.[29]

The procession snaked its way through winding streets and it was, according to a surviving eighteenth-century drawing, so enticing to watch, that people stood on rooftops to catch a glimpse of the king. Tapestries and banners to celebrate the occasion were hung from houses along the route, and clerks, craftsmen, and priests stood outside 'with their crosses ... and in their best ornaments'.[30] Along the way, masses of cheering crowds hailed Edward as a 'young King Solomon' – a reference to the tenth-century King of Israel, who built the first temple of Jerusalem.[31] This reinforced the clear hope – and indeed, expectation – of the people that Edward would continue the Protestant Reformation that his father had begun thirteen years prior. After nearly five hours, the procession finally reached its end at Westminster Palace, where Edward would spend the night before his coronation. He was apparently so exhausted from the ride that ambassadors were ushered passed him and asked to speak 'as few words as possible' to him as they departed Westminster.[32]

The next morning noblemen arrived at Westminster by seven o'clock 'in their best array', as instructed the previous evening.³³ Edward concisely summed up the day's following events in his *Chronicle*, describing that he:

> came into Westminster Hall, and it was asked [of] the people (whether they would have him to be their) King, who answered, "Yea, yea." Then he was crowned King of England, France, and Ireland by the Archbishop of Canterbury and all the rest of the clergy and nobles, and anointed with all such ceremonies as were accustomed, and took his oath, and gave a general pardon, and so was brought to the hall to dinner.³⁴

A more detailed account of the day begins with Edward's nine o'clock journey by river from Westminster to the court of augmentations inside Whitehall Palace, where he was dressed in 'a gown of cloth of silver embroidered with rubies and diamonds, girdled with white velvet and Venetian silk, on top of which was a white velvet cloak threaded with Venetian silver'.³⁵ Yet another procession (this time entirely on foot) assembled there in ceremonial clothes and caps of state. Somerset carried the king's crown, Suffolk bore the orb, and Dorset held the sceptre. Lisle – assisted by the Marquess of Northampton and Thomas Seymour – stood behind the king and carried his heavy train.³⁶ The lengthy procession – similar in structure to the previous day's order – made its way from Whitehall to Westminster Abbey, with Edward walking serenely beneath a canopy. They arrived to find the abbey decked out in its ceremonial finest, with fresh rushes covering the floors and cloths of arras hanging from the choir.³⁷ A platform at the end of the aisle near the altar had been erected to hold the white throne – St Edward's chair – covered in damask and gold. Thoughtfully, two cushions had been placed upon the wooden seat, to compensate for the short stature of the nine-year-old king.

The *Liber Regalis*, a fourteenth-century manuscript that dictated the order of a coronation, was mostly followed on this occasion. However, given the 'tedious length' of the ceremony, the Privy Council had decided to abbreviate certain parts, out of fear that it might 'weary and be hurtsome peradventure to the King's Majesty being yet of tender age fully to endure and bid out'.[38] In total, the usually-twelve-hour-long coronation lasted around seven hours, and allowed Edward a few moments of rest.[39]

Archbishop Cranmer led the coronation, reading the address as the king was presented to the congregation. As was expected, the audience shouted, 'God save King Edward!' before the coronation oath was administered. Cranmer had altered certain texts of the oath, which he explained next in a sermon prior to the anointing. With a nod to the Reformation that was well underway in England, he asserted that the oaths taken by the new king were not 'to be taken in the bishop of Rome's sense'. This was, of course, the first such coronation of an English king – as the country's ties with Rome had been severed for over a decade. The archbishop next made a striking comparison to yet another biblical figure (following the references to King Solomon from the previous day), when he cited the Old Testament in his sermon, directed to Edward:

> Your majesty is God's vice-gerent and Christ's vicar within your own dominions, and to see, with your predecessor Josiah, God truly worshipped, and idolatry destroyed, the tyranny of the bishops of Rome banished from your subjects, and images removed. These acts be signs of a second Josiah, who reformed the church of God in his days ... For example, it is written of Josiah in the book of Kings thus: "Like unto him there was no king before him that turned to the Lord with all his heart, according to the law of Moses, neither after him arose there any like him." This was to that prince a perpetual fame of dignity, to remain to the end of days.[40]

This was an incredibly anti-Catholic coronation, and the comparison between himself and the biblical Josiah must have been a poignant one for Edward, who had already been fanatical about the Protestant Reformation for years through his studies. He was the first monarch to have been born to inherit the title of Defender of the Faith, established by his father – bearing no allegiance to the 'corrupt' Church of Rome. His rule would be absolute in a way that no other king's before had been, and one can imagine the young Edward's chest swelling a bit as the words were spoken about him. He had large shoes to fill – a total Reformation to finish – and his people were counting on him to abolish any remnants of the old faith. He was England's 'second Josiah'.

Next, Edward was anointed with holy oils, for which he donned a crimson satin shirt and ermine coat.[41] He was given three swords to represent his three kingdoms of England, Ireland, and France. Following this, three crowns were placed upon his head – including the crown of King Edward the Confessor, the imperial crown, and a special new crown just for this occasion. A gold ring to represent his commitment to the country was then slid onto his finger. The orb and sceptre, along with St Edward's staff and spurs, were placed into his hands, and he needed assistance in order to bear the load. Finally, a *Te Deum* was sung, and the lords paid homage to their new king – including Somerset, who knelt before him and swore his life and limb to Edward's service – before the vast procession filed out of the abbey.

The Great Hall at Westminster was the site of the dinner that Edward refers to in his *Chronicle*. It had been repainted and decorated for the grand occasion, and a rich cloth of estate covered the king's seat at his high table. This was possibly one of Edward's favourite parts of the entire day, where he was served an elaborate feast and a herald announced his new title to the masses that celebrated him. The festivities of the occasion continued onto Whitehall later in the evening – including more feasting, pageantry, and gaming – and then for another two days beyond that. Thomas Seymour was particularly successful in a number of jousts held in the new king's honour, and for the most part, the festivities impressed all who attended – apart from Van der Delft. He claimed that the entertainments were 'unremarkable', though it is possible that he simply harboured resentment at not having been invited to the coronation.

With the coronation complete and the crown firmly on the new king's head, it was a new age in England – and an uncertain one, at that. What would Edward VI's reign look like, and how would religion be affected after the late Henry VIII's break with Rome? Was a marital alliance with Scotland to be had, or would the country be engulfed in a war with one of the devoutly Catholic European countries, such as France or Spain? And just what kind of king would the young Edward prove to be?

As he was only nine years old, the beginning of his reign was – albeit unintentionally – also the beginning of Somerset's 'reign'. At this point, he was around forty years old, tall, and conventionally attractive for the time.[42] Having risen to prominence in Henry VIII's court upon the rise of his younger sister, Jane Seymour, in 1537, he was the closest blood relation to the new king, and there were likely few people that Edward trusted more. With Somerset's new position as Lord Protector, Edward would have had every reason to believe that his uncle had only his and England's best interests at heart. In truth, the degree to which Somerset could exercise his own agenda and power at the opening of Edward's reign was quite limited. He still relied on the majority's agreement within the regency council for anything that he might wish to do. With Paget still his right-hand man, and Wriothesley very much his conservative nemesis, there was still enough of a balance within the council to keep the Lord Protector in check. Opposition existed even within his own evangelical faction. Van der Delft could already see 'some jealousy or rivalry' between Somerset and Warwick, noting that:

> Although they both belong to the same sect they are nevertheless widely different in characters: [Dudley] being of high courage will not willingly submit to his colleague. He is, moreover, in higher favour both with the people and with the nobles than [Somerset], owing to his liberality and splendour.[43]

In comparison, Somerset was 'not so accomplished in this respect, and is indeed looked down upon by everybody as a dry, sour, opinionated man'.[44]

Though Warwick might have harboured resentment against Somerset – as well as a general difference in character – it was not he who posed the greatest threat to Somerset's power in these early days of Edward VI's rule. It was the conservative Wriothesley, who had supported Somerset's appointment to the Protectorate but nevertheless vehemently disagreed with him on principle and feared his influence growing to unprecedented heights. Somerset was keenly aware of this resistance, and probably had a plan to bring Wriothesley down even before the king's coronation. After all, Wriothesley's position as Lord Chancellor afforded him the honour of holding the Great Seal – which was stamped upon every royal patent and official legal document. How would Somerset rule through Edward if he did not also control the Great Seal – or at least hold significant influence over its keeper?

Two days prior to the coronation, Somerset had commissioned four lawyers to hear cases against Wriothesley, and soon after, the council determined that he should be removed from his post, on charges that he had sold some of his offices to delegates.[45] Wriothesley was charged on 5 March, and his indictment – read by Somerset – included the following accusations:

> he had not only menaced divers of the said learned men ... but also used unfitting words to me, the said Protector, to the prejudice of the King's estate, and the hindrance of his Majesty's affairs. What danger might ensue if the great seal of England, whereby the king and realm might be bound, should continue in the hands of so stout and arrogant a person as durst presume at his will to seal without a warrant.[46]

For what it was worth, though Somerset understandably viewed Wriothesley's downfall as a personal victory, the latter claimed to have accepted the conviction and agreed to step aside so as not to excite 'divisions within the realm'.[47]

Divisions, however, certainly began to grow. Other conservatives on the council – including Gardiner and Arundel – were aggravated by Wriothesley's fall, and the evangelical members could see that they might very well pose a threat to the Lord Protector. Perhaps realizing the obstacles he was likely to face against his rivals, Somerset called a meeting of the Privy Council, and on 12 March, with only seven members in attendance, he gained majority votes that granted him extraordinary new powers. A new commission was formed and granted full authority for the extent of the young king's minority. Somerset was given extended authority to decide matters 'both private and public, as well in outward and foreign causes', to add or remove members of the council at his will, and even act without its approval. This last change, in particular, was such a deviation from the intention of Henry VIII's will that it was almost laughable how completely Somerset had taken matters into his own hands.[48]

What were Edward's own personal views of Somerset's control and authority in his government? The fact that we cannot know his thoughts on such a significant matter has been the cause for much debate and frustration among historians throughout the centuries. Edward makes no mention in his *Chronicle* of the immense power that Somerset held, despite noting his appointment as Lord Protector. He does not share any of his thoughts, and not a single contemporary chronicler notes any such mention from Edward on the subject. It is probably safe to assume, however, that the young – and somewhat naïve – king was being assured that many, if not all, government happenings were better handled by the experienced hands of Somerset and the rest of the regency council. It is not unreasonable to think that his uncle might have insisted that Edward would learn all of this in time, as his education continued, and he grew in maturity and understanding of government business. Very likely there was no cause for concern in the nine-year-old's mind. Why shouldn't he trust that his uncle had the most noble of intentions, and would only help Edward to succeed? Indeed, Edward probably felt relieved to have such an experienced man guiding him and the government and was much happier instead to continue the pursuits of his boyhood – most notably, his studies. He would learn to be king in time, under his uncle's meticulous tutelage.

Before long, however, when Van der Delft reported back to Emperor Charles V of the goings-on at the English court, he barely mentioned King Edward at all. It was Somerset who seized the attention and conducted all the business of government. In one particularly ostentatious move (as early as 10 February, in fact), he ordered that two gilt maces should be carried before him when he walked.[49] In another, through correspondence with the French King Francis I, he brazenly referred to him as 'brother' – a term used only between friendly kings.[50] He even raised his own annual salary to 8,000 marks (the equivalent of £1.6 million in today's money). And if all that were not already enough, Somerset also ensured that only his supporters were allowed the most intimate access to Edward. By appointing his own brother-in-law, Sir Michael Stanhope, as one of the king's Gentleman of the Privy Chamber, Somerset was taking further steps to ensure that those closest to the king were those in his own pockets – keeping him and his power safe from any who might one day attempt to force him out of the spotlight.

Most concerning of all, perhaps, was that within months of Edward's coronation, it was Somerset who signed royal warrants and letters patent on the boy king's behalf. Paget made a clumsy excuse for this when questioned by the French ambassador, claiming that the king was in the process of learning a new signature for himself, as it must change now that he was king. He assured the ambassador that, in future, it would be only the king who signed such documents. But this was difficult to believe when one could easily look around the court of late summer 1547 to find that Edward VI was virtually nowhere in sight. Instead, it was Somerset who stood front and centre – probably just as he had intended.

Chapter 6

England's Josiah

While the Protestant Reformation in England had its origins during Henry VIII's reign, it was Edward's reign that was determined to see these religious changes through to an exceptional degree. His coronation had already disrupted the precedent – having been a decidedly anti-Rome affair and making it absolutely clear that Edward VI, as Defender of the Faith and Supreme Head of the Church of England, owed the pope no allegiance. Because of this, he was powerful in an entirely different way than any other English king before him had been at the time of their own coronations, and Archbishop Cranmer's words had made the expectation of him quite clear. The reference to Josiah of the Old Testament showed just how important it was to the English people (and notably, to the evangelicals who surrounded Edward) to further the Protestant cause and 'build a new temple' as his biblical predecessor had done. The hope was that Edward's regime would make even more powerful and decisive strides than had been made during the reign of Henry VIII – removing all traces of sinful Catholic idolatry, dismantling and dissolving corrupt monasteries, and persecuting any who opposed the new way of religious thinking.

In order to understand this expectation of Edward VI's reign and the desire for further reform in England, it is important first to have a clear view of the state of religion at the time of Edward's crowning. The religious landscape in England following Henry VIII's separation from the Catholic Church had been confusing and difficult for the general populous over the last decade. This was largely due to the fact that Henry's own personal religious convictions had been changing and evolving through the last several years of his life. At first, when he had decreed that England was no longer beholden to the pope, he had simply replaced Rome's authority with his own – while not actually changing any theological interpretations. All that he had truly desired at the outset of the Reformation was full control – thus removing the pope's power over him and his personal decisions (namely, his marital choices).

However, while Henry had claimed the title of 'sole protector and supreme head of the English Church', Bishop Fisher had added the caveat 'as far as the law of Christ allows', after some debate. In 1534, the Dispensations Act ensured that payments would cease to be made to Rome in return for dispensations according to canon law. These now were to be secured from the Archbishop of Canterbury. That same year, the Act of Supremacy declared that the king would take on the role of visiting monasteries under question throughout his realm, in order to 'repress, redress, reform, order, correct, restrain, and amend all such errors, heresies, abuses, offences, contempts, and enormities'.[1]

There were, of course, still a few exceptions to Henry VIII's authority. For instance, he could not consecrate bishops (though he could and did appoint them), and he could not administer the sacraments. His control over the English Church, though, was otherwise immense. Anything that the Roman Church had previously exercised authority over – such as marriages – were now to be 'finally and definitively adjudged and determined, within the king's jurisdiction and authority, and not elsewhere'.[2] In 1535, Stephen Gardiner had reinforced the new concept of royal supremacy and the king's divine authority in his book *De vera obedientia* (which translates to 'About True Obedience'), in which he argued that English subjects owed the king their absolute submission, not only as citizens, but as devoted Christians. Though he would later come to regret these words and subsequently retract them, he wrote the following about King Henry VIII's status:

> All sorts of people are agreed upon this point with most steadfast consent, learned and unlearned, both men and women: that no manner of person born and brought up in England hath aught to do with Rome. All manner of people receiving and embracing the truth with one whole consent acknowledge, honour, and reverence the King for the Supreme Headship of the Church upon earth. They bid the Bishop of Rome farewell.[3]

In 1536, Henry had decided that perhaps some theological changes were necessary after all. He commissioned the Ten Articles of 1536 – the Church of England's first statement of doctrine. The first five articles pertained to biblical creeds and 'things necessary to our salvation'. It was within these articles that he rejected four of the Catholic Church's seven sacraments, choosing to acknowledge only three: the eucharist, baptism, and penance (confession and absolution by a priest). He also affirmed the real presence of Christ in the bread and wine of the Mass.[4] Articles six, seven, and eight concerned the topic of honouring and praying to saints – which seemed to be somewhat murky territory for Henry and his religious advisors. In general, praying for saintly intercession was deemed to be acceptable, so long as 'it be done without any vain superstition'.[5]

Leaning only slightly towards the radical ideology of Martin Luther – who had begun preaching against the Catholic Church some twenty years earlier – Henry believed that the grace of God could be partially earned through one's faith, but not solely, as Lutherans taught. Not quite willing to let go of this particular piece of Catholic doctrine, he still insisted that a man's faith must be coupled with charitable works in order to gain himself a place in Heaven. Purgatory was another problematic concept. By early 1538, he no longer viewed it as a location for souls to linger until final judgment, but rather a vague concept that should encourage the faithful to pray for the dead, 'merely out of charity because the dead are part of the body of Christ, like us'.[6]

Also that year, Henry had begun his mission of eradicating superstition, idolatry, and hypocrisy. Thomas Cromwell wrote the Royal Injunctions of 1536, which 'restricted the use of images in worship and the veneration of the saints, called for the destruction of shrines and commanded an end to the practice of pilgrimage'.[7] His right to visit potentially corrupt monasteries – granted in 1534 – initiated a similar undertaking to dissolve such monasteries that he deemed unworthy. This, in particular, had a devastating effect on religious life in England. Following the Pilgrimage of Grace – a northern rebellion against the Crown organized by Catholic sympathizers – more than eight hundred religious houses were closed in four years.[8] Within just four more, all traditional monasteries, nunneries, and friaries throughout England and Wales would be extinguished.[9]

Though it had seemed that Henrician England was becoming fervently evangelical throughout the 1530s, the king was nothing if not inconsistent in his policies. Evidently never quite sure of the correct belief system (despite the many religious publications, laws, and persecutions during the latter years of his reign), Henry VIII could somehow justify the 1540 hanging, drawing, and quartering of three devout Roman Catholics, while also ordering the burning of three heretical reformers for believing in the theory of grace through faith alone.[10] Just two years prior, he had 'called a halt to theological experimentation' and ordered John Lambert burnt at the stake for denying Christ's real presence in the eucharist.[11] It seemed, depending on the year, the month, or perhaps even the week, that no one was truly considered 'safe' in their religious beliefs, so long as Henry VIII was undecided about what 'reform' truly meant.

By 1539, Henry had begun backing the conservatives once again, while he simultaneously determined that the sacrament of penance had not been instituted by God. One of the champions of Henry's reformation, Thomas Cromwell, was condemned for treason and heresy and executed in 1540. This was swiftly followed by the king's fifth marriage to Katherine Howard of the conservative faction. Even further confusion arose with the Act for the Advancement of True Religion in 1543, which restricted the classes of people who were allowed to read English bibles – prohibiting 'women, artificers, apprenticers, journeymen, serving men under the influence of yeomen, husbandmen, and labourers' from so doing.[12] Strikingly, this new decree was passed by Parliament only five years after Henry VIII's order that an English bible should be placed in every parish church throughout the country. To sum up, the religious tides turned constantly by the end of Henry's reign, and no one was able to predict in which direction the pendulum might next swing.

Most interestingly, at the heart of England's Protestant Reformation origins was, ultimately, a conservative king. For all of Henry VIII's attempts to re-align his theological interpretations away from Catholic doctrine, the most important moments in his life point to a man who undeniably continued to adhere to many aspects of Catholic teaching. He cherished his rosary and maintained that the Mass should continue to be celebrated in its traditional Latin form.[13] In his will, he ordered that Requiem Masses be said in order to deliver his soul to Heaven (perhaps illuminating a deep-rooted belief in purgatory after all), and left £666 for the poor to pray for his soul.[14] Aside from this, his will opened with the words, 'In the name of God and of the glorious and blessed Virgin our Lady Saint Mary.'[15] Dr Suzannah Lipscomb asserts that 'the language of the will leaves us with no sense of a man about to press further into Protestant reform,' deeming his a 'special, idiosyncratic religious position; reform coupled with fairly orthodox Catholic theology'.[16]

It is possible that Henry VIII had not intended to make England any more evangelical than it was at the time of his death, and he would not have seen his son as a fervently anti-Catholic Protestant reformer. Certainly, he would have wanted Edward to recognise his unique position as Supreme Head of the Church – an honour and title created by his father – but his will indicates no special instruction or desire for the reformation to continue with renewed vigour upon his death.

However, with a large number of evangelicals forming the late king's inner circle – and thus, the regency council for Edward VI – it is little wonder why the Reformation movement gained such ground, or why such emphasis was placed upon Edward as England's 'second Josiah'. Archbishop Cranmer, for one – who had championed King Henry's reformation efforts since the early 1530s – certainly chose to believe that the late king's silent wish had been to establish a truly Protestant government through his son. Somerset and his supporters were all evangelical in their beliefs, and the young king himself had been raised under the tutelage of renowned Protestant teachers – many of whom had been appointed by yet another reform supporter, Queen Katherine Parr.

Hopes for Edward – the young, impressionable, malleable new king – were quite different than they had been for the aging Henry VIII. It has been the opinion of many historians through the centuries that Edward's evangelical councillors orchestrated the next steps of the Reformation under Edward VI's name – seeing this as their chance to finally make the religious impact they so desired on their country. However, such a view of the councillors' total control ignores the reality of Edward's own Protestant fanaticism – which he had proven already in the years leading up to his coronation. His education had created within him a desire to debate scripture and condemn the pope, above taking part in any other childhood activity. His own religious beliefs had led to him chastising his much-older sister Mary for her Catholic piety. Edward was no pushover or marionette for which his councillors could pull the strings when it came to matters of religion. On this subject, he was dedicated and devout – determined to be just what the country, and specifically, Archbishop Cranmer in his coronation sermon, hoped he would prove to be.

His Protestant passion continued once he was king – as he enjoyed long, complex sermons and scribbled notes in Greek as he listened. He continued to write about the sinfulness of the Catholic Church and defended his own royal supremacy in England. So devout that it was once rumoured that he had refused to stand on a bible in order to reach a high shelf, he was lauded by the Scottish reformer, John Knox, for being 'that most godly and virtuous King that has ever been known to have reigned in England'.[17] He was supported totally by Archbishop Cranmer, who believed that 'the Christian's primary duty was to strengthen the power of the king, and [he] was prepared to sacrifice all other doctrines in order to accomplish this'.[18]

Though Edward was undoubtedly passionate, it is undeniable that Somerset also was enthusiastic about Protestant reform. He was, in fact, an extremely earnest evangelical who saw it as God's will that he had been charged with the king's care and upbringing. He patronized Protestant ministers and dined with the Protestant Bishop of Worcester, Hugh Latimer, in 1539. He shared his radical ambitions with his second wife, Anne Stanhope, who had been suspected of supporting the fanatically Protestant Anne Askew – burnt at the stake years earlier for her heresy.[19] In Somerset's eyes (and in his own words while speaking to God), he was a 'shepherd for thy people' and a 'sword-bearer for thy justice'.[20] He issued a prayer to mark the occasion of his promotion to Lord Protector, and the text shows his true feelings about the high estate he found himself in – for God's service:

> O my Lord and my God, I am the work of thy hands: thy goodness cannot reject me. I am the price of thy Son's death Jesus Christ ... I am written with the very blood of Jesus; thy inestimable love will not cancel then my name. For this cause, Lord God, I am bold to speak to thy Majesty. Thou,

Lord, by thy providence has called me to rule; make me therefore able to follow thy calling.[21]

Perhaps due to Somerset's influence, reform progressed quickly following Edward's accession – with some churches being stripped of their saintly images and statuary before Henry's body had grown cold in its grave. While under the old king's reign idols had been condemned, much of the traditional framework of Catholicism had continued to be honoured and respected. Now, however, it was deemed time to 'go forward in these matters, the opportunity of the time much better serving thereunto than in King Henry's days'.[22] As Edward's coronation homily had decreed – that God should be 'truly worshipped, and idolatry destroyed, the tyranny of the bishops of Rome banished from your subjects, and images removed', the stripping of any trace of traditional Catholicism began with fervour swiftly following Henry VIII's burial.[23] Idols were now taken down and smashed to pieces, so as not to distract the minds of impressionable parishioners away from the beauty of the scriptures.[24] By July, official rulings against idols and images were issued, and even Cranmer was concerned about the speed at which things were progressing.[25] Van der Delft described the events taking place at the English court as 'strange' – noting that 'the people are beginning to adhere strongly to the sects', and Edward's councillors appeared 'to vie with each other as to who can abuse most strongly the old religion'.[26]

If reform supporters saw King Edward as a 'second Josiah', they also viewed Somerset as his worthy guide in the mission to bring about God's plans in England. The poet William Forest dedicated one of his works to the Lord Protector in 1548, drawing stark comparisons to the last known Lord Protector – Richard, Duke of Gloucester, and later Richard III. The poem stated that Somerset was 'not Richard rager of cruelty, to whom the fourth Edward his children betook', but rather a 'true Theseus'.[27] This sentiment was echoed by the general public, who viewed Somerset as having been ordained by God to steward the king in bringing his Reformation to fruition. He was not there to destroy Edward as Richard III had destroyed his own nephew. Somerset was seen instead as a godly man with holy, reformist intentions.

With the conservative faction largely snuffed out by Somerset and his supporters, he was virtually unstoppable on the council – and most would not have tried to stop him anyway. He was the giver of gifts, honours, and titles, after all, and most of the powerful men at court had him to thank for their privilege and position. But if there was one man who still stood against Somerset, it was his own brother, Thomas Seymour, the Lord Admiral, who had long since resented his older brother's prestigious place as Lord Protector. Standing up for the late king's wishes, he had verbally questioned Somerset, saying, 'It was not the King's will that dead is that any one man should have both the Government of the King… and also the Realm.'[28] Unsatisfied with his positions of Lord High Admiral and Baron Sudeley, and the measly £200 left to him by Henry VIII, he evidently determined that taking a royal bride would be the next best path to power.[29]

There were contemporary reports and rumours that he had contemplated three possible marriages – to Henry VIII's fourth wife, Anne of Cleves, as well as princesses Mary and Elizabeth (the latter was twenty-five years his junior). Unsurprisingly, however, Somerset was not in favour of his younger brother's plans, and sharply rebuked him for setting his sights on Princess Mary, saying 'neither of them was born to be King, nor marry King's daughters.[30] King Edward, however, encouraged his uncle Thomas in his interest in Mary, declaring that the match would be for her soul's benefit – its purpose being 'to change her opinions'.[31] For this reason, he also showed favour upon the Anne of Cleves proposal, but despite this royal permission for either case, the council (namely Somerset) forbade such a match.

Thomas Seymour was warned not to push matters, and so he angrily stormed away in pursuit of a different marital avenue – though this one was hardly any less offensive.

Years earlier, probably sometime between 1542 and 1543, Seymour had kindled a romantic relationship with Katherine Parr, who had evidently returned his affections and hoped to marry him before being 'overruled by a higher power'.[32] Now, a thrice-widowed thirty-four-year-old, the Queen Dowager was a free woman once more – and a very wealthy and high-ranking one at that.[33] And so, by late spring of 1547, the Lord Admiral was paying visits to her residences in Chelsea and Hanworth, clearly intent on wooing her once again. Apparently keen to rekindle their romance, Katherine exchanged heartfelt letters with him when they were apart and welcomed him to spend nights with her in the country, though she was certainly aware of the risks they were taking regarding this new affair. She reportedly warned him, 'When it shall be your pleasure to repair hither, ye must take some pain to come early in the morning, that ye may be gone again by seven o'clock.'[34]

However, word soon reached the households of Katherine's family members, and before long they were discussing the potential for marriage. Though she had her reservations, she had fallen deeply in love with him again, after years apart, and had assured him that she would happily become his wife if he were to ask her. It was all the encouragement he needed. Sometime during the last two weeks of May, the two were wed in a secret ceremony, and then faced the frightening reality of informing the king and council. Upon informing Princess Mary of their marriage they were faced with a less-than-enthusiastic reaction, with Mary declaring it 'strange news' – in essence she was telling her stepmother that it was fine if Katherine was happy, though she admitted to knowing nothing of 'wooing matters'.[35] In private, she was infuriated by the match and blamed Katherine for the affair and its dishonour upon the late king, her father. Now Seymour had to tell Edward – but better than simply telling him, he reasoned, he should make the king believe that it had been his own idea.

Like a schoolboy, Seymour used a Gentleman of the Privy Chamber, John Fowler, to subtly question the king about whether or not he was surprised that his dashing uncle had not yet taken a wife. After the possibilities of Mary, Elizabeth, and Anne of Cleves had been mulled over, Seymour persuaded Fowler casually to mention the prospect of the Dowager Queen. Becoming more serious, he pressed further by telling Fowler that if Edward would support the match, he should write a letter to Katherine. Somewhat ingeniously, Seymour himself masterminded this letter – visiting his nephew in private and guiding him as to its wording. Dated 25 June, the finished letter gave the impression that the young king was all but commanding Katherine to marry his uncle. Clearly Edward had no notion that the two had already secretly married, and that Seymour was saving his own skin with this act of deceit. Most crucially, the letter stated that King Edward would protect the union of Katherine and Thomas from the wrath of Somerset – and so Seymour was untouchable for the moment.

As expected, Somerset was furious to learn the news. Hearing that his brother had sought the king's permission to marry the Dowager Queen – and that it had been granted – only enraged him further. Even Edward noted in his diary that 'the Lord Protector was much offended'.[36] Somerset's wife, Anne Seymour (née Stanhope), Duchess of Somerset, was equally incensed; she hated Katherine Parr and considered herself a higher-ranking lady now that she was married to England's Lord Protector. For what it was worth, Katherine returned Anne's loathing in equal measure, nicknaming the duchess simply 'hell'. She had reason enough to dislike the Lord Protector too, together with her husband; he had been made the most powerful figure in England and had usurped her expected place as Queen Regent. Now, as he refused to hand over the jewels and sentimental valuables that Henry VIII had left for his sixth wife, as well as leasing out her own lands without her consent, Katherine joined Thomas wholeheartedly in opposing him. So began the stirrings which would soon enough lead to the disastrous clash of the Seymour brothers – the result of their unavoidable angry, embittered struggle for ultimate power.

Chapter 7

Brotherly Rivalry

Where was Edward in all of this, as his uncles quarrelled and secret powerful marriages were taking place behind his back? The evidence points to an unhappy and sulky boy, who felt he was being mismanaged in these first few months as king. He complained of how severe his uncle Somerset was with him, and how he allowed him only few treats and pleasures. He suffered under his strict tutors and grumbled about not having enough money to do as he liked or to reward those who attended and entertained him. In short, he did not feel much like a king at all – and though he certainly did not realize it at the time, this fact had swiftly become a pawn in Thomas Seymour's power play. Determined to win his young nephew's favour over Somerset, he had begun gifting the young king with money – sometimes as much as £40 in 'pocket change', which would be the equivalent of over £19,000 today.

In reality, Edward was financially provided for quite well; he had received a reported £1,448 9s 2d for his Privy Chamber expenses, as well as a personal gift of £213 from Somerset himself.[1] While this was admittedly far less than the funds supplied to his late father's Privy Chamber, there is little reason to believe that he was suffering for lack of money. Still, to reward generously with gifts of money was a matter of dignity and honour for a king, and was a crucial aspect of Edward VI's identity. The fact that he felt he was not given sufficient funds to to dispense as gifts clearly bothered him, to the extent that the Lord Marquess of Dorset reported that, 'The King's Majesty has divers made his money unto him, saying that my uncle of Somerset dealeth very hardly with me … that I cannot have money at my will. But my Lord Admiral both sends me money and gives me money.'[2] Edward felt that in Somerset's eyes, he was a 'beggarly king', which gave Seymour the perfect opportunity to gain an advantage over his ambitious and all-too-powerful brother. He played on the king's insecurities regarding his coffers, reminding him of Somerset's stinginess, and promising to provide for him through John Fowler. His payments soon became so regular and expected, that Edward felt comfortable enough to write to him at his new home in Chelsea, saying, 'My lord, I recommend me unto you and the Queen, praying you to send me such money as ye think good.'[3]

During much of this time during the late summer of 1547, Somerset was otherwise occupied with diplomacy and military pursuits. The situation with Scotland had remained tense and unpredictable since before Henry VIII's death, and any conquests and battles fought against the Scots had only resulted in their numbers and strength growing, once the English had returned home. Now, secure in his position as Lord Protector, with Edward VI comfortably settled in London, Somerset determined that his next act must be to establish English-armed garrisons in Scotland. By late August, he was ready to depart north, along with sixteen thousand troops and eighty ships along the coast. When he reached Berwick, he made a conditional peace offering – still contingent on acceptance by the Scots of the marriage betrothal between Edward and Mary, as well as their willingness to become united with England through their acceptance of the reformed evangelical faith. Of course, both of these offers were soundly refused, at which point Somerset felt he had no choice but to draw battle lines at Pinkie Cleugh.

It was a disastrous military defeat for Scotland, which lost roughly half of its 30,000-man army in the battle on 10 September. The English forces had numbered only around 17,000, making this a crushing and decisive victory. According to Van der Delft, Somerset's men reportedly took another 2,000 Scottish prisoners, while 'the dead bodies lay as thick as a man may note cattle grazing in a full replenished pasture'.[4] William Patten shared the victorious news with Edward at Oatlands Palace, and the young king was ecstatic – especially when informed of the Catholic priests and monks who had been cut down among the Scottish soldiers. He reasoned triumphantly, 'We fight for the cause of God, they for that of the pope.'[5]

Suspicious of what his brother might be getting up to in London behind his back, following the victory Somerset hurried home – leaving his costly garrisons in place in Scotland – only to find that he had another problem on his hands. Reform of English churches had already gained dangerous momentum – and though the destruction of idols and images had been both ordered and encouraged by Somerset, he nevertheless recognized that such actions were already becoming overzealous and problematic. While churches were being whitewashed, their statues and stained glass smashed to pieces and burnt in city-wide bonfires, attacks on the Holy Sacrament were also taking place. Catholics who attempted to fight back were jailed, and many chose to flee England. Assaults on churches continued through the autumn, leading to an attempt by the government to quell the overenthusiastic destruction of holy places – and especially the Sacrament. In November, Parliament passed the 'Act against Revilers of the Sacrament and for the Communion in both kinds', threatening to harshly punish anyone who abused the Host. This was followed by another proclamation in late December against such acts, but by this point the chaos and ruin was truly unprecedented and now saw no end.

Meanwhile, Somerset was still pushing forward with other aspects of reform – such as the dissolution of some 4,000 charitable foundations and chantries – or bequests left in wills for priests to say Masses on behalf of departed souls.[6] This Act was based on the denouncement of the doctrine of purgatory, a firm facet of Somerset's and Edward VI's Reformation, and its wording mocked the very intention of such endowments in the first place: 'Phantasising vain opinions of purgatory and masse satisfactory, to be done for them which be departed.'[7] But while at face value the abolishment of chantries appeared a valiant step in the right direction of reform, the fact should not be overlooked that it was a convenient way for Somerset to recover some of the English funds lost in his Scottish war. It was certainly a nice alternative to increasing taxes on the king's subjects, and there can be little doubt that the zealous king was enthusiastic about anything that appeared to be furthering the Protestant cause. This was, indeed, a convenient solution to some of Somerset's financial problems. As might have been expected, the money collected from these abolished chantries was not put towards endowments for schools and charities, or the 'provisions of pensions for redundant priests', as the Chantries Act itself promised.[8] Instead, the roughly £610,000 collected was used for the Crown's purposes – indeed, to recover from the enormous expenses of military involvement in Scotland, and to help pay for the expensive garrisons set up there by Somerset.[9] In fact, the number of resulting 'new' schools created by Edward VI, as they have been known through the centuries, were actually miscalculated and grossly misrepresented. Though some certainly were established during this period, many were actually founded in the years before and after Edward's reign.[10]

While Somerset controlled every aspect of Edward's government – from the military pursuits to the passing of religious acts and desecration of churches – he desired even more power. He sought to have a bill passed by Parliament that would allow him to serve as Lord Protector not only until Edward VI reached the age of eighteen – but until an undetermined time that the council might deem appropriate for the king to rule on his own. With Edward's rule having not even been established for a year, Somerset was fast trying to secure a completely unregulated amount of power over him – something which his younger brother was not keen to allow.

While Seymour had been gaining the young king's favour during Somerset's absence in Scotland – and through most of the summer of 1547 – he now knew that he required more than just his nephew's willing ear. He had bribed him with monetary gifts for months, making Edward beholden to him, and now he had a proposition. Seymour had begun lobbying for support to become Governor of the King's Person – a role which would split some of the Lord Protector's offices and claim some of the power over the king for itself. No doubt he considered this a reasonable request to make at the time, sure to be supported by his loving nephew – and yet, Edward hesitated to sign the proposed bill during a private audience with Seymour. He had been told before to wait for the council's approval before signing anything, and so he insisted that he must wait. This decision was firmly supported by John Cheke – the tutor who had always been an influential and well-respected figure in the young king's life. Cheke had reason to doubt Seymour's intention and warned Edward against signing anything that could give the man more power.

But Seymour was not the sort of man to give up easily, and as he continued regularly to gift Edward with sums of money, his nephew's resolve faltered slightly with time. Giving his verbal agreement to his uncle's proposition, he instructed Seymour to leave the bill with Cheke, who would deliver it to him to be signed at a later time. Cheke, however, refused to present the bill to the king, still staunchly against Seymour's plans. When he reminded Edward of the gravity of the situation, the king was remorseful for having ignored his tutor's previous instruction. He assured him that, 'The Lord Admiral shall have no bill signed or written by me.'[11]

In addition to his gifts of money and not-so-subtle attempts to win governorship of the king, Seymour had also been working to arrange a marriage for his nephew almost since he had first taken the throne. Already the guardian of the king's sister, Elizabeth, since his marriage to Katherine Parr, another young lady had joined the household at Chelsea several months prior – none other than Lady Jane Grey, the daughter of Henry Grey, Marquess of Dorset. In February, Seymour had utilized the services of a go-between – a man in his employ named John Harington, who was also a companion of Dorset. Dorset recalled that Harington:

> [s]howed me that the admiral was likely to come to great authority and, as the king's uncle, might do me much pleasure, advising me to report to him and enter more into his friendship. He advised me to allow my daughter Jane to be betrothed with the admiral, saying he would have her married to the king.[12]

It was probably a combination of Seymour's flattery that Jane was 'as handsome a lady as any in England', as well as his tempting loan of £2,000 (£615,000 today) which had convinced Dorset to send Jane to Seymour Place in the first place – whether or not he had truly believed there was a chance she could really become Edward's consort.[13] Dorset was a patient man as it turned out – aware that Seymour could do only so much, as he was not the king's Lord Protector, and ultimately Somerset contained all the veto power in England. He had agreed to let Jane reside in the Dowager Queen's household along with Seymour, trusting that marriage discussions might be taking place behind the scenes.

In fact, they did, but only briefly. John Fowler was sent by Seymour to broach the subject with Edward, who apparently flatly refused and showed no interest at all in marrying Jane; (to be fair, he was still only nine years old). These conversations were yet another reason for John Cheke's suspicion and disapproval of the Lord Admiral. When he caught wind of such talk, he was alarmed and took the matter straight to Somerset – along with the knowledge that Seymour had been paying the king sums of money for months. None of this helped Seymour's case in the eyes of his brother, or much of the court, and by the end of 1547 he was growing ever more desperate to determine a path ahead.[14]

In the early months of 1548 he thought he had figured it out – and his dangerous solution was to lead a rebellion against his brother. He had worked to befriend a number of noblemen over the months – including the Marquess of Dorset, the Earl of Rutland, and even the Earl of Southampton, Thomas Wriothesley. According to Sir William Sharington, Seymour was quite proud of himself, believing that 'he had more gentlemen that loved him, than my Lord Protector had'.[15] He had purposely sought out the support of men who were embittered towards his brother, and had ordered them to bolster their castles and gather troops of men to his cause. This was not an inexpensive task, of course. Soldiers, supplies, and equipment were estimated to cost him around £7,500 (£2.4 million today), but in order to acquire those funds, Seymour needed only to turn to Sharington, an under-treasurer of the mint in Bristol.[16]

Meanwhile, Somerset's Reformation raged on. Henry VIII's Act of Six Articles – a reassertion of Catholic doctrine and denouncement of heretical teachings – was swiftly repealed, now allowing for the unrestricted reading of English bibles. Protestant books – many of which had been formerly banned – were now widely published and spread throughout the country. Somerset's own chaplain printed tracts against the Mass, though fervent Catholics continued to fight back as – and *if* – they could. One such Catholic who found herself in an uncomfortable position was the king's much-older sister, Mary, who had once known a very warm and loving relationship with him. Now, as she watched altars stripped of their finery, traditional Latin replaced with English in both bibles and church services, she saw everything she valued crumbling under her brother's rule – or rather, as she knew, her uncle's government.

She wrote passionately to Somerset and reminded him of the 'godly order and quietness' of her late father's reign, which painted a stark contrast to the chaos and disorder of the present day. She displayed concern for her young, impressionable brother and feared he might be led astray and into heresy without his own awareness. Somerset, in answer, feigned astonishment at her apprehensions, assuring her that the majority of England supported the reform. He warned her – albeit politely – that she was free to continue to worship as she pleased, so long as she did not meddle in the government's work or challenge her brother's wishes and kingly authority. Put firmly in her place, Mary wisely decided to bide her time and heed her uncle's advice for the time being.[17]

Meanwhile at Chelsea, as Seymour continued to plan the challenge he would mount against his brother (as well as working to gain the necessary funds), there was another bit of familial drama taking place that would cause his character to come further into question. Few people had known that, for nearly the entirety of Princess Elizabeth's residence with Thomas and Katherine, he had been growing more and more inappropriate in his conduct with her.[18] Katherine (Kat) Ashley, the princess's governess, reported later that throughout the summer months and into the autumn of 1547, the Lord Admiral had crept into his fourteen-year-old niece's bedchamber at early hours in the morning 'in his nightgown, barelegged in his slippers' to bid her good morning and often 'strike her upon the back, or on the buttocks familiarly ... and if she were in her bed, he would put open the curtains, and ... make as though he would come at her'.[19]

Further reports indicate that Seymour attempted to kiss his niece, tickled her many times, and spent far more time alone with her than would be considered seemly. For much of this inappropriate behaviour towards Elizabeth, his wife appears to have been either oblivious or indifferent – at least until one particularly strange encounter in the gardens at Hanworth, when Katherine was an accomplice to the foul play. In this case, Seymour noted his distaste for his niece's black dress, and directed Katherine to hold the princess still while he sliced it to shreds. Later when Kat Ashley could remain silent no longer and approached Seymour about his conduct towards the princess, Seymour displayed no remorse or apology, instead exclaiming, 'God's precious soul! I will tell my Lord Protector [how I am slandered], and I will not leave off, for I mean no evil.'[20]

While Katherine had either maintained ignorance or a cautious acceptance of her husband's behaviour, matters changed abruptly in late spring 1548. The head of Elizabeth's household, Thomas Parry, gave a second-hand account from Kat Ashley:

> The Queen, suspecting the often access of the Admiral to the Lady Elizabeth, came suddenly upon them, where they were all alone [he having her in his arms]: wherefor the Queen fell out, both with the Lord Admiral and with her Grace also ... and, as I remember, this was the cause why she was sent from the Queen.[21]

When Elizabeth was sent to stay with Sir Anthony Denny in early summer, Katherine was pregnant with the Lord Admiral's child and had good reason to be rid of any competition for her husband's affections. Her parting words to her niece were reportedly cool and cautioning in tone and let her know what her misconduct might have done to her reputation. As Chris Skidmore points out, it is perhaps more telling that Elizabeth 'answered little' in response to such warnings.[22]

As Seymour's reputation continued to dwindle, Somerset carried on fighting his own battles in London – no doubt well-aware of the goings-on at his brother's home away from court. In addition to the stripping of churches and spreading of the reformed gospel, landowners fought over enclosing common lands and inflation caused landlords to raise their rents – causing civil unrest throughout much of the country. The Rough Wooing in Scotland, had continued to cost the English, thanks to Somerset's garrisons stationed in the north which required regular funds. The English coin continued to be debased as the Lord Protector struggled to finance his questionable decisions – and the final blow came on 7 July 1548, when it was announced that Mary, Queen of Scots was betrothed to the Dauphin of France, and thus the main reason for England's involvement in Scotland had come to nothing, after all. In short, Somerset was not having an easy time of things either.

But things took an even more negative turn for his brother when, six days after the birth of his daughter, Mary, named for the king's sister, his wife of little more than a year succumbed to puerperal fever and died on 5 September. Katherine's death shocked many, as it had been assumed that she was coming out of her fever before taking a sudden turn for the worse. Certainly, Seymour was stunned and left suddenly alone with his newborn daughter, but his mother, Margery, came swiftly to assist with the infant. Katherine, only thirty-seven years old, was honoured with the first Protestant burial of an English queen. She was buried on 7 September in St Mary's Chapel on the grounds of Sudeley Castle, with Lady Jane Grey acting as her chief mourner.[23] In the days following the funeral, the widowed Seymour struggled to determine how to move forward without Katherine, and even considered dismantling her household and giving up on the ambitious path he had been forging for the past year-and-a-half. Ten days following the funeral, he wrote to Lady Jane's father, 'I was so amazed that I had small regard either to myself or to my doings.'[24]

It seemed that soon, however his focus returned to Elizabeth, and there was at least one man – her servant, Thomas Parry – who had reason to believe that the Lord Admiral hoped to rekindle his acquaintance with her. He attempted to use Parry as a go-between in order to ask after his former ward, reportedly even daring to ask, 'whether her great buttocks were grown any less or no?'[25] According to Parry, Seymour contemplated marrying Elizabeth yet again, though he acknowledged that his brother would never allow it – just as he had not the year prior. Resigned, he apparently told Kat Ashley, 'I look not to lose my life for a wife. It has been spoken of, but it cannot be.'[26] Elizabeth, for her part, appeared to show no interest in her uncle now that she had been away from his household for some months. She declined sending a letter of condolence to him regarding his wife's death, even when it was suggested that it would be a kind gesture. She appeared to want little to do with the man who had caused her own reputation to come under question, and who had soured her relationship with her stepmother in those precious final months of Katherine's life. Even if Somerset had agreed to the possible marriage, Elizabeth may very well have refused Seymour.

As late summer cooled to autumn, other council members began to feel uneasy about Seymour's renewed ambition and seemingly underhanded actions. A few of them, including Warwick, brought up their concerns with Seymour himself, but he shrugged them off and denied any malicious intent against his brother's protectorship. But by November, he apparently realized that he was in need of greater support than ever, and he sought out private audiences with his nephew once again. He visited him at Hampton Court, reminding him that in just a few years' time, he would be in charge of his own government and no longer in need of a Lord Protector. 'Nay,' was Edward's response, which must have startled Seymour. By the end of the month there was more reason for concern related to the Lord Admiral's behaviour; he appeared to be making unusual preparations at Holt Castle. Great sums of money – coming once again from Seymour's good friend, Sharington, were pouring into his coffers as he stocked the castle with food and drink. At last, it seemed as if his months-long preparation to rise up against his brother's rule might be reaching its climax, and that he intended to use Holt as his stronghold. The most shocking rumour of all, arising from Seymour's previous conversations with John Fowler earlier that year, indicated that he was strategizing how to get the king into his possession and keep him at the castle – possibly planning to hold him in custody as part of his rebellion.

Somerset had been catching wind of these suspicious activities through the noblemen who reported back to him, including Warwick, Russell, and Wriothesley. In January 1549, he had decided that enough was enough – he would give his brother a chance to explain himself and settle the bitterness between them. But when he summoned him to his presence, Seymour wrote back hastily that he would only meet in the presence of the full council.

On 19 January, Seymour's desperation and foolhardiness reached new heights when he infiltrated the king's privy garden late at night, sneaking into the palace and reaching the door to his nephew's bedchamber, accompanied by two servants. Alerted to the sudden and unexpected intruder, Edward's spaniel began barking protectively before Seymour could reach the sleeping king. Pistol in hand, Seymour shot and killed the dog on the spot, abruptly awakening Edward's guards who leapt into action against him, as they yelled 'Murder!' The dog, described by one of the guards as 'the most faithful guardian of the King's Majesty', lay lifeless as the stunned and traumatized king rose from bed to find his uncle surrounded by armed guards, claiming his innocence and insisting weakly that he had only intended to ensure Edward's security.[27] Despite these protestations everyone surmised that Seymour had been intent on kidnapping the king and mercifully had been deterred by the dog.

The following morning at eight o'clock Seymour was arrested. While it is extremely unlikely that he had meant his nephew any harm, this situation did not show him in a favourable light. Word immediately spread throughout Europe that Seymour had 'attempted, by an unheard-of treachery and cruelty, to destroy with his own impious hands, in the deep silence of the night, our innocent king.'[28] Somewhat surprisingly, Seymour remained assured of his own innocence and apparently did not fear the consequences of his actions even as he was rowed by barge to the Tower of London. He spoke rather defiantly about the situation, insisting that 'they cannot kill me, except they do me wrong. And if they do, I shall die but once. And if they take my life from me, I have a master that will at once revenge it.'[29] However, after only a few weeks of imprisonment, he began to doubt his 'many friends' at the court, feeling that he had been forgotten after all.

Meanwhile, anyone close to the Lord Admiral was under question – including Elizabeth, and even the king himself. Edward confessed that his uncle had been giving him money behind the Lord Protector's back for months, and had even tried to persuade him to sign bills without the council's consent. One-by-one, noblemen shared what they knew of the Lord Admiral – including his months of bragging about the wealth that bought him noble alliances and friendships, his plotting to marry one of the princesses, and even his bolstering of forces to overthrow Somerset's position.[30] Wisely, Elizabeth distanced herself from any negative association with her uncle to the best of her ability – taking the matter straight to Somerset and insisting that she never would have considered accepting a marriage proposal without the consent of the king and council.[31] Thomas Parry and Kat Ashley lost their positions over the ordeal, and evidence and testimony was collected for nearly a month, until finally on 24 February, the council declared their findings

King Henry VIII, second monarch of the Tudor dynasty and initiator of the Protestant Reformation in England, waited twenty-eight long years into his marital life for a legitimate son who would survive infancy. Prince Edward would grow up in the shadow of his illustrious father, ever seeking to please him and acquire the fatherly attention he so craved. (Hans Holbein the Younger; Courtesy of Wikimedia Commons, CC Public Domain)

Jane Seymour, Henry VIII's third queen and mother of Edward VI, would live less than two weeks following the birth of the son who would seal her legacy as Henry's 'true wife and queen'. (Hans Holbein the Younger; Courtesy of Wikimedia Commons, CC Public Domain)

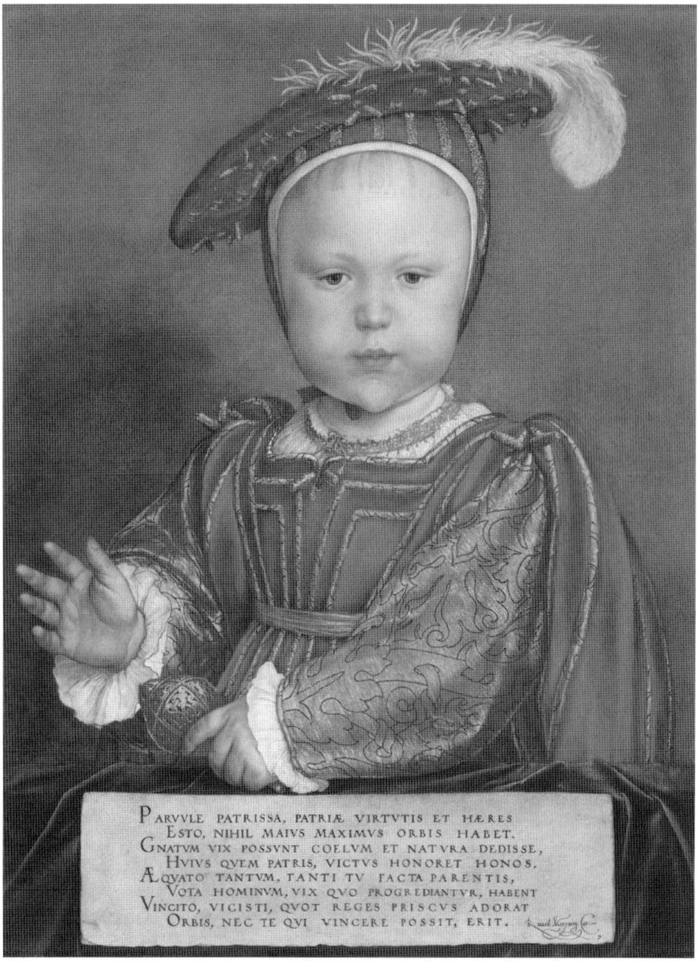

'Little one, emulate thy father and be the heir of his virtue; the world contains nothing greater. Heaven and earth could scarcely produce a son whose glory would surpass that of such a father ...' reads Richard Morison's Latin inscription in this infant portrait of Prince Edward. This painting was gifted to King Henry VIII for the 1539 New Year, and probably depicts Edward when he was around one year old. (Hans Holbein the Younger; Courtesy of the Andrew W. Mellon Collection, National Gallery of Art)

The 'Family of Henry VIII' portrait presents a stark message to the world about the core members of Henry's family, as he viewed them. An eight-year-old Prince Edward stands to his right, while his demure, obedient wife, Queen Jane, sits to his left. His two legitimate daughters, Mary and Elizabeth, are symbolically separated from both himself and the throne of England by the columns surrounding him. (Artist Unknown, c. 1545; Courtesy of Wikimedia Commons, CC Public Domain)

A posthumous portrait of the core Tudor family, featuring (from top left) the founder of the dynasty, King Henry VII, and his wife, Elizabeth of York, King Henry VIII and his 'true' wife, Jane Seymour, and finally, Prince Edward front and centre. In this portrait, the likeness between father and son – both in dress and stance – is unmistakeable and entirely intentional. (Remigius van Leemput, date unknown; Courtesy of Wikimedia Commons, CC Public Domain)

Katherine Parr, Henry VIII's sixth wife, became the only maternal figure of Edward's life. The four-times-married champion of Protestantism was a strong supporter of Edward's reformist education and shared a close bond and affection with her stepson, as evidenced by several letters shared between the two. Following the death of Henry VIII in 1547, Katherine was disappointed to learn that she would not be appointed Regent of Edward's government, and made a rather ill-fated decision to marry the Lord Admiral Thomas Seymour – firmly positioning herself against the majority of the council and Edward's government. (Master John, date unknown; Courtesy of Wikimedia Commons, CC Public Domain)

The 'Badge of Prince Edward', illustrated in John Leland's *Genethliacon illustrissimi Eaduerdi principis Cambriae* (1543), featuring the traditional heraldic symbolism of the Prince of Wales – a gold coronet encircling three white ostrich feathers. As a member of the Tudor dynasty and an extension of the House of York, the Sun of York surrounds the badge. The abbreviation 'EP' represents the Latin *Edwardus Princeps*, and the German motto *Ich Dien* translates as 'I serve'. (Courtesy of Wikimedia Commons, CC Public Domain)

This well-known portrait by William Scrots features Edward as Prince of Wales, posing in the Queen's Drawing Room at Windsor Castle. The likeness to Henry VIII is prominent, from the dark penetrating eyes to the golden-red hair. Even the stance is reminiscent of that of his father. (c. 1546; Courtesy of Wikimedia Commons, CC Public Domain)

Princess Elizabeth, Edward's elder half-sister by four years, remained close with her brother throughout childhood and into his reign. The two were educated similarly, both showing impressive aptitude in their studies, and received high praise from several of their shared tutors. They frequently exchanged gifts and letters, and their shared interest and passion for the Protestant Reformation held their sibling bond much tighter than the tenuous bond between Edward and his much elder half-sister, the Catholic Princess Mary. Elizabeth and Edward would continue their regular warm correspondence and visits until his death. (William Scrots, c. 1546–7; Courtesy of Wikimedia Commons, CC Public Domain)

Eighteenth-century artist James Basire engraved this depiction of Edward VI's coronation procession from the Tower of London to Westminster. The scale of the massive procession is notable as it extends across the entire length of the engraving. Edward is shown beneath a golden canopy at its centre. (c. 1787; Courtesy of Wikimedia Commons, CC0 1.0)

A print of the coronation medal produced to celebrate Edward VI's coronation in 1547. The Latin inscription reads 'Edward VI by the grace of god King of England, France and Ireland, defender of the faith and the supreme head on earth of the Church of England and Ireland …' (Courtesy of Wikimedia Commons, CC Public Domain)

This painting of Edward by William Scrots features the red and white roses of Lancaster and York, symbols of the two warring houses whose thirty-two-year-long conflict culminated in the founding of the Tudor dynasty. It also depicts sunflowers facing away from the sun and instead towards the boy king – a reference to his power. The painting was commissioned by the Stanhope family, the in-laws of Edward's uncle, Edward Seymour, Duke of Somerset. (c. 1550; Courtesy of Wikimedia Commons, CC Public Domain)

Portrait of Edward Seymour, 1st Earl of Hertford and later Duke of Somerset under King Edward VI. Upon his nephew's accession, Seymour named himself Lord Protector of the Realm and attempted to lead Edward's government from 1547 until his beheading for treason in 1552. Often referred to as 'the good duke', he has been characterized as having had largely good intentions during his time in power, though several of his poor decisions caused England's government and economy to suffer. (Artist and date unknown; Courtesy of Wikimedia Commons, CC Public Domain)

Portrait of King Edward VI, attributed to William Scrots. Here Edward is sitting upon his throne, finely attired in a gown lined with ermine, with the collar of the Order of the Garter over his shoulders. Notably, as a king who would strive to further the Protestant Reformation, he holds a bible in his right hand. (Date unknown; Courtesy of Wikimedia Commons, CC Public Domain)

The official signature of King Edward VI. (Courtesy of Wikimedia Commons, CC Public Domain)

Painted in 1550 by William Scrots, this portrait of Edward VI likely depicts him at a time when he felt he was starting to come into his own. At about 13 years old, Edward stands regally, holding a pair of gloves. At this time, marriage negotiations were underway and he was three years away from the age of majority – yet, sadly, fewer than three years away from his untimely death. (Courtesy of Wikimedia Commons, CC Public Domain)

This portrait of Archbishop Thomas Cranmer, by an unknown artist, is probably a posthumous representation of the man in his later years (possibly depicting him shortly before his execution in 1556). Cranmer was the architect of the Protestant Reformation in England, having authored both versions of the Book of Common Prayer during Edward VI's reign. He became a Protestant martyr under Queen Mary I. (Date unknown; Courtesy of Wikimedia Commons, CC Public Domain)

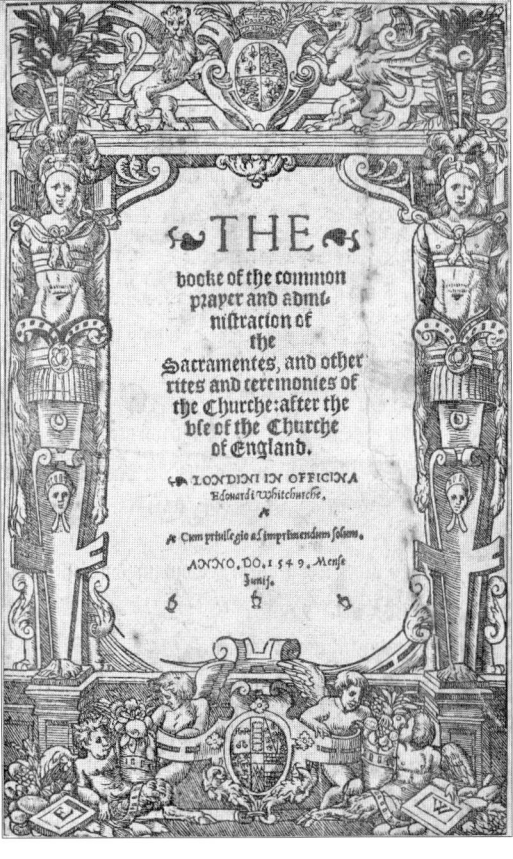

The first iteration of Archbishop Cranmer's Book of Common Prayer was published in 1549, followed by an unpopular Act of Uniformity. This book took small steps away from the traditional Catholic liturgy and introduced a more Protestant flair to church services in England. It was reviewed and deemed heavily flawed by several prominent reformers, who argued that the Book did not go far enough to espouse progressive, anti-Catholic ideals and the service structure. It was thus revised and republished in 1552. (Courtesy of Wikimedia Commons, CC Public Domain)

'A man of much wit and very little judgement' were the words written by Princess Elizabeth upon Thomas Seymour's execution in 1549. Seymour became Lord Admiral upon Edward VI's accession, but he coveted the power of his brother, the Duke of Somerset, which culminated in ill-contrived plots and scheming against the council. He was ultimately arrested and charged with more than twenty counts of treason before his execution by axe. Having enjoyed, for a brief time, a very close and affectionate relationship with his royal nephew, Seymour's death garnered little sympathy from Edward, who made only a cursory mention of it in his Chronicle. (Nicolas Denisot, c. 1547–9; Courtesy of Wikimedia Commons, CC Public Domain)

Twentieth-century painting by Ernest Board depicts Bishop Hugh Latimer preaching to Edward VI at Paul's Cross. The impassioned Latimer reaches towards the young king, as Edward watches stoically and thoughtfully. Lengthy Protestant sermons flourished during Edward's reign but were later shortened under Elizabeth I, several years later. (c. 1910; Courtesy of Wikimedia Commons, CC Public Domain)

Another representation of Hugh Latimer preaching to Edward, first published in John Foxe's *Acts and Monuments*. Here, Latimer preaches from a pulpit erected in the Privy Garden at Whitehall while Edward watches from an upstairs gallery window. (c. 1563; Courtesy of Wikimedia Commons, CC Public Domain)

John Dudley, Earl of Warwick and later 1st Duke of Northumberland, succeeded in ousting the Duke of Somerset from power in late 1551, becoming Edward VI's Lord President of the Council until the young king's death. Nicknamed 'the bad duke', Northumberland was seen as a ruthless, overly ambitious hothead who could not be trusted, and who was accused of fatally poisoning Edward VI (though there is no evidence for this). He was beheaded for treason shortly after Mary I took the throne, due to his efforts to displace her from the line of succession and establish his new daughter-in-law, Lady Jane Grey, as England's queen. (Artist and date unknown; Courtesy of Wikimedia Commons, CC Public Domain)

'My devise for the succession …' These words introduce Edward's most notable official document, in which he rearranged the order of succession shortly before his death. Knowing that allowing his sister Mary to succeed him would result in a complete reversal of the Reformation progress his reign had accomplished, he instead bestowed his crown upon 'L' Jane and her heires masles', (his cousin, the Protestant Lady Jane Grey and her male heirs). (Courtesy of Wikimedia Commons, CC Public Domain)

A posthumous engraving of the ill-fated Lady Jane Grey, Queen of England for less than two weeks upon Edward VI's death in 1553. According to her own words, she had never desired the crown for herself and knew it to be Mary Tudor's right. Unwilling to convert to Catholicism upon Mary's triumphant return to London to claim her throne, Jane Grey was executed on 12 February 1554, along with her husband, Guildford Dudley, and father-in-law, the Duke of Northumberland. (Willem van de Passe, c. 1620; Courtesy of Wikimedia Commons, CC Public Domain)

An official portrait of Queen Mary I of England, shortly following her accession to the throne, after Lady Jane Grey's brief reign as queen. Mary's sole purpose as monarch would be to halt the Protestant Reformation's progress in England and revert many of the changes made under her brother. She would become known throughout history as 'Bloody Mary', as she sent more than 280 Protestants to be burnt at the stake for their heresy during her short reign. In 1558, upon her death, the crown would pass to her Protestant half-sister, Elizabeth. (Antonis Mor, c. 1554; Courtesy of Wikimedia Commons, CC Public Domain)

Queen Elizabeth I, painted nearly ten years after her accession. She returned many of the Protestant features of Edward's reign to the country, following the brief Catholic resurgence under her sister. While she was decidedly not quite so fervent in her Reformist ideals as her younger brother had been, many of the tenets of his religious policy were carefully crafted and finalized to create a Church of England very similar to the church attended by modern-day Britons. While the Protestant Church established under her reign would prove (largely) to flourish, many of its foundations were laid during the prior reign of Edward VI. Elizabeth would reign successfully until her death and the end of the Tudor dynasty in 1603. (George Gower, c. 1567; Courtesy of Wikimedia Commons, CC Public Domain)

that Thomas Seymour was guilty of treason. Thirty-three charges had been brought against him and his nephew had the final word – if only as a matter of formality. Upon hearing the council's evidence and verdict, Edward replied authoritatively,

> We do perceive that there is great things objected and laid to my Lord Admiral mine uncle – and they tend to treason – and we perceive that you require but justice to be done. We think it reasonable, and we will well that you proceed according to your request.[32]

Following the king's words, the council was reportedly overjoyed – maintaining the illusion that Edward held any real power over the verdict, as if they would not have proceeded in convicting Seymour regardless. On 5 March 1549 Seymour was formally declared guilty of high treason against His Majesty and sentenced to death on Tower Hill. It was his own brother – not the king – who signed the death warrant, his signature apparently 'so shaky that it is almost illegible.'[33]

It is, of course, impossible to know Edward's own personal feelings on the matter, as he is reported to have said very little. Aside from his statement 24 February, he also told his council, after the final verdict had been read, 'without further molestation of myself, or of the Lord Protector ... I pray you, my Lords, do so.'[34] While we can assume that this was an emotional moment for an eleven-year-old boy who was witnessing the ruination of a once-beloved uncle, he reportedly showed no outward evidence of sadness. Perhaps he was being swayed behind the scenes by Somerset's own feelings of betrayal, with emphasis being placed on Edward's personal safety and the great danger he may have been subjected to, at the hands of his evil uncle. Whatever the truth, this was Edward's first glimpse of the treachery and deceit of men so close to the throne, and it must have been a very uncomfortable time for him – whether he sympathized with Seymour in those final days or not.

Far from being willing to give up his last shred of ambition, from his prison cell in the Tower Seymour reportedly scribbled a note to Elizabeth and Mary which was secreted in the soles of his shoes, and which encouraged them to unite and rise against their brother. He had intended for his servants to collect his shoes on the scaffold and so deliver them to the princesses, but alas, even this final plan was thwarted. He was executed on 19 March before his servants were able to fetch the shoes, and once dead the treasonous note was discovered. To the end, Thomas Seymour appeared to have been convinced by his own purity of intention, even penning a poem about his faithfulness to the king in his final days. Those who knew him, however, remained unconvinced after his execution. His nephew, who had once been so enchanted by Seymour's generosity and fun-loving spirit, wrote in his diary only one short sentiment when recounting the events of early 1549: 'The Lord Sudeley, Admiral of England, was condemned to death, and died the March ensuing.'[35] Elizabeth, who had experienced a complicated relationship with the Lord Admiral, perhaps said it best when she was informed of his execution. She reportedly observed, 'This day died a man of much wit, and very little judgment.'[36]

With Seymour's death, Somerset had one fewer problem on his hands, but that wasn't saying much. While Edward VI was still very much governed by his uncle and the regency council, all was not peaceful and well throughout England. Religious tension and violence against churches and the Catholic sacraments continued. Riots ensued over land enclosures as the value of English coins lessened due to the Lord Protector's poor fiscal policies and military pursuits. Meanwhile, the council that had once revered him now critically questioned his judgement and ability to govern, especially in the aftermath of Seymour's treason and the close call they had all witnessed when he almost succeeded in kidnapping the king. Somerset's reputation as the 'goodly Duke', and his vast authority, had been badly damaged in the downfall of his brother, and as spring 1549 approached, he grappled to maintain the power he had so easily attained at the beginning of the king's reign.

Just two years into Edward VI's kingship tensions were high, much of the country was in turmoil, and once-powerful noblemen were falling from grace and meeting with the executioner's axe. And this was only the beginning.

Chapter 8

How Far the Mighty Fall

At the same time that the Lord Admiral Thomas Seymour was meeting his gruesome end, other notable figures of Edward VI's government were hard at work developing a staple of his reign and the English Reformation as a whole. Since September 1548, Archbishop Cranmer had been holding meetings to debate and ultimately create a uniform liturgy for the English Church. As religious reform had been spreading through the country relatively unbridled for over two years, it was time to bring some order to the new way of theological thinking. The English language had already replaced the traditional Latin throughout parish services since the beginning of Edward VI's reign, in order to include the less-educated laity in the understanding of God's holy word. Now Cranmer determined that it was appropriate to standardize the Edwardian theological doctrine, establish English as the official language of the Church of England, and create some religious order in a country that had been suffering through turmoil and confusion for years. His goal – and ultimate result – was the Book of Common Prayer of 1549.

Meetings to discuss and construct this critical book were held at Chertsey Abbey in Surrey, as well as Windsor Castle, and though the total list of participants in these discussions has been lost to history, we know that they consisted fairly equally of both progressive evangelicals and traditional conservatives. Though it was perhaps not a unanimous agreement, it was decided in the autumn of 1548 that this new book would replace the Latin liturgy of Roman Catholicism – although it is worth noting that Cranmer himself did not wholly object to the use of Latin in all circumstances of worship.[1] An element of Roman doctrine that he was moving further away from, however, as was becoming more evident in his discussions at the end of 1548, was that of the corporeal true presence of Christ in the eucharist. Prior to this, more evangelical 'heretics' had been burnt at the stake than were Catholic sympathizers – and this was largely due to those reformers' desecration and dishonour of the eucharist.[2]

But for years, Cranmer had been learning from European reformers and theologians who increasingly had been challenging the interpretation of the Lord's real presence in the bread and wine of holy communion. He had been in discreet contact with the German reformer, Martin Bucer, since the early 1530s – their correspondence growing in frequency during the latter-half of the 1540s. They discussed topics such as transubstantiation and the adoration of the eucharist, and their relationship grew ever closer as Cranmer established England as a country of refuge for evangelical exiles from the Continent, in late 1547.[3] Two such refugees, Peter Martyr and Bernardino Ochino, made an even deeper impression upon Cranmer's view of the real presence, when the former presented him with a letter on the subject, believed to have been written by John Chrysostom – Archbishop of Constantinople and an Early Church Father of the fifth century.[4] These conversations, letters, and in-person meetings with well-known European leaders of the Reformation led to Cranmer publicly stating his position against the Western Church's view of the eucharist. Thus the Book of Common Prayer became a vehicle not only to entrench English as the primary language of the Church, but also to expound an entirely reformed doctrine for the country's new faith.

According to Cranmer's Church of England (and by association the Church of England of Edward VI), the eucharistic presence of Christ was merely spiritual. In addition, the sacrament of penance (an element of Catholicism that had been retained in Henry VIII's Ten Articles of 1536) was rejected, due to its principle of placing a priest between the faithful and God. So too the Catholic belief that Confession required some act of good work as a means of contrition (the very definition of 'penance'), which contradicted the Protestant belief in 'grace through faith alone.' Of course, the concept of purgatory was also omitted from the Book of Common Prayer – it was definitively not a belief of the reformed church. According to Cranmer, immediately following his or her death a person would either be granted access to heaven or cast into the pits of hell – without the in-between limbo (purgatory) as asserted by the Catholic Church. These theological positions successfully gained a majority of support from Edward's Parliament, which had approved the publication of the book in late December 1548.

From the beginning of 1549, once the general public was aware that the Book of Common Prayer would be placed in every church and forced upon them, the text was greatly controversial. The book changed everything about worship in England – including the ways in which a priest was expected to stand when handling the eucharist and chalice. Now, although 'the consecration was retained, there was no suggestion of sacrifice, and elevation of the bread and wine was forbidden.'[5] No longer would he pause reverently while elevating the host for the congregation to adore – facing east towards the site of Golgotha as the Catholic rites instructed. Now he should face the people, showing no special veneration for the merely symbolic communion; according to Cranmer, 'Our faith is not to believe Him to be in the bread and wine, but that He is in heaven.'[6] Robert Parkyn, a parish priest near Doncaster, was particularly scandalized by this attack on the holy sacrament, writing, 'In many places of this realm (but specially in the south parts, as Suffolk, Norfolk, Kent and Wales, etc.) neither bread nor water was sanctified or distributed among Christian people on Sundays, but clearly omitted as things tending to idolatry.' He went on to complain further:

> Yea, and also the pyxes hanging over the alters (wherein was remaining Christ's blessed body under form of bread) was despitefully cast away as things most abominable ... uttering such words thereby as it did abhor true Christian ears for to hear, but only that Christ's mercy is so much, it is [a] marvel that the earth did not open and swallow up such villainous persons.[7]

These and more impositions on the mass were enacted as a result of the publication of the book, and soon afterwards the Act of Uniformity was passed by Parliament, which demanded obedience to the new way of religious thinking as well as the abolition of the ancient Latin rite.[8] The answer to this was not positive in many parts of the country, though the champions of reform seemed determined either to ignore or downplay the severity of the violent reactions. Rebellions and riots spread throughout Hampshire, Oxfordshire, Buckinghamshire, and North Yorkshire – with more serious uprisings in the West Country. Bucer described the state of progress, saying, 'Things are for the most part carried on by the means of ordinances, which the majority obey very grudgingly, and by the removal of the instruments of the ancient superstition.'[9]

While the speed and intensity of reformation had certainly begun to pick up, England had already seen great religious change over the past several years – and certainly within the two that Edward had been king. About a year prior it had been determined that candles should no longer be carried on Candlemas, and ashes would not be applied to the faithful's foreheads on Ash Wednesday. Palms were forbidden to be carried in celebration of Palm Sunday, and other similar Catholic celebratory rituals were also done away with.[10] Bishops were deemed official by the mere signing of the king's letters patent, and the 1414 Act for the Burning of Heretics (namely anti-Catholics) was abolished and dismissed by this now very anti-Catholic government.[11] Somerset, Cranmer, and perhaps Edward VI himself had been quick to abolish many aspects of the Roman faith in England – but the Act of Uniformity of 1549 was the first instance of real government crack-down. Any man of the cloth who dared refuse to adhere to the writings and doctrine of the Book of Common Prayer would face a prison sentence of at least six months – the third offence consigning him to a lifetime behind bars.[12] According to the Act, all churches and ministers were expected to have purchased and be adhering to the Book of Common Prayer by Whitsunday (9 June), or else risk such punishment and depravity of their positions.[13]

The general public's reaction to the imposition of this new book was, as might be expected, a negative one. While one of the purposes of the book was likely to have been an attempt by Cranmer to stifle the chaos and dissent around the country, it in fact had the opposite effect, sparking further rebellion and protest among several regions. One striking example took place in the Cornish parish of Bodmin, where rebels reportedly yelled defiantly, 'Kill the gentlemen, and we will have the Six Articles up again and ceremonies as they were in King Henry VIII's time!'[14] Another example of protest took place on 10 June, when parishioners of Sampford Courtenay in Devon approached their priest and asserted that 'they would keep the old and ancient religion as their forefathers before them had done.' [15] Martin Bucer continued to pay the will of the people little mind, however.

One such citizen who was troubled by the introduction of the book and the subsequent Act of Uniformity was Edward's sister, Mary. She had been shown leniency by Somerset in her Catholic sympathies thus far, but as soon as the Act was passed, she received a warning from the Lord Protector that she, too, would be expected to conform to the new ways by Whitsunday. Even her cousin – the Holy Roman Emperor, Charles V – warned her not to make an enemy of Somerset as reform swept through England, and yet Mary was emboldened by this challenge to her devout faith. She wrote back to Somerset in the spring of 1549, accusing him of usurping her brother's power and dismantling the will of her late father. Unfortunately for Mary, her refusal to acquiesce to the new doctrine not only irritated Somerset – it infuriated Edward, who took her words as an insinuation that she believed him too young to think for himself or have religious convictions that were entirely his own. He became more determined than ever to convert his stubbornly-papist sister to the reformed faith, and it was at this point that their sibling bond began to fray and weaken beyond repair.

But Mary was the least of Somerset's troubles in the summer of 1549. He was now facing increasingly violent rebellions against his policies regarding enclosures and landownership, as well as a number of new taxes on livestock. Between late May and June, he attempted to placate angry rebels to no avail, and by the beginning of July their land and fencing grievances combined with religious confusion and dissent led to armed revolts against the evil Lord Protector.[16] People were not only fighting for their lands – they were unemployed, struggling to make ends meet, and unable to afford the rents that had risen to unreasonable heights in recent years. In fact, the financial situation in England was growing increasingly dire, and this was due to severe inflation caused by Somerset's debasement of the English coin, which 'blushed for shame' according to Hugh Latimer's Lenten sermon that year. While such debasement had already begun during the final years of Henry VIII's reign, it was continuing with wild abandon in

Edward's, and causing enormous strain on the country's economy. Over the previous five years, food prices in London had risen by almost ninety per cent, and the continuing invasion of Scotland was costing England upwards of £200,000.[17] The general populous was poorer and more miserable than they had been in recent years, and who else could be to blame for their troubles but the man at the helm of the minority king's government?

It was not long before the council was beginning to blame Somerset and his questionable decisions as Lord Protector. Only two years into the reign of King Edward VI and already there was public discontent and financial hardships – the likes of which the English people had not seen in recent memory. Somerset's insistence on bringing the Scottish to heel in the ongoing 'Rough Wooing', his hasty pursuit of reform, as well as his sympathy for the poor and lowly had all invited protest and disgruntlement around the realm, and as the English people displayed their disapproval, so too did the very men Somerset relied on for support.[18] Nevertheless, Edward VI continued to look to his uncle for guidance – and Somerset remained, rather unwisely, unfazed. Nobles throughout the country were ordered to quell their local protests as best they could, as Somerset insisted the disorder would die down.

However, a revolt which started in Wymondham on 8 July would prove to catch his attention. Yeoman Robert Kett led roughly 16,000 angry rebels through Norfolk to storm the city of Norwich and defeat the royal army in a staggering assault that the Lord Protector had not seen coming. While Kett was subsequently captured, tried, and hanged for treason, his infamous 'Kett's Rebellion' would live on as one of the most notable uprisings of Edward VI's reign – and it certainly contributed to the ever-shrinking good opinion of the Lord Protector. After valiant attempts to ignore the discord around the country, Somerset could no longer deny that traitors needed to be dealt with. Towards the end of July, he had written to Lord Russell, 'Sharp justice must be executed upon those sundry traitors which will learn nothing but by the sword.'[19]

Yet another complication arose in the summer of 1549, however, as King Henri II of France declared war on England and distracted Somerset from the rebels who marched through Norfolk, Suffolk, and

Cambridge. As he dealt with the French siege on Boulogne, the Earl of Warwick faced rebels head-on in August. He led forces out of London and sent orders for his own residences throughout the country to be armed and defended.[20] Though he attempted unsuccessfully to reason with and pardon Kett's dissenters a number of times, he ultimately ordered his men not to take the rebels for men, but 'brute beasts imbued with all cruelty'. More than two thousand of Kett's men were killed in this final stand-off, while only forty (approximately) of the king's men were lost. Shortly afterwards, Kett himself was taken prisoner, and the whole victory was a feather in Warwick's cap.

The motives behind Robert Kett having led this infamous rebellion have been debated by historians ever since – with one popular theory pointing to Lady Mary's possible involvement. At this point, it was no secret that she had been adamantly against the religious doctrine-turned-law earlier in the year, and in mid-July, the council claimed to find proof that, 'Certain of [Mary's] servants are reported to be chief in these commotions.'[21] Of course, she denied any participation in the rebellion, and no one could directly prove otherwise. Still, the suspicion only increased the king's wariness of his sister, and further set Somerset against her.

Crushing Kett's Rebellion took a great economic toll on Edward's coffers, for which the public would soon answer with rising taxes. This financial burden placed on the government became yet another strike against the Lord Protector in the eyes of many noblemen, who now doubled down in their questioning of his ability to maintain law and order. While his strong position had already begun to waver in the face of his late brother's treason, he now faced increased scrutiny from his peers, who simultaneously looked to Warwick as a hero in quelling the rebellion. Thus, Somerset's hold on ultimate power and the title of Lord Protector was growing ever more tenuous, and in late summer Paget sent a scolding letter to him, indicating the council's feelings:

> Every man of the council have misliked your proceedings ... would to God, that, at the first stir you had followed the matter hotly, and caused justice to be ministered in solemn fashion to the terror of others.[22]

In the same vein, he warned:

> Unless Your Grace will debate with other men and hear them say their opinions, that will ensue whereof I would be right sorry, and Your Grace shall have first cause to repent.[23]

As summer faded to autumn, Van der Delft reported to the Holy Roman Emperor that the council was split and restless for change, despite Somerset's assertions to the contrary. It seemed that the Lord Protector was existing in his own reality – choosing to ignore the dissatisfied grumblings of the rest of the council. However, while he chose to keep his head in the sand, he was growing increasingly paranoid about his peers' loyalties, nonetheless. Two gentlemen could not speak quietly to one another without Somerset suspecting plots of treason. In truth, he was right to be concerned, even if his outward disposition indicated no such fear. Warwick had been growing increasingly discontented with the government for months – his head swelling from the admiration of those around him in the aftermath of Kett's Rebellion. When in early autumn he approached the Lord Protector on behalf of a neighbouring family who had lost one of its members in defence against the rebels, he was flatly refused – being told that there was nothing to give them in return for their service and loss. This appears to have been the deciding moment for the earl. It was time to bring Somerset down.

Warwick still had the backing of his troops from Norfolk at his disposal, and it took little convincing to acquire the support necessary to plan a coup against the Lord Protector. Nearly everyone was disenchanted with him – angry with his economic policies and the gross inflation that the realm had suffered over the previous two years. The average prices of food were now double what they had been during the final years of Henry VIII's reign, rebellion and civil disquiet plagued several regions of the country, and the king's coffers were dangerously near empty. In addition, Somerset's foreign policy had been disastrous – including his expensive and ultimately pointless conflict with Scotland, as well as war with France, precipitated by his failure to maintain the English hold of Boulogne.[24] While the council had once been confident in their leader, they now viewed Somerset as the Crown's enemy. Even the king had begun to grow resentful of his once-beloved uncle – perhaps convinced by Somerset's emotionless response to his brother's execution that Somerset truly was the evil man he had been warned about the late Lord Admiral. Forced out of his own government's matters of state, and with strict routine imposed upon him, Edward made no secret of his own displeasure with the Lord Protector. Thus, the council determined to dismantle the power held by Somerset.

Warwick knew he needed to gain even more support if he was to defeat Somerset, and the key to his success possibly could be found in the conservative faction. Staunch Catholics would surely be keen to move against the zealously Protestant Lord Protector, and so he reached out to Princess Mary for support – only to be flatly refused, as she distrusted him greatly. Nevertheless, he certainly used her name in gaining the conservative support he needed, claiming that if they were successful in taking down Somerset, Mary might become regent over her younger brother's government.[25] Such a move would certainly turn the country back towards Rome, and what better way to tempt traditional councillors than with such a tantalizing prospect? In truth, of course, Warwick had no intention whatsoever of returning the country to Catholicism, as many of his new supporters might have hoped. He rather deviously convinced men to join his cause by whatever means necessary, knowing full well that their support was his only means to a successful – and powerful – end. Following secret meetings towards the end of September, the plot was arranged while Somerset was out hunting in Hampshire with his wife, Duchess Anne. When on 1 October he returned to Hampton Court, he signed a series of warrants that granted various military payments – totalling around £16,000.[26] Little did he know that he – a man who had long held sympathy for the poor – had been tricked into thinking the money would go to the 'many poor men [who] did daily cry out to him for money,' as Paget had indicated.[27] In reality, he was funding the coup that was planning to destroy him.

Somerset had no idea what was being planned behind his back, but the first days of October indicated that something was amiss. Warwick refused to see him, and the armies of Lord Russell and Sir William Herbert were still absent – having been sent west to subdue rebellion, but since expected back at court. Somerset became paranoid that indeed some conspiracy might be afoot, and he desperately wrote to his councillors to bring everyone together. He was positioned well at Hampton Court, where the king was in residence. If he had Edward in his sights and grasp, he still had full control against whatever threat might move against him.

And move against him it did. In the early hours of the morning, news reached the palace of hundreds, if not thousands, of horsemen swarming the city. It was determined that they had gathered at Warwick's London home of Ely Place, at which time their motive may have become clear to Somerset. Troops were ordered to arm Hampton Court by any means necessary against Dudley's army, while the king – likely stunned and confused by the flurry of activity – noted in his diary that 'people came abundantly to the house.'[28] The palace was a hive of anxiety as Somerset prepared to defend himself and the king, and in the few days following he planned for his own troops to descend upon London and stave off any threat before it reached the palace. At some point it must have become clear to him that Hampton Court was not the safest location for them to remain, and he decided in a rather brazen move to whisk the king away to the stronghold of Windsor Castle.

His next actions were eerily reminiscent of the grave mistake his brother had made the previous year when he had attempted to barge into Edward's rooms under cover of darkness. Now, Somerset dared to burst into the royal bedchamber and drag the sleeping king from his bed at about nine o'clock in the evening. He ordered him dressed and delivered to the courtyard where the Lord Protector's troops waited to escort him to Windsor. Edward was none too pleased by the way he was being handled. Relegated for two-and-a-half years already to being treated like a child instead of a king, he was now even less in control of his own person than ever before. However, there must have been at least a part of him that truly believed the Lord Protector's claims that he was in danger, as he was seen riding out of Windsor with a small sword, exclaiming to those around him, 'My vassals will you help me against those who want to kill me!'[29]

Once he arrived at the dreaded castle (which he reportedly hated), he reportedly said, according to the gentlemen of his chamber, 'Methinks

I am in prison.'[30] He also described the night in his own writing, 'That night, with all the people, at nine or ten o'clock at night, I went to Windsor, and there was watch and ward kept every night.'[31] The staff at Windsor was ill-prepared for the king's arrival, and there were reports that the royal retinue had been despatched without any provisions – including food. It was a scramble to organize the castle and lodgings for their stay, but the Lord Protector had more pressing matters at hand. He needed to ensure that he was safe from Warwick and his men, and that the new stronghold of Windsor Castle was secure against anyone who threatened him.

But Warwick's army of men claimed to mean no ill towards Somerset; they maintained that they sought only to air their grievances to him and the king, regarding the current state of affairs. Now that the Lord Protector had acted in such a suspect manner – shuttling Edward away to Windsor – the council wrote to inquire after their young king's well-being: 'We mean nothing else but the surety of his Majesty's person,' the letter said, adding:

> If the Duke of Somerset would at any time have heard our advices, if he would have heard reason, and acknowledged himself a subject, our meaning was to have quietly communed with him for redress of all things without any disturbance of the realm.[32]

However, Somerset could not be convinced so easily that Warwick and his supporters pursued anything but violence against him. He wrote back hotly that if it was violence they were after, he would oblige them – insinuating his confidence in God's will for his own victory and his noble cause to 'preserve the King's Majesty's person, his realm and subjects.'[33] He sent other frantic letters, beseeching noblemen for their loyalty and support in protecting the king. Meanwhile, the number of Warwick's supporters in London increased, and it seemed the only solution to this impasse would be bloody civil war. In an already-chaotic England filled with discontent and disturbance, even Somerset knew better than to let such a thing happen. The final nail in his coffin, so to speak, were the words he was reported to have uttered on 9 October, 'that if the lords intended his death, that the king's majesty should die before him.'[34] Once his enemies caught wind of these treasonous words (if indeed they were spoken), their mission was even clearer. One of Somerset's former supporters, Sir Philip Hoby, played a crucial role as a secret agent of Warwick's men, feigning loyalty to Somerset while simultaneously passing messages between the waiting councilmen and Paget, Cranmer, and even the king. It was not long before Somerset had given up the fight, allowing Paget and Cranmer to call off his servants, and submitting humbly to the council's representative, Sir Anthony Wingfield, when he arrived at Windsor to arrest him two days later.[35] He apologized to his nephew, assuring him that he had never intended any hurt, but instead had only ever tried to protect him. Edward offered no comfort or words of support, and so Somerset turned his attention elsewhere – to his ally-turned-enemy, Warwick – with a hastily-written letter:

> My Lord, I cannot persuade myself that there is any ill conceived in your heart as of yourself against me; for that the same seemeth impossible that where there hath been from your youth and mine so great a friendship and amity betwixt us, as never for my part to no man was greater, now so suddenly there should be hatred; and that without just cause, whatsoever rumours and bruits, or persuasion of others have moved you to conceive; in the sight and judgment of almighty God, I protest and affirm this unto you, I never meant worse to you than to myself; wherefore my lord, for God's sake, for friendship, for the love that hath ever been betwixt us or that hereafter may be, persuade yourself with truth, and let this time declare to me and the world your just honour and perseverance in friendship.[36]

It appears that Edward – despite his irritation with his uncle's recent behaviour – was troubled and conflicted by the goings-on around him. He swiftly wrote a letter of his own to the council members who had opposed the Lord Protector, beseeching them to work together as his late father had intended, and to deal more gently with Somerset than he assumed they were inclined to. His letter reads:

> As far as our age can understand ... we do lament our present estate being in such an imminent danger; and unless God do put it into the hearts of you there to be as careful to bring these uproars unto a quiet ... we shall have cause to think you forget your duties towards us, and the great benefits which the King our lord, and father, of most noble memory, hath employed on every one of you. For, howsoever you charge our said uncle with wilfulness in your letter ... we trust that both you and he may continue ... without superstition, by a friendly determination and agreement among yourselves ... Each man hath his faults; he his and you yours; and if we shall hereafter as rigorously weigh yours, as we hear that you intend with cruelty to purge his, which of you all shall be able to stand before us?[37]

While some historians question the possibility of Cranmer or Paget's hand in Edward's writing of this letter (as they were known to have desired the council's gentleness in their dealings with the Lord Protector and had written separately to them in an effort to spare his life), it seems that this letter follows a similar style to those previously identified as Edward's own writing. It is not far-fetched to assume that he held a certain fondness for the uncle who had been his chief guardian and mentor for the past few years, or that he felt saddened and concerned for his sudden undoing. To assume that he himself did not pen this letter to the council – or conceive of its message himself – only perpetuates the hyperbolic caricature of the 'child king', allowing him no emotion, care, or intelligent thought that was entirely his own. As he witnessed the abrupt arrest of his Lord Protector and uncle, why shouldn't we expect that the nearly twelve-year-old-king would have truly desired Somerset to live and work peaceably with the council, to correct any wrongdoing that had been committed, and to avoid the bloody execution that his brother had faced only months earlier?

On 14 October, Somerset was escorted by three hundred armed guards from Windsor to the Tower of London, where he was housed with several members of his household, as well as his private secretary, Sir Thomas Smith. There he faced twenty charges of treason set forth by his former friends, who accused him of everything from bankrupting the country to bullying his colleagues. As Somerset awaited his fate Edward was conveyed back to Hampton Court, appearing shaken, according to Van der Delft, though he regally led a procession of a thousand horses through the streets of London.[38] Meanwhile, the council was scurrying to ensure that the king's security was heightened, and to create some new order among them. It was Wriothesley who took the lead – seeming to take a page from Somerset's book by promising favours to anyone who supported him. Whether he was after the title of Lord Protector is up for debate, but he certainly appeared to settle himself nearest the king and assume the spotlight in Somerset's wake.

According to a contemporary version of events, Edward became confused regarding Somerset's location once he was settled back at court. In the presence of the former Lord Protector's wife, the Duchess of Somerset, Edward asked innocently, 'Where is my uncle?' – to which she replied that he was a prisoner in the Tower, and that the council was determined to kill him. Astonished, Edward exclaimed, 'Jesu! They told me the Duke was ill – why have they taken him prisoner?' He questioned Cranmer, who attempted to placate him by reminding him of the fear of Somerset's instability: 'We feared that he might kill you ... If my lord had not been imprisoned, great harm had been done.' But Edward was adamant, insisting, 'The Duke never did me any harm ... He went to the Tower of his own will, it is a sign that he be not guilty.'[39]

There is, of course, some debate as to the authenticity of this exchange, but it does add colour to the already-believable theory that Edward was truly concerned for his uncle's welfare. He had already written his letter to the council upon Somerset's arrest, and now that he was made aware of the full extent of the danger his uncle might face, he was resolute that no harm should come to him. He insisted upon seeing Somerset, though Warwick initially balked at the idea. It apparently became clear, however, that the only way to secure the young king's favour was to placate and humour him, and so the ambitious Warwick supposedly addressed the council soon after, saying, 'We must return good for evil. And as it is the

King's will that the Duke should be pardoned, and it is the first matter he hath asked of us, we ought to accede to His Grace's wish.'[40] Once again, the legitimacy of this story is in some question, but it remains convincing enough in light of the fact that no immediate action was taken against Somerset while he sat in the Tower, and Warwick did not directly pounce upon the title of Lord Protector. Instead, he appeared to bide his time – slowly gaining the king's friendship and trust as he plotted his next move – knowing that while Somerset's star had so swiftly fallen, there was now plenty of room enough for his own to rise.

Chapter 9

Changing Tides

John Dudley, Earl of Warwick, had learned through watching his predecessor that the path to victory and power did not necessarily rely on the title of 'Lord Protector'. Instead, as his influence increased over the regency council and his relationship with the young king grew and developed, Warwick recognized the power he could wield simply by making others believe that he was the antithesis of the evil Somerset. He rejected the title of Lord Protector, instead naming himself *primus inter pares*, or 'first among equals', and Lord President of the Council – which he somehow reasoned was a fairer position than the one Somerset had held.[1] He would allow his colleagues on the council more freedom to rule the government as he simply offered suggestions from the sidelines.[2] King Edward – previously shoved into the background of state affairs by the former protector – would be brought more into the fold, allowed to attend his own council meetings and have a voice in conversation (though situations such as these may well have been staged).[3]

Perhaps in part due to his care to include Edward in the running of his own country, Warwick was granted the title of Admiral by the end of October 1549, and he rewarded the king in turn with gifts of money and even looser restrictions on his schedule and duties. It would have seemed at the time that he had learned from both the Seymour brothers – precisely what not to do from Somerset, and how to gain the king's favour and obedience, per the late Lord Admiral. Sure enough, Edward was drawn ever closer to Warwick in the weeks following Somerset's removal from the council, and it was not long before he appeared unable to refuse him anything he wanted. By the end of November, Warwick was effectively ruling as Somerset had – albeit through a different name and by slightly different tactics. Determined to gain and maintain even more of the king's good opinion, he placed several friends in positions close to the sovereign, both within the royal household and the privy council. In addition, he had attained Paget's 'great friendship' during the organizing of Somerset's downfall, and as a result more powerful friendships followed – such as that of the Lord Chancellor, Richard Rich.[4]

In the months prior, the Catholics had been afforded a relatively promising glimpse of hope that their religion might be restored as the preferred faith in England, when Warwick had flattered and appeased them in his mission to destroy Somerset. Now, however, as his victory had become well-established, he had no intention of following through on the promises he had made. Ultimate success in Edward VI's government meant aligning with the Protestant faith and plans for reformation – and Warwick himself was an anti-papist, anyway. By continuing to dissolve religious houses and chantries as Somerset had started, Warwick could ensure his favour with the king by padding the royal coffers – and he would reap the benefits himself by adding to his own. The conservative noblemen and council members were quick to catch wind of Warwick's deviousness, though, and it was not long before Arundel was communicating with Princess Mary, who swiftly shut him down in order to remain firmly outside of the political drama. When Warwick discovered this sly attempt by Arundel to gain royal Catholic support, he barred him from the council and later placed him under house arrest.[5] While Protestants viewed Warwick as an 'intrepid soldier of Christ [and] the thunderbolt and terror of the papists', Catholics now feared how much further he might take the Reformation.[6]

In fact, Warwick planned to take the Reformation much further, indeed – so much so that even Cranmer was slightly concerned, as he had always intended more tolerance and caution in planned reforms than the new President of the Council appeared to have adopted.[7] Warwick was determined to move apace in his destruction of Catholicism in England, speedily appointing two evangelicals to the council in Arundel's place – Thomas Goodrich, Bishop of Ely, and Henry Grey, Marquess of Dorset.[8] By doing so he gave his own faction the majority of control over the council which allowed his plans to move forward – probably to the young king's pleasure. With Christmas 1549 came the order to all bishops to burn every Catholic book and to proclaim the message of reformation.

Passionate evangelicals were ecstatic that Somerset's end had not also been the demise of the spread of the Protestant faith, and so Warwick's support and influence continued to grow. Once again, he took a page from Somerset's book by rewarding his loyal council members with gifts of land, money, and elevations to the peerage.

But as all seemed well for Warwick at court, a rumour swirled that Somerset might be released from the Tower of London on New Year's Day, as a token of the king's fondness and forgiveness. Wriothesley, whose health had been deteriorating over the past few months, could not countenance the idea of Somerset returning to power – but neither could he stomach Warwick's rule. Both men were his enemies; each had done his part effectively to destroy conservative control of the government. When in December Wriothesley was given the task of visiting Somerset daily in the Tower, to question him regarding the articles with which he was charged, he saw this as an opportunity to take down both his enemies. One day, upon exiting the Tower grounds, he remarked, 'I thought ever we should find them traitors both, and both are worthy to die by my advice.'[9] But he made the mistake of directing this comment to William Paulet, who hastily warned Warwick. In turn, Wriothesley was called out at the next council meeting as he read out his argument for Somerset's execution. A heated Warwick rounded on him, jumping up and accusing him of seeking both Somerset's blood as well as his own (reportedly while gripping his sword). He ordered the house arrests of Wriothesley and all his supporters – including Sir Richard Southwell, Sir Thomas Arundell and Sir Edward Rogers, who were also fined upwards of £500 (£125,000 today).[10] Soon after, in February 1550, Henry FitzAlan, Earl of Arundel (not to be confused with Sir Thomas), was heavily fined and removed from his post of Lord Chamberlain when Sir Andrew Dudley found him removing the bolts and locks on the doors at Westminster Palace. Certainly, in Warwick's view, the conservatives posed a massive threat, and they needed to be destroyed.

Far from court, the king's elder sister remained well-informed of the goings-on under Warwick's effective rule. Mary, who had previously shown some favour towards him, could see clearly enough that his true colours were showing through, and that he had no affection or loyalty towards Catholics such as herself. With Somerset still imprisoned, she could not be certain that she would be afforded the same reluctant liberties to practice her faith in private, as she wished to do. She feared that any and all leniency that the previous Lord Protector had shown her might swiftly be revoked now that Warwick was in control. Consequently, she began to plan her departure from England, hoping that her cousin, Charles V, might help her. She was to be disappointed, however, due to the latter's fears that Mary would be renouncing any chance of ruling England in the future if she left the country at that time. He brushed off Mary's plea for help, indicating that it would be too difficult and risky to assist her. This left a helpless Mary confiding in Van der Delft that she would wait 'not without apprehension' to see what her future might hold.[11] King Edward, if he had known of his sister's feelings, would likely have had little sympathy for her plight. He was delighted with Warwick's enthusiasm for continued reform and had begrudgingly looked the other way for the previous two years, regarding his sister's religious beliefs.

Both of the king's sisters were invited to court for Christmas of 1549, but while Mary elected to remain at her own house in London during the festivities and joined her brother for a short time only), Elizabeth was delighted to visit with him. Notably, the once-fashionably-dressed teenager now opted for plain black garments that signified her Protestantism, and she carried her prayer books with her wherever she went.[12] In stark contrast to the vibrant colours and ornate jewellery that her sister preferred, Elizabeth's new style certainly pleased the ever-fanatical king, as well as their tutor, Roger Ascham. He noted around this time that, 'With respect to personal decoration, she [Elizabeth] greatly prefers a simple elegance to show and splendour, so despising the outward adorning of plaiting the hair and wearing of gold, that in the whole manner of her life she rather resembles Hippolyta than Phaedra.'[13] According to Van der Delft, the sixteen-year-old Elizabeth was 'continually with the King' following her arrival at court on 19 December, and was evidently successful in recovering her reputation from the scandal with the late Lord Admiral, which had tainted her reputation the previous year.[14] While Edward had been momentarily stunned by the stories from Chelsea some months prior, it seemed he no longer cared one way or another regarding the affairs of his sister's heart.

He was becoming a rather priggish and pompous king, focused nearly entirely on matters of religion.

Following Christmas, once Elizabeth was returned to Hatfield, she received confirmation that her relationship with her brother was solidified and stronger than ever, when he wrote to her requesting her portrait. She replied graciously:

> The face, I grant, I might well blush to offer, but the mind I shall never be ashamed to present. For thought from the grace of the picture the colours may fade by time ... yet the other nor time with her swift wings shall overtake ... And further, I shall most humbly beseech your Majesty, that when you shall look on my picture, you will vouchsafe to think that as you have but the outward shadow the body afore you, so my inward mind wisheth that the body itself were often in your presence.[15]

While Warwick still held the most powerful cards of any man on the council, his problems were far from over. By mid-January it was looking more likely that Somerset would be released from the Tower, though he was also formally deposed as Lord Protector at this time. On 6 February 1550, he was brought in front of the council to receive King Edward's pardon for the thirty-three charges to which he had admitted and was ordered to remain under house arrest at the king's pleasure.[16] Four days prior, Warwick had been named Lord Great Master of the Chamber, which afforded him an enormous amount of access to the king, as well as control of the royal apartments. As 'first among equals' and Lord President of the Council, Warwick knew that he had a fine line to toe, in order not to make the near-fatal mistake that Somerset had made by abusing his authority and turning the rest of the council against him. A more equal and agreeable system needed to be established, and the king's councillors needed to present a united front. Paget delivered a speech called 'Advice to the King's Council' on 23 March, detailing these exact expectations, and beseeching everyone to work together for the king's good and for the sake of the country.[17]

By mid-spring, it appeared that Warwick was willing to do almost anything to maintain this good will and spirit among his colleagues, even when it came time to see Somerset at court. On 12 April 1550, the former Lord Protector visited the king at Greenwich and dined with Warwick directly afterwards. This caused some confusion about Somerset's position and the likelihood of his return to power, as relayed from Van der Delft to the Holy Roman Emperor: 'Some say he will be President of the Council, others that he will be Governor of the King's person; however that may be, there is apparently a great likelihood of his return to high authority.'[18] Sure enough, by the end of the month Somerset had fully returned to court; on 7 May he rejoined the council; and on 11 May he was re-admitted to the Privy Chamber.[19] It seemed, despite Warwick's subtle advances, that Somerset was still the man best fit for ultimate control at Edward's court.

It is difficult, however, to know the king's own mind when it came to Somerset's return. For the past several months, he had been growing ever closer with Warwick, who forged passionately ahead with plans for reformation, much to the young king's approval. Though he possibly still held a fondness for his uncle, he could also be forgiven for harbouring some amount of unease following the unsettling events of the previous October. His own words on the subject are nondescript and emotionless, as he wrote only, 'My Lord Somerset was (Delivered [of] his bonds) and came to court.'[20] Edward returned Somerset House to the duke, and approved of a marriage between Somerset's daughter, Anne, and Warwick's son, John, for mid-summer that year. It seemed he was trying his best to maintain peace among his councillors, having been shocked and frightened by what might happen when discord and disorder was left to germinate.

Warwick was certainly no fool during this time, and he played his cards exactly right. With Somerset back in the picture, Warwick made a show of retreating quietly and conducting more of his business from home. He feigned ill health, though he remained in constant contact with the king, and continued to stage tournaments and amusements for Edward, keen to remind him often that he had his best interests in mind. Meanwhile, although Somerset may have been tricked into believing that all was on course to resume as it had been some seven months prior,

Van der Delft was not so easily duped. He wrote to the Emperor, 'The Earl of Warwick is absolute master here, and the Lords of the Council are under his orders. They go daily to his house to learn his pleasure; nothing is done except by his command.'[21]

Mary certainly knew who was in charge, too, as she had been tormented by Warwick since the New Year. While she had previously hoped for a possible avenue of escape from England in the form of marriage with the Catholic Dom Luis of Portugal, Warwick had prevented the union by declining to supply her dowry.[22] The council was reminded in early spring of Somerset's previous promise to allow Mary to worship through the mass in private, but Warwick was icy in his discussions with Van der Delft on the topic. He scoffed passionately, 'You talk a great deal about the Lady Mary's conscience … You should consider that the king's conscience would receive a stain if he allowed her to live in error.'[23] He refused to uphold the agreement that Somerset had allowed, knowing full well that by standing up for the king's preferred religion, he was further securing Edward's affection for him. Still, Mary continued quietly to celebrate the mass as she had always done, albeit behind the council's back.

As Warwick picked fights with Mary and Van der Delft he also tightened security around the king, now that Somerset was under the same roof. In late April, Edward wrote that he had five grooms constantly attending him, as well as three outer Privy Chamber gentlemen – two who slept on pallet beds in the royal bedchamber – and knights standing guard within his apartments.[24] Yeomen of the Guard were also increased from one hundred to four hundred men, and sixty 'men of arms' were stationed around the palace. Anywhere the king might go first required inspection by one of his ushers – including the roofs and floors – in order to ensure that there were no hidden doors or passageways through which someone might smuggle him away.[25] Clearly, Warwick took Edward's personal safety extremely seriously, perhaps to some extreme.

In addition to the king's physical safety, he also took a special interest in his education and pastimes, making significant alterations to Edward's schedule. Under Somerset, the young king had undergone long, rigorous days of coursework, academic reading, and scholarly debate, with little to no time for play or sport. But Warwick was different – again, probably due to his effort to win Edward's affection. He wanted the king to spend time riding, exercising, and learning how to handle weapons. He encouraged hunting, tennis, and hours spent in the tiltyard – though he 'never neglected his studies'.[26] Warwick paid special attention to those who were instructing Edward, particularly regarding matters of religion, and though he was rather lenient regarding the king's free time and physical pursuits, there were still strict rules to follow when it came to his studies. His tutors were replaced as necessary, and religious books were carefully screened before the king had access to them, and nothing – not even the impressive reformist treatise *De Regno Christi*, written by Martin Bucer – could be presented to Edward without first passing through the hands of the council.[27]

Edward's education continued to thrive under Warwick, and by this time he had a full and fluent understanding of the Latin language and was successfully translating Greek texts, according to Cheke. Impressed upon seeing him, Roger Ascham gave this description of Edward's scholarly abilities, in the spring of 1550:

> The ability of our prince equals his fortune, and his virtue surpasses both. In eagerness for the best literature, in pursuit of the most strict religion, in willingness, in judgement, and in perseverance, he is wonderfully in advance of his years. I consider him fortunate in that he has had John Cheke as the instructor of his youth.[28]

It was around this time that *Edward's Chronicle* came into being, as Cheke encouraged the king to keep a diary in which to record the events of his life and reign. The argument for Edward starting to write his *Chronicle* at this time lies within the very structure of the document – with longer and more general description (often in the third person) making up the first three years of his reign, and more thorough and frequent entries going forward from April 1550. It appears that Edward was reviewing his few years as king, detailing anything he could remember as part of his writing assignment – and structuring his writing very much like some of the famous contemporary English history chroniclers – before beginning his nearly-daily notes.[29]

Throughout the summer of 1550, it seemed Edward was very much enjoying the freedoms he was granted by Warwick and he began exercising his own (new) free will to ignore those who dared attempt to bridle him. He was warned by men like Hugh Latimer and Thomas Lever to avoid frivolous pursuits – despite Warwick's permission – and to remain focused on the main task at hand: the Reformation. He was urged not to fall into the dangerous traps of the heart, as his father had done, which might cause 'much whoredom and divorcing', as well as to limit time spent with carefree adolescents such as Barnaby Fitzpatrick, Edward's closest friend.[30] But the twelve-year-old king was becoming increasingly confident at doing exactly as he pleased, now that he was being afforded the ability to do so. He often ignored such warnings and instructions – opting to transform his Privy Garden into a bear-baiting arena or racking up gambling debts while playing at cards and chess. He excitedly wrote about bear and bullbaiting, as well as hunting, in a few *Chronicle* entries from May.[31] In these ways, he continued to prove that he was every inch the late Henry VIII's son – valuing material goods, expensive finery, and a healthy dose of fun. The fact that he could now turn a blithe eye away from those who disapproved of his activities only furthered his appreciation for and loyalty towards the Earl of Warwick – much to the latter's satisfaction.

Unfortunately, on 21 June, one of our best sources for details of Edward's court – Ambassador Van der Delft – passed away, just one month after leaving court to return to Flanders. This sudden event came after he had discussed another possible escape attempt with Princess Mary, who remained desperate to flee England to find religious safety on the continent. He had shared with Mary that the new ambassador to the English court, Jehan Scheyfve (meant to replace him that month anyway), was ignorant of her hopes to escape, and so Van der Delft himself would be able to return quietly to England to secretly convey her out of the country. However, as his health rapidly deteriorated in June, he made known the details of the plot to those around him. When Charles V heard of Van der Delft's death, he instructed Scheyfve's secretary, Jean Dubois, to return to England to accomplish the deceased former ambassador's plans. It seemed there might be hope for Mary's escape after all.

But this escape plan went awry when Mary, in a very inconvenient case of cold feet, delayed Dubois when he arrived to collect her in Maldon, disguised as a merchant sailor occupied with shipping corn from the Netherlands. She was afraid to leave, questioning her decision to abandon her birthright – especially as her controller, Sir Robert Rochester, reminded her that astrologers had recently predicted the young king's death within the next year. If such were to happen, then Mary could be queen. Her indecision cost them their chance to flee unnoticed, and within days the council was aware of a suspicious foreign ship docked in the Maldon harbour. Dubois narrowly escaped arrest, but Charles V decided that no further attempts would be made to assist Mary to flee her current situation. Meanwhile, spies were placed in her household and Warwick's men ensured that she was well-guarded and observed, as they now suspected that she intended to leave England. More desperate for help now than ever, Mary pled with the new ambassador, Scheyfve, to help her retain her ability to celebrate the Catholic mass – something she feared would be stripped from her. However, Scheyfve proved frustratingly less helpful than Van der Delft had been, in part due to his struggles with the English language. He made no progress in fighting for Mary's interests, and the council insisted, 'She would have to put up with the new religion introduced by the king, or she might rue it.'[32] The emperor was insistent, even if his words to Scheyfve had little effect. He wrote in September:

> You will declare that you have special orders from us to request [the council] to leave the said Lady Mary, our cousin, in full liberty to practice and observe her religion, on the same terms as those her father approved, until the King her brother is old enough to give his orders on the subject ... You will persist in your request at all costs. Give them plainly to understand that, if they decide otherwise, we will not take it in good part, or suffer it to be done.[33]

If the council was making Mary's life difficult, Edward had little sympathy for her plight, especially once he had recovered from a brief and mysterious but reportedly grave, illness between October and

November 1550. This short period had left his council – particularly Somerset and Warwick – in a tizzy of anxiety as they feared the young king's untimely death, and thus a halt to the progress of the Reformation. In early November, Scheyfve wrote that tensions between Somerset and Warwick had grown to uncomfortable new heights, and that as a result, 'there are deep causes of discord among the members of the council. Some take Warwick's side, others my Lord of Somerset's.'[34] But with the end of November came a fully recovered king, and as he returned to attend to his studies and appear at council meetings, the previously reported friction between the two most powerful men at court seemed to fizzle. This gave everyone cause to breathe a sigh of relief, except perhaps for Mary, who now found herself more at odds with her brother than ever before.

In fact, Edward appeared entirely devoted to turning his elder sister's heart against her stubborn Catholic faith, even when certain of his council members tentatively questioned how truly harmful it would be to allow her to continue hearing mass within her private home. He was incensed that any of his most trusted men would suggest that he turn a blind eye to idolatry, referring to it as 'the evil thing I will not allow'.[35] He proceeded to write her forceful letters over the next several months, perhaps further emboldened by his new position – sitting on his own council and overseeing matters of state, which he had begun doing in August. He was truly feeling like a king, now that Warwick was allowing him some semblance of control, and he would not be disobeyed by anyone – least of all his sister. On 28 January 1551, following another happy Christmas celebration with his loyal sister, Elizabeth, he penned a letter – perhaps with the help of his council –to send Mary a blistering message of his disapproval:

> Your near relationship to us, your exalted rank, the conditions of the times, all magnify your offence. It is a scandalous thing that so high a personage should deny our sovereignty, that our sister should be less to us than any of our other subjects is an unnatural example; and finally, in a troubled republic, it lends colour to factions among the people ... Truly, sister, I will not say more and worse things, because

my duty would compel me to use harsher and angrier words. But this I will say with certain intention, that I will see my laws strictly obeyed, and those who break them shall be watched and denounced.[36]

The letter was written two months before Mary visited the king at Westminster. Prior to seeing him in person, she had replied passionately to her brother's scathing warnings, writing that the contents of his letter 'have caused me more suffering than any illness even unto death, because your Majesty accuses me therein of being a breaker of your laws, and moreover of inciting others to do likewise.'[37] Edward remained unmoved, and her subsequent visit in March was evidently particularly frustrating for him – a clear contrast to the times he shared with Elizabeth. He devoted an entire paragraph to the event in his *Chronicle*, writing:

> The Lady Mary, my sister, came to me to Westminster, where after salutations she was called with my Council into a chamber where was declared how long I had suffered her mass in hope of her reconciliation and how now, being no hope, which I perceived by her letters, except I saw some short amendment, I could not bear it. She answered that her soul was God['s] and her faith she would not change, nor dissemble her opinion with contrary doings. It was said I constrained not, her faith but willed her not as a king to rule but as a subject to obey. And that her example might breed too much inconvenience.[38]

This meeting accomplished nothing more than to further separate the siblings from one another – as Edward and his council demanded that Mary renounce her faith, while she argued in return that their late father had allowed her to worship and hear the mass as she had always done, and that things ought to be left as they had been at the time of his death. When Edward shot back the retort that it was he who was king now, and that it was his laws that must be obeyed, Mary challenged his ability rightly to judge such important matters due to his tender age. Finally, she asserted that she was more than willing to die for her cause if there be a need, to which a stunned Edward replied that he desired no such sacrifice from her. There was to be no resolution found at Westminster that day, and so Mary departed for home – no closer to reconciling with her brother, and certainly no surer of her ability to legally continue practicing her faith.

Edward's patience had long since run out, as he had already written in his *Chronicle* the previous December that 'there were letters sent for the taking of certain chaplains of the Lady Mary for saying mass, which she denied.'[39] He and his council were making little headway in their attempts to control her, though he was determined to continue – even when a warning came from Charles V in late March, in which he threatened war against England if his cousin was not granted the freedom to hear mass. Edward's council began back-pedalling, suggesting that he might reconsider.[40] Obstinate even to the point of passionate tears, Edward insisted that he would not be persuaded in this matter – and this impressed Cranmer to the point of confronting Cheke about his young, zealous pupil. 'Ah! Master Cheke,' he said to him, 'you may be glad all the days of your life, that you have such a scholar, for he hath more divinity in his little finger, than all we have in all our bodies.'[41]

For the moment, peace was restored. With an unhappy Mary returned home (likely to continue hearing mass in secret), Charles V seemed too distracted with other diplomatic engagements to make good on the threat he had issued to Edward. There would be no war for now, but it was far from the end of the young king's problems. Malcontent, disorder, and rioting threatened to resume across the country, and hostility smouldered once more, much closer to home. It seemed that Warwick and Somerset were at odds again. The two men continued vying for ultimate political power as the king's right hand – and as spring 1551 approached it was difficult to predict which one of them would be victorious.

Chapter 10

A King Rises; A Duke Falls

It did not take long before the entire council was once again aware of the bitter rivalry between Warwick and Somerset, as they openly argued in council meetings and the former took any and every opportunity to degrade the latter's position. In the early spring months, Warwick's men were granted promotions while he assumed the position of earl marshal – previously held by Somerset. Scheyfve wrote in April that 'it seems that what was taken from the Duke has been given to the Earl', and although it was openly declared by one of Somerset's servants that his master was better qualified to lead the king's council – not least because he was King Edward's uncle – it seemed that Warwick was still putting his rival down at every opportunity.[1]

Warwick was a formidable opponent, and as various noblemen at court had been burnt by him in the past, Somerset was warned not to provoke him any further. But the former Lord Protector could take only so much disrespect after having come so far from his fallen state, in just over a year. Somerset was not going to lose his hold on the council – and certainly not the king – without a fight. Before long, it was suspected that the ill-treated former leader of the council was plotting something; he had begun to seek the support of conservatives at court, by championing Princess Mary's cause. While Warwick now led the reformist faction, Somerset's hand was forced into cajoling the Catholics, and by so doing he gained the support of the Earl of Derby, among others.

At this point, the fervour of Somerset's own Protestant faith can be called into question. It became clear in the spring of 1551 that he was willing to play both sides in order to gain – and retain – political power. While he had been a powerhouse of reformist passion over the previous few years, he now joined forces with the conservatives to bring about either his own renewed Lord Protector status, or the regency of Princess

Mary – in which case, the religious flavour of the country would surely turn decidedly Catholic. Even Scheyfve confirmed in his writings to Charles V that Somerset 'would not object to abandoning the new religion and taking up the old again', which seems a far cry from the Lord Protector who had previously encouraged the reformation efforts with such vigour and pace that it had made even Archbishop Cranmer uncomfortable.[2]

Whether or not Mary was involved in such plotting is difficult to know, given her distrust of Somerset, and also her severe hatred of Warwick. In any case, it did not take long for Warwick to become aware of Somerset's plans to lead a conservative army against him. And there is evidence that he may have suspected his rival's plans for some months already. By mid-April, hundreds of mounted armed guards were positioned in London, and cities across the country were commanded to be on guard against crime and suspicious activity. Even the king knew something was amiss, when he penned the following entry in his *Chronicle* on 15 April: 'A conspiracy opened of the Essex men who within three days after minded to declare the coming of strangers and so to bring people together to Chelmsford and then to spoil the rich men's houses if they could.' Then, the following day he wrote: 'Also [a conspiracy] of Londoners who thought to rise on May Day against the strangers of the City; and both the parties committed to ward.'[3] That same night, a man was found near Warwick's London home brandishing a bloodied sword, and it was suspected that an assassination attempt against the earl might have been thwarted.

There were plenty of signs pointing to Somerset's possible involvement in the threats against the council and Warwick in particular, and by the end of April men who were suspected of plotting with the former Lord Protector were being hauled in for interrogation. It was a difficult thing to prove, however, and even King Edward was fooled into thinking that no serious harm had been caused – or would be perpetrated – from the conspiracies and threats of the previous weeks. He wrote in his diary at the end of April that his council had closeted together for a period of three days in order 'to show agreement among them, whereas discord was bruited, and somewhat to look to the punishment of talebearers and apprehending of evil persons.'[4] To his mind, the council had come together to move forward from the momentary chaos, and all would be all right from there. In fact, Edward's council was more divided, fractured, and paranoid than ever, and nearly everyone – from the reformers who sought refuge in England to the ambassadors who reported to their masters on the continent – could see that the tension at Edward's court had once again risen to uncomfortable heights. Daniel Barbaro, the Venetian ambassador, wrote that, 'Everything is going daily from bad to worse.'[5] But for the moment, talk of the planned uprisings and possible assassination attempts were put to bed, and it seemed that business as usual was the way forward.

Edward, for his part, was thriving – despite the drama. He had been King of England for over four years, yet was only now coming into his own – allowed to take his seat among the council and have a hand in state affairs for the first time in his reign. Warwick – apparently having learned from the late Lord Admiral how to please, flatter, and befriend the young king (and having seen by Somerset's example how not to overstep the mark), had been allowing Edward more and more insight into the goings-on of his government over the past several months, yet spring 1551 is the first occasion on which we see some of the first fruits of Edward's progress in his kingship studies.

It was then that he wrote his first treatise on reform and the societal functioning of England. This text – a judgment on the various social classes, as well as a proposed remedy for all the wrongs and evil-doings he identifies – illustrated a largely dismal view of the kingdom and its inhabitants. Some of his suggested solutions to the realm's maladies included 'good education', 'good laws', the 'punishing of vagabonds and idle persons', and 'encouraging the good', among others. He was harsh in his criticism of the impoverished and lowly – even the farmers, merchants, and husbandmen. He even had a bone to pick with the nobles, faulting them for failing to increase their rents while their own expenses rose, which would lead to further destruction. About criminals, nomads, and gypsies, he had the severest words: 'The vagabonds ought clearly to be banished as is the superfluous humour in the body, that is to say, the spittle and filth.'[6]

His attitude towards the poor certainly diverted from that of Somerset's, and it was becoming clearer, now that Edward was in his fourteenth year, that he was becoming more like his late father with each passing day. His enjoyment of many of Henry VIII's favourite pastimes – including listening to and playing music, hunting, tennis, gambling, and taking part in armed tournaments – had increased as he had begun to feel more like the king he was. Throughout the spring and early summer, he detailed many of his games, sports, and tournaments in his *Chronicle* – celebrating his victories ('The first day of the challenge at base, or running, the King won'), and begrudgingly admitting his losses ('I lost the challenge of shooting at rounds …').[7]

Sheyfve reported that summer that the king 'practices the use of arms every day on horseback, and enjoys it greatly', and he reportedly spent much of his time – when not embroiled in his still-rigorous studies – enjoying a number of amusements and entertainments at numerous palaces.[8] These kingly pursuits, combined with a more active role in the affairs of government, certainly bolstered the thirteen-year-old king's confidence and sense of royal self. The portraits painted of him between 1550 and 1551 depict a young king who perhaps viewed himself as a new and improved King Henry VIII. His taste for fine clothes and embellishments clearly matched those of his predecessor, and the shrewd, pointed expression on the boy's face paints an eerie similarity to the appearance of his late father. Even his stance – hands on hips, ankle turned out – is nearly identical to the stance of Henry VIII in his most famous Holbein portrait. Edward was clearly coming into his own by mid-summer 1551, and anyone at court might have confidently assumed that he was close to taking the reins of government fully for himself – perhaps under Warwick and the council's supervision – but as a king in his own right, regardless. Even Bishop Hooper declared, 'He will be the wonder and terror of the world if he lives.'[9] A new Henry VIII indeed, and at such a time there was surely little doubt that the strong, healthy king would live a long and full life. There was no doubt whatsoever that when the time came, he would provide sons to carry the Tudor dynasty well into the future.

This notion may have been thrown into some doubt, however, when the sweating sickness descended upon London. Edward recorded in his *Chronicle* on 9 July:

> At this time came the sweat into London, which was more vehement than the old sweat. For if one took cold, he died

within three hours, and if he escaped, it held him but nine hours, or ten at most. Also, if he slept the first six hours, as he should be very desirous to do, then he raved and should die raving.

The 'old sweat' to which Edward referred had struck London three decades prior, and already this new visitation appeared more deadly than that recalled by the king's elder subjects and councillors.[10] Two days later, Edward was writing that the infection had grown so much as to kill seventy people in London the previous day, and one hundred and twenty at the time of his writing. He recorded that some of his own attendants had fallen ill and died, and so he was moved to Hampton Count with 'very few with me'.[11] In fact, the 'sweat,' as it was called, would ravage England for the next three months and claim the lives of two of Edward's close friends, the brothers Charles and Henry Brandon, aged thirteen and fifteen – the sons of the late Duke of Suffolk. According to Henry Machyn:

> for there died in London many merchants and great rich men and women, and young men and old, of the new sweat … the sixteenth day of July died of the sweat the two young dukes of Suffolk of the sweat, both in one bed in Cambridgeshire.[12]

Edward was said to be devastated at the loss of his friends, and he penned a discourse on the tragic subject soon after, though he made no mention of it in his *Chronicle*.[13] Across England mass graves were hastily dug for the swift burials of several hundreds of bodies, and as if the devastation of the disease was not difficult enough, the aggression of the sweating sickness proved to be another opportunity for frustrated Catholics to rail against the Reformation. God was punishing England and England alone, as it was noted by Hooper that, 'None other nation [was] infected therewith.'[14]

It was not only disease, destruction, and devastation at play in the summer of 1551, however. Romance was also a topic of discussion – or rather, a new marriage arrangement for the young king. The royal bride who had been the goal of the seven-years-long 'Rough Wooing' – for which far too many English and Scots had died – was now contracted to marry Francis, the young dauphin of France. England's great fear that Scotland would align itself with France – thanks to Mary's mother, Mary of Guise – had proved true and it was time for Edward to look elsewhere for a wife. It hardly took any time at all, for when the Marquess of Northampton travelled to France, conversation was reopened regarding a possible marriage agreement between Edward and King Henri II's daughter, Elizabeth of Valois.[15] As the sister of Francis, who was now betrothed to Mary, Queen of Scots, Elizabeth provided the opportunity for an alliance with France which, while unexpected, would prove beneficial to England's diplomatic interests. Her dowry was the cause for some debate, but 200,000 ecus was finally agreed upon, even when Pope Julius III threatened to excommunicate Elizabeth if she married the Protestant king. Clearly, her father – who was, of course, Catholic – was unconcerned. He agreed that the marriage would go ahead in six years' time, when Elizabeth was the acceptable marriageable age of twelve.[16]

The sweat in London slightly complicated the arrival of the French envoys in London in mid-July, in order to visit with Edward, but nevertheless their stay evidently made an impact on the king, who wrote extensively about it in his *Chronicle*. In addition to entertainments, banquets, music, hunting, and gaming, on 16 July Edward was invested as a Knight of the Order of Saint-Michel (the highest order of chivalry in France at the time). This occasion was an opportunity for Edward to dazzle the French envoys with his magnificence – bedecked in luxurious garments and dripping with costly jewels – looking every inch a king that their Elizabeth would be lucky to marry. They were, reportedly, quite impressed, describing him as 'an angel in human form'.[17] The envoys were also showered with expensive gifts – including an especially valuable ring from Edward's own finger – before they returned home to France, and it was soon afterwards that William Scrots set to work painting a new portrait of the English king for his intended. This painting, which can still be viewed on its original canvas in the Louvre, featured a version of Edward as a proud and regal young man – a king who now attended his own council meetings, discussed matters of state, and entertained foreign diplomats. In late summer 1551, this portrait illustrated the king that Edward believed himself to be, and who all of Europe – perhaps especially, France – should have held in awe.

Under Warwick's guidance, Edward's education in matters of state increased as the summer progressed and he found himself reaching the end of his formal studies. His tutors were dismissed in August, and that same month he ordered the name of one of his father's ships, 'The Great Harry' to be renamed 'The Great Edward'.[18] He was within only a few years of ruling in his own right, his confidence had grown enormously over the previous year, and he was taking steps to ensure there was no mistaking just who was in control. But while he showed a great interest in the running of government and organization of his council, Edward's attention turned again in mid-August towards his disobedient sister. He determined again that Mary may not attend mass or hear private masses in her home, and by the end of the month two of her servants had been arrested and committed to the Tower, as a warning.[19] Two days later, Lord Rich, Sir Anthony Wingfield, and Sir William Petre travelled to her Essex home of Copt Hall to deliver yet another message from Edward. Her answering words surely infuriated her brother even more, as she once again defied his wishes and questioned his ability to instruct her in such matters, due to his young age:

> his Majesty shall find me ready to obey his orders in religion: but now in these years, although the good sweet king have more knowledge than any other of his years, yet is it not possible that he can be a judge in these things. For if ships were to be sent to the seas, or any other thing to be done touching the policy and government of the realm I am sure you would not think his years yet able to consider what were to be done: and much less … can he in these years discern what is fittest in matters of divinity.[20]

Edward was once again insistent, even when Charles V instructed Sheyfve to protest to the council on the Holy Roman Empire's behalf. It would do no good. No one was above the king's laws – and yet very little would be done to move against Mary. Even her imprisoned servants would be quietly released in time, and she would go ahead hearing mass in her private residences.

Meanwhile, there were more pressing matters to worry about. As the sweat ravaged on, the financial state of England continued to decline as well. Rising inflation continued to plague the country, and Warwick responded to this crisis by further debasing the coin. There were also rumours that, once again, Somerset might be up to no good – away from court for a time to escape the sweating sickness. While no one knew precisely what he might be planning, five hundred foreign mercenaries were employed to join the royal guards to defend the king and council.[21]

As it turned out, Somerset did have men ready to fight against Warwick, as one of his followers admitted in early October. A good two thousand men had been readied to move against Somerset's enemies in London. But his plans may not have rested wholly on an armed insurrection. Sir Thomas Palmer – a friend of Warwick's – claimed at the time that Somerset actually planned to invite his rival to a banquet, only to have him killed.[22] Edward himself wrote about this in his diary, noting, 'Sir Thomas Palmer came to the Earl of Warwick ... whereupon in my Lord's garden he declared a conspiracy. How at St George's Day last, my Lord of Somerset ... went to raise the people.' He went on to write that, 'A device was made to call the Earl of Warwick to a banquet with the Marquis of Northampton and divers other[s] and to cut off their heads.'[23]

Warwick needed to move quickly in order to beat Somerset at his own game. As some English chroniclers suspected, his next move – that of bestowing upon himself a dukedom – may have been in order to raise himself to the same level as Somerset, and thus mount a serious challenge.[24] Whatever the reason, on 11 October at Hampton Court he was created Duke of Northumberland. In addition, he granted titles to several of his friends – perhaps to ensure their support in the movements to come. According to Edward, Henry Grey, Marquess of Dorset, was created Duke of Suffolk, William Paulet was named Marquis of Winchester, Sir William Herbert was made Earl of Pembroke and Lord of Cardiff, and three gentlemen of the Privy Chamber were knighted.[25] Somerset, of course, grew all the more suspicious of Warwick's (now Northumberland's) intentions. Even Scheyfve wrote soon after the ceremonies, 'I have heard from a trustworthy source that the Duke of Somerset is again going to be arrested, and that the plot is being very secretly woven by the Earl of Warwick and his party.'[26]

Edward wrote on 14 October 1551 that Somerset 'suspected some ill' and said as much to Secretary Cecil, who ensured him in return that, 'If he were not guilty he might be of good courage.' These, as it turned out, were ominous words. Just two days later, Edward added to his *Chronicle* that Somerset was apprehended after dinner at Westminster and taken once again to the Tower, followed the next day by his wife and a number of associates– all for 'devising these treasons'.[27] He had, indeed, been accused of treason and conspiracy against the council, and was alleged to have plotted to take control of the Tower of London and its armoury. Whether or not this was true, Northumberland now had his enemy exactly where he wanted him, and Edward appears to have done little to intervene when hearing of his uncle's second arrest.[28] However, Sheyfve described Edward as having 'become very thin and weak during the last season' and suspected that he may have been 'deeply distressed'.[29]

In fact, it is difficult to know what Edward's personal feelings were, regarding Somerset's arrest. Certainly, he had grown closer to Northumberland in previous months, and it is very likely that he had been convinced of his uncle's guilt in plotting against him and threatening his safety. The fact that we have little evidence of the king's opposition to Somerset's imprisonment in 1551 (compared with our evidence for his incarceration in 1549) may indicate that Edward's mind had turned against Somerset and was set on other, arguably more important, matters. He was fourteen years old now, after all – the age of majority, at least in the case of his cousin, James V of Scotland. He had been playing a more active role in government for months now, learning underneath Northumberland's guidance, and perhaps was placing much of his trust in the new duke.

Interestingly, even as he reached what would have been considered the age where he could sign official state papers himself, he allowed Northumberland's man, John Gates, the ability to utilize the dry stamp with Edward's signature instead. As had been the case several years ago with the signing of Henry VIII's last will and testament (among other official papers), this was reason for some – perhaps many – to suspect foul play and fraud.[30] But Edward saw himself very much in charge, despite the use of the dry stamp – which, of course, his father had also used. He was brazen in his expectations of his councillors to bow to his every demand and sign every bill that he sent to them. When he disagreed with a bill that was set before him, he made no hesitation in refusing to sign it – proving that he viewed himself as no one's puppet, despite Northumberland's agitation.[31]

The attitude throughout the realm regarding Somerset's situation was mixed. Some joined in the chants of 'traitor', claiming that he had grown far too haughty and entitled in the time since Henry VIII's death, while others continued to regard him as 'the good duke' who had been woefully wronged by Northumberland and his cronies. Many feared and hated the new duke – which Sheyfve reported back to the emperor, saying, 'Indeed the matter is kept alive by the hatred borne towards the Duke of Northumberland and his party by many lords ... who are saying quite openly that the Duke of Somerset is being unjustly accused.'[32] Meanwhile, Edward was clearly kept apprised of the interrogations in the Tower. He recorded in his *Chronicle* that William Crane had confessed on 26 October to the location of the supposed banquet where Northumberland and his friends would have had been murdered. He also wrote that Lord Strange confessed to having been ordered by Somerset to 'spy in all matters of my doings and sayings and to know when some of my Council spoke secretly with me'.[33]

In addition to these, Arundel also admitted to some involvement in Somerset's conspiracy – acknowledging that the original plan had been to arrest Northumberland and some of his allies on the council, though he claimed never to have intended any harm against any of the councillors' bodies. In early November, none other than Northumberland himself interrogated Somerset in the Tower – questioning him about his motives, plans, and communications. Unfortunately, Somerset's responses to these questions have not survived the centuries, but whatever was said served only to grease the wheels, as preparations for his trial were well underway.

The trial took place on 1 December from eight o'clock in the morning until three o'clock in the afternoon. He was conveyed from the Tower to Westminster at five in the morning, to avoid the massive crowd gathering to see him, and as he was tried by his peers – who accused him of everything, from seizing the king's person to plotting to murder Northumberland; from threatening Edward's own safety to aiming to take control of the Tower of London's arsenal. Somerset denied every single charge laid against him. Adamantly, he refused to confess to any treason, and insisted that any claim made against his character was a malicious lie or an incomplete story lacking sufficient witnesses. Edward himself recorded the trial and his uncle's responses (at least, what he was told of them) with a lengthy entry in his *Chronicle*:

> He answered he did not intend to raise London, and that swore the witness[es] [who] were not there. His assembling of men was but for his own defence. He did not determine to kill the duke of Northumberland, the Marquis, etc., but spoke of it and determined after[ward] the contrary; and yet seemed to confess he went about their death.

After the long trial with crowds gathered outside Westminster, the final verdict was read aloud. As Edward recorded, 'the Lords acquitted him of high treason' – much to the delight of the waiting crowds.[34] The guards standing at the entrance to Westminster Hall left their axes pointed downwards (a known symbol for the defendant's innocence), and the waiting masses of Somerset's supporters erupted with cheers.[35] Even Edward, who overheard the noise, insisted that 'he had never believed Somerset could be a traitor'.[36] However, though the duke had not been convicted of high treason, the remainder of his sentence did not bear good news. As Edward would continue to record in his *Chronicle,* the lords 'condemned him of treason felonious, and so he was adjudged to be hanged'.[37] He had broken the law against the gathering of unlawful assemblies and thus would die, regardless of his innocence of treason against the Crown. Horrified, Somerset fell to his knees as the verdict was read. He begged Northumberland's pardon – as well as that of several other lords – and before he was led away, Northumberland gave a chilling (and insincere) response to his condemned enemy:

> Duke of Somerset, you see yourself a man in peril of life and sentenced to die. Once before I saved you in a like danger,

nor will I desist you now, though you may not believe me. Appeal to the mercy of the King's Majesty, which I doubt not he will extend to you. For myself, gladly I pardon all things which you have designed against me, and I will do my best that your life may be spared.[38]

It was widely suspected at the time, and indeed in the years following, that Somerset's trial and subsequent execution would not have come to pass without Northumberland's scheming hand. The two men's bitter rivalry was no secret, and there appears to be ample evidence of Somerset's plotting in the spring of 1551 to bring down his nemesis – though historians through the centuries have been divided as to whether or not he truly intended to murder Northumberland. It is more likely that Somerset aimed merely to unseat him from the power he held over the king, and wanted to reclaim the title and prestige that he had enjoyed only a few years prior. If not for Northumberland's insistence that Somerset needed to be wholly destroyed, it is altogether likely that the latter would not have met the fate that he did. He was no traitor, after all, and many who viewed the trial of December 1551 would later whisper about Northumberland's heavy-handed ministrations and concocting of 'evidence' and witnesses. Even he claimed to know that he had blood on his hands, as it was reported in later years that his rival's death haunted him, and the memory of his own part in Somerset's execution was something he regretted until his own death. Whether or not that was true is, of course, impossible to know. Northumberland, after all, was not known in his life for his genuine nature or sincere intention.

Regardless of Northumberland's sincerity or lack thereof, there were many throughout England who railed against the Duke of Somerset's conviction. Northumberland and the rest of the council effectively shut those negative voices out, however, and by Edward's own account, the Christmas season passed happily at court despite his uncle's imprisonment and impending death. He wrote extensively in his *Chronicle* about merrymaking through tournaments, banquets, and festivities, and though Scheyfve seems to have noticed that the young king was 'grieved and sombre about the imprisonment of his uncle', he remained unmoved in his resolution that Somerset should die according to his charge.[39] It is probable that Northumberland was spurring him on to see the execution through, sooner rather than later, and on 21 January 1552, Edward signed Somerset's death warrant himself. That same day, he sent word to the Tower to inform his uncle that he would not die by hanging after all, but rather by the more merciful act of beheading the following day.

At eight o'clock in the morning on 22 January, Somerset was led to the scaffold on Tower Hill, amidst a large gathering of people. If any of them still held out hope that the king would pardon his uncle and return him to favour for a second time in two years, they were to be sorely disappointed. As he approached the scaffold, Somerset knelt and prayed silently, before addressing the crowd with his final speech:

> Masters and good fellows, I am come hither to die; but a true and faithful man as any was unto the King's Majesty and to his realm. But I am condemned by a law whereunto I am subject, and are we all, and therefore to show obedience I am content to die; wherewith I am well content, being a thing most heartily welcome unto me; for the which I do thank God, taking it for a singular benefit as ever might have come to me otherwise. For, as I am a man, I have deserved at God's hand many deaths; and it has pleased his goodness, whereas He might have taken me suddenly, that I should neither have known Him nor myself, thus now to visit me and call me with this present death as you do see, where I have had time to remember and acknowledge Him, and to know also myself, for the which I do thank Him most heartily. And, my friends, more I have to say to you concerning religion: I have been always, being in authority, a furtherer of it to the glory of God to the uttermost of the power; whereof I am nothing sorry, but rather have cause and do rejoice most gladly that I have so done, for the mightiest benefit of God that ever I had, or any man might have in this world, beseeching you all to take it so, and to follow it on still; for, if not, there will follow and come a worse and great plague.

A brief scuffle of activity ensued, following a sudden and loud booming noise. Onlookers shouted in hopeful relief that the king was pardoning Somerset – that he would, in fact, be spared the axe that waited only feet away from him as he addressed the crowd. But as a few moments passed and no pardon came, Somerset continued gravely:

> There is no such thing good people, there is no such thing. It is the ordinance of God thus for to die, wherewith we must be content, and I pray you be quiet for I myself am quiet and make you no stirring and I pray you now let us pray together for the King's majesty to whose Grace I have been always faithful, true and most loving subject, desirous always of his most prosperous success in all his affairs and ever glad of the furtherance and helping forth ward of the common wealth of this realm.[40]

The rest of Somerset's speech acknowledged his altercations with men of the regency council, and his desire for their forgiveness. As he neared the end, he made one final request of the rowdy crowd who had interjected their cries of anguish and support throughout his oration:

> Now I once again require you, dearly beloved in the Lord, that you will keep yourselves quiet and still, lest, through your tumult, you might trouble me. For albeit the spirit be willing and ready, the flesh is frail and wavering, and, through your quietness, I shall be much more quiet.[41]

The beheading was swift and Somerset's body was thrust into a cart and wheeled away to the chapel within the Tower grounds, while onlookers openly wept for the former Lord Protector – the man whom they believed to have been so horribly wronged by 'the bad duke'.

But with this execution, Northumberland's quest for dominance over the council – and of Edward – was complete. Within another month, several of Somerset's allies would also die by the axe, while others would suffer merely the destruction of their careers. The political landscape was irrevocably changed with Somerset's fall, and even two of the men central to the king's Reformation – Cranmer and Ridley – had watched, horrified, as events had unfolded. The citizens of England – though many had not been supportive of Somerset's rule in previous years – feared the future and held even less trust and hope for the current administration of the boy king's government. The only one who seemed (at least publicly) unaffected, was Edward himself. The affairs of court proceeded as normal, and with only rare exceptions, even in private, Edward did not divulge his own personal thoughts on the matter of his uncle's execution.

Instead, he wrote rather matter-of-factly in his *Chronicle* on 22 January, 'The Duke of Somerset had his head cut off upon Tower Hill between eight and nine o'clock in the morning.'

Chapter 11

The Second Prayer Book

As the Duke of Somerset's days had become numbered towards the end of 1551, other changes were afoot concerning Edward VI's government. These went unnoticed by the general populace who were mesmerised by the nobleman's dramatic and violent fall. These changes were religious, and they were driven by Bishop Hooper's examinations of parish clergy just two years after the Book of Common Prayer had been issued and mandated across the country. His findings in 1551 were dismal, proving to him that only seventy-nine of the three hundred thirty-one clergymen he observed 'were satisfactory from a reformist point of view'. More than half of them did not know the full list of the Lord's Commandments, while two-thirds could not reference passages from scripture in defence of the Creed.[1] Church attendance had decreased significantly, and even King Edward himself had noted recently that much of the new mandated liturgy was ignored in parts of the country.[2] Due to the original Book remaining somewhat traditional with regard to certain elements of worship – particularly the medieval vestments, choral singing, and indications as to where the priest should stand and gesture when handling the Eucharist – Hooper found that many members of the clergy were teetering dangerously on the edge of orthodoxy.[3]

This was unacceptable, given how far they had come with reform in England, and how quickly it was spreading throughout parts of Europe. The Book did not go far enough for Hooper's liking, and it was obvious to him and other fervent reformers that it toed the line of Catholicism in an its efforts to avoid outright offence to the traditionalists. Instead, it upset virtually everyone and pointedly offended the reformers. Martin Bucer had been in full agreement with Hooper, having also found fault – or rather, at least sixty faults – in the 1549 Prayer Book, which he had documented just prior to his death in February 1551.[4] It was Cranmer's hesitation about ploughing ahead too arduously, so soon into the young king's reign, that was largely to blame for the tone of the book. He had known at the time of the original writing that the reform's progress needed to be handled somewhat delicately, and that much of the country would not immediately be on board with the changes. And of course, he had been right about that. The reception of the book in 1549 had been anything but universally positive, and riots and rebellions in the name of traditional Catholicism had plagued parts of England ever since. However, in those two years, popular theological thought had adapted and changed, and by the time Hooper was noting his disappointment in the clergy, and Bucer had listed his grievances with the still-too-Catholic Book of Common Prayer, even Cranmer suspected that it might be time to revise the writing to support the ever-reformed ways of thinking.

In 1548, during the writing of the original book, nearly all theological thought had supported the real presence of Christ's body and blood in the eucharist. This was not entirely the case in 1551; sermons on the spiritual (rather than literal) presence in the bread and wine were becoming more and more commonplace, as progressive religious thought wafted over from the Continent. Much of this perhaps was due to the reformist refugees who had recently made their homes in England, but it was also hastened by born-and-bred Englishmen like Secretary Cecil, who had 'organized a series of formal disputations on the eucharist' by the autumn of that year.[5] Indeed, the main subject of this revision – which was probably encouraged by Hooper and Knox and authored by Cranmer and Ridley – concerned the celebration and adoration of the eucharist, and the absolute restructuring of holy communion, which was renamed 'The Order for the Administration of the Lord's Supper'.[6] When Knox showed some concern over the concept of kneeling communicants, a section of the Book called the 'Black Rubric' was added to assure people that kneeling at the Communion did not imply any sense of adoration of the bread and wine.[7] In fact, it went on to argue firmly against the notion:

> Whereas it is ordained in the book of common prayer, in the administration of the Lord's Supper, that the Communicants kneeling should receive the holy Communion: which thing

> being well meant, for a signification of the humble and grateful acknowledging of the benefits of Chris, given unto the worthy receiver, and to avoid the profanation and disorder, which about the holy Communion might else ensue: Lest yet the same kneeling might be thought or taken otherwise, we do declare that it is not meant thereby, that any adoration is done, or out to be done, either unto the Sacramental bread or wine there bodily received, or unto any real and essential presence there being of Christ's natural flesh and blood. For as concerning the Sacramental bread and wine, they remain still in their very natural substances, and therefore may not be adored, for that were Idolatry to be abhorred of all faithful Christians. And as concerning the natural body and blood of our saviour Christ, they are in heaven and not here. For it is against the truth of Christ's natural body, to be in more places than in one, at any time.[8]

It is likely that the book was already being revised and rewritten by autumn. It was finalized in April 1552, though there is no record of Edward having played a part in its writing at all.[9] He certainly would have known of the work being done and supported it wholeheartedly, given his passion for the cause. But by then he was embroiled in other matters – drafting bills and other 'weighty matters' to be set before his council and taking part in nearly every meeting.[10] A passionate Protestant to his core, he had the business of government to attend to, as well as learning to be king –instructed and guided by Northumberland. Still, his convictions were no less strong than they had ever been, and even though he did not take a formal role in the editing of the Book, Scheyfve reported later in 1552 (rather disappointedly) that Edward was just as passionate about the faith as ever he had been. He would even refuse (on behalf of his plagued conscience) to attend the christening of the Imperial Ambassador's newly born son that following autumn, due to the ceremony being a Catholic one.[11]

In fact, that spring saw Edward making several plans to further religious change in England and, in particular, to make a positive impact on the poor. He had already established two new charitable foundations that February, as well as a hospital and a school for impoverished children. He had grand ambitions to enforce a new pledge upon the Knights of the Order of the Garter in the coming months – one that bound them to 'the truth wholly contained in the Scripture'.[12] He was busier than ever and growing more frustrated by the day that he was still a king in name alone until he reached his majority. There was plenty of work – especially as it related to the Protestant cause – to be done, and as he was still very much a champion for Protestantism, he clearly trusted Cranmer to assume the brunt of the work relating to the revisions of the Book of Common Prayer. The result would later be considered 'the greatest single achievement of [his] reign.'[13]

Robert Parkyn, the devout Catholic priest who had already demonstrated quite a large bone to pick with the 1549 version, would later describe the blasphemy in the 1552 Book of Common Prayer as being 'brought to pass only to subdue the most blessed sacrament of Christ's body and blood'. He went on to lament, 'Oh, how abominable heresy and unseeming order was this, let every man ponder his own conscience.'[14] The book decreed that ordinary bread would be used in church services, the vestments would be altered to break with the ornamentation and decadence of Catholic priests' garments, and nearly every element of the mass relating to the handling and adoration of the eucharist would be entirely rewritten. Even the leftovers – whatever bread and wine was not consumed during holy communion – were directed to go home with the clergy at the end of the day ('the curate shall have it to his own use').[15] Such a thought was a sacrilegious abomination in the eyes of a traditionalist.

While the issue of transubstantiation was the main focus of the 1551-52 revisions, it was not the only subject altered by the new Book. The sacraments of baptism and confirmation were also updated, and Parkyn recorded his distress that there was no longer any recognition of extreme unction or prayers for the dead in any official format.[16] Restrictions on singing during church services were also enforced, and all these updates were reiterated with the 1552 Act of Uniformity that coincided with the revised Book, just as with the original 1549 version. The Act presented the updated Book as a clarification to its precursor, and – in the words of Hooper – was meant to 'produce services which could be less easily dressed up as Catholic.'[17] All these denouncements of the traditional Roman faith would be even more ardently condemned with the New Articles of Religion, being drafted by Cranmer around the same time as these revisions. These Forty-Two Articles would be a great departure from the Six Articles published during Henry VIII's reign – of which transubstantiation had been listed first and most importantly among the three articles pertaining to the mass.[18] Though the Act of 1539 had intended to 'abolish the diversity in opinions' on matters of religion, the Forty-Two Articles of 1553 would crack down decisively on anabaptist heresies and Catholic superstition – decimating any notion of the significance of purgatory, the invocation of saints, or the value of 'good works'.[19] They would reach the masses a few months after the revised Book of Common Prayer, which would be issued in the early months of 1553.

These religious writings would become a hallmark of Edward VI's short reign – and yet, he had very little to do with either of them. In fact, while work on the Book was well underway in early April 1552 Edward's health was suddenly a matter for concern. He wrote in his *Chronicle* on 2 April, 'I fell sick of the measles and the smallpox,' though it was probably only the former, as there is no evidence that he suffered the hallmark pockmarks of smallpox.[20] He recovered swiftly and was described by Scheyfve as being back to his cheerful self by the end of the month.[21] His sister, Elizabeth, wrote to him to express her relief at his full recovery from the perilous disease, but there is no record of a similar sentiment sent by Mary – who may have been aware of the modifications being made to the already-Protestant books and acts that had been published earlier in her brother's reign.[22] Edward was returned to the business of government in early May, and he gave his royal assent to Cranmer's Forty-Two Articles in June, paving the way for them to be formally submitted to the council three months later.[23]

Edward was on the precipice of true power – so close to reaching the age of majority which would allow him to rule in his own right, and he was a quick learner in affairs of state. He was taking great pleasure in standing at the helm of his council and – whether truly wielding any real authority or not – certainly acting like the king he was swiftly becoming. In fact, such a quick learner was he that the council – with

Northumberland's blessing – had come together to settle on the official date that Edward would assume his majority rule. Upon his sixteenth birthday in October 1553, Edward would govern his realm in his own right.[24]

But in the meantime, there was one thing that would make him feel even more like a king, and which would formally introduce him to the citizens he ruled. A two-month royal progress was planned for midsummer, and on 15 July, Edward and his retinue departed London for the south.[25] The scale of the progress was enormous –at one point it numbered around four thousand men and horses before it was trimmed down to a manageable one hundred and fifty. According to Edward this was due to there being 'little meadow nor hay all the way as I went.'[26] They stopped at Guildford, Petworth, Cowdray, Halnaker, Warblington, Waltham, Portsmouth, Southampton, Beaulieu, Christchurch, Woodlands, Salisbury, Wilton, Winchester, and Reading before the progress concluded on 15 September at Windsor Castle.[27] Edward and his followers supped, gamed, and hunted all the way around these southern counties, and he wrote fairly extensively about their stops and the visits he made into the towns. Towards the end of August, he wrote to Barnaby Fitzpatrick that he had been 'occupied in killing of wild beasts, in pleasant journeys, in good fare, in viewing of fair countries, and rather [having] sought how to fortify our own than to spoil another man's.'[28]

Upon the conclusion of the progress in early autumn, however, the joviality of the king's travels came to a skidding halt when Northumberland's ongoing health issues began to plague him once more. What he suffered was likely a stomach ulcer, and the relapse into poor health sent him into a dark depression. He began lamenting his place on the council – the very position he had fought so hard to attain at Somerset's expense over the past two years. He wrote in September: 'His Majesty's choice of Councillors is, in my opinion, very well appointed, all save myself, who neither hath understanding nor wit, meet for the Association, nor body apt to render his Duty any ways, as the will and heart desireth.'[29] In addition to his illness, he was massively unpopular – which he knew, but generally cared little about. He was aware at the same time of multiple additional threats of uprising and plots against the

Crown, which he warned the council to take seriously as he rested and recovered. And these were not his only problems. England was still in extraordinary debt – the worst financial position the country had been in since the dawn of the Tudor period, and the disgruntled Northumberland decisively blamed 'the wilful government of the late Duke of Somerset'. In just ten years, the country's military expenses had totalled nearly £3.5 million – the equivalent of £684.6 million today – due to 'that man's unskilful protectorship', which caused Edward's government to be 'plunged into wars whereby his majesty's charges were suddenly increased to the point of 120 to 140 thousand pounds a year.'[30]

It was not only Somerset's military expenses from the years of the Rough Wooing to blame for England's economic woes, however. Bad harvests in 1550 and 1551, as well as the coin debasement of 1549 and 1551 'had also contributed greatly to the country's plight.'[31] Parish finances were suffering too, because as services had become simpler and church adornment grew plainer, the numbers of parishioners in attendance decreased – consequently leaving less money for those parishes. The funds gifted to local churches had decreased ever since Edward had taken the throne – with around seventy per cent of northern subjects leaving bequests to churches during the final seven years of Henry VIII's reign, falling to only thirty-two per cent under Edward. Likewise, in the counties of Lincolnshire and Huntingdonshire, while two-thirds of people had made benefactions to their local parishes in 1545, only ten per cent did so in 1550.[32] Parishioners – so heavily impacted by inflation, bad harvests, unemployment, and unaffordable rents – refused to tithe, which further harmed the state of the churches' coffers. To add insult to injury, the 1552 Act of Uniformity acknowledged that church attendance had reached crushing lows, bankrupt churches had fallen into decay and disrepair, and there was a noticeable shortage of priests, as recruitment to the Order had all but ceased in the face of reform and financial hardships.[33] Overall, it was not a prosperous time to be an Englishman, to say the least.

As if matters were not bad enough, after a brief period of enjoying his sporting and gaming pursuits at both Windsor and Hampton Court, within a month of the end of the royal progress Edward had grown weak and sickly yet again. In late October, the council was desperate to learn the cause of the young king's affliction, so they hired the Italian physician and astrologer, Hieronymus Cardano, to provide answers through the casting of Edward's horoscope. Edward himself – while likely not the one who summoned Cardano to his privy chamber – had an interest in astrology. He had once written, 'What is more natural than understanding of the principles, the sky, the constellations, the stars, the planets through the courses of which our bodies … and all grasses, flowers, trees, grains, wines and all others are governed and ruled?'[34] His interest in the stars was, of course, grounded in his faith, as he also remarked, 'Astronomy proclaims the works of God, from which he is revealed to men.'[35]

While Cardano spoke highly of Edward's intelligence and maturity, with his 'excellent wit and forwardness, being yet but a child,' he also provided a helpful physical description of the fifteen-year-old king. He was 'of stature somewhat below the middle height, pale-faced with grey eyes, a grave aspect, decorous and handsome' but also 'rather of a bad habit of body, than a sufferer from fixed diseases'. He noted that Edward had a 'somewhat projecting shoulder-blade' though he clarified that 'such defects do not amount to deformity'.[36] Edward was also described as suffering from poor hearing and eyesight – a detail which was already known at the time. He had his own pair of spectacles and dabbed an elaborate concoction of herbs onto his eyes, with a feather, whenever they bothered him. This herbal remedy reportedly consisted of red fennel, sage, powdered peppercorns, wine, honey and 'the water of a man-child that is an innocent' (a young boy's urine).[37] With those ingredients, one cannot help but wonder whether Edward's eyes were not worse off – and certainly more painful – after having such a mixture applied to them.

When it finally came time to cast Edward's horoscope (a long process that reportedly took a hundred hours), he declared that the king would live a long life. He would experience some illness in his thirties and again in his mid-fifties, but the astrologer saw no great cause for concern with Edward's current weakened state.[38] He would no doubt recover and live several, largely healthy, decades more. This would, of course, prove absolutely false, as poor Edward would be dead in just nine months' time.

Indeed, throughout the remaining months of 1552, Edward grew steadily worse. He developed a violent racking cough, lost his appetite, and became increasingly bloated and uncomfortable. Blood had begun to accompany the phlegm that dislodged from his diseased lungs – a tell-tale sign of consumption (tuberculosis), for which there was no cure.[39] It is around this time that we see the end of Edward's contributions to his *Chronicle*, as his last entry was made on the 28 November. He never makes mention of his illness, or even Cardano's visit to court. Perhaps it was comforting for the ailing king to distract himself by writing of military pursuits on the Continent, as those details make up the last several entries and end rather abruptly with the note of Paget being fined '£6,000, and £2,000 diminished, to pay it within the space of [blank] years at days limited'.[40] Meanwhile, the revised Book of Common Prayer had come into use on 1 November, garnering not even the briefest mention in the *Chronicle*.[41]

Although it was likely being whispered at court by December that the king may be in peril of his life, Northumberland chose to go forth with the regular Christmas festivities. Celebrations went ahead at Greenwich, for which Edward was present, but Northumberland's own illness and depression maintained its hold over him. He wrote to Cecil:

> Now, by extreme sickness and otherwise constrained to seek some health and quietness, I am not without a new evil imagination of men. What should I wish any longer this life, that seeth such frailty in it? Surely, but for a few children which God hath set me, which also helpeth to pluck me on my knees, I have no great cause to desire to tarry much longer here.[42]

The year 1553 began with Edward's already-hacking cough having 'grievously increased'.[43] It must have appeared to many at court that he was likely nearing death. People were already speaking of him in such a way, as evident by John Cheke's letter to Heinrich Bullinger early that year. In the letter, he praised the young king's work and all that he had accomplished in his short reign, noting that he was 'debilitated by long illness':

[he] [h]as accomplished at this early period of his life more numerous and important objects, than others have been able to do when their age was more settled and matured. He has repealed the act of the six articles; he has removed images from the churches; he has overthrown idolatry; he has abolished the mass, and destroyed almost every kind of superstition.[44]

Perhaps partly due to the king's illness, Princess Mary accepted an invitation to pay him a visit at court for the first time in two years, and she arrived on 10 February. Notably, she was greeted quite differently than ever before, with the council waiting to welcome her at the gates 'as if she had been Queen of England'. She was 'more honourably received and entertained with greater magnificence' than Ambassador Scheyfve had ever witnessed, and this might have been due to the fact that, without any heirs of Edward's young body, Mary was quite obviously next in line to the throne.[45] No one had expected that they might need to prepare for her accession upon the untimely death of the king, but now they were staring that possibility squarely in the face. Now, many of them were surely thinking that they had years of mistreatment to atone for, in order to establish themselves in her good graces, should the need arise.

Indeed, the need was looking likelier by the day, as Edward's condition continued to worsen. He now suffered from a fever and chill that kept him from welcoming Mary into his presence for three days after her arrival at court.[46] She was understandably distressed at the sight of her ailing brother and, mercifully, the conversation between the two of them remained light, without mention of their religious differences. As Mary left his bedchamber following their brief meeting, Scheyfve noted that several members of the council – most notably, the Duke of Northumberland – 'did duty and obeisance to her, as if she had been Queen of England'.[47] She surely knew her time was fast approaching, and anyone could see that the consumption-ridden young king would not long remain on the throne. His physicians cautiously guessed that he might live until September, and that didn't give Northumberland much time to get himself on a comfortable footing with the soon-to-be Queen of England.[48] If Mary acceded to the throne, Northumberland would be ruined. The Reformation's progress in England would be halted, the parish churches would be returned to their popish idolatry and superstitious mass, and all the work of the past six years would be for naught. After all the trouble he had given the king's sister for her private masses and insistence on practicing her own faith in her own home, Northumberland had a high hill to climb if he was ever to ingratiate himself with her, and so he found himself at a critical crossroads. Should he sacrifice the work he had done on behalf of the evangelicals and fall at Mary's feet in supplication? Or should he find a way to fight against her?

In truth, Northumberland had probably already been planning his next scheme for some time before he verbalized it in April 1553. By doing so he would redirect the course of the Tudor dynasty. Threatened with the loss of his own position, he needed to act swiftly and decisively to maintain his power – with or without King Edward.

Chapter 12

Devise for the Succession

On 1 March, Edward took part in the annual opening of Parliament, but immediately following the ceremony he shed his velvet and ermine and crept back into bed, not to appear again for over a fortnight.[1] At the end of the month, as the weather began to warm, it was reported that the king might be starting to regain some of his energy, and he was allowed to spend more time outdoors. Though historians are unsure of the exact time, it is assumed that this brief revitalization of his health precipitated his sitting down to pen his will. Perhaps this was put to him as a 'just in case' scenario, as none of his advisors would have dared speak the very real possibility that he was, in fact, quite close to death.

However this idea may have been presented to him, we can be quite sure that Northumberland had a heavy hand in it. As he continued to envision the dark future of a possible Queen Mary of England, he began to set his sights on other avenues for the succession, and he meant to force those ideas upon Edward. The only way for Northumberland's own interests to be preserved was to ensure that Mary never touched the throne. But how could she be ousted from the line of succession without her younger sister, Elizabeth, also being removed? Elizabeth and Edward had always been close – but according to Henry VIII, as Northumberland recalled, it had been Edward's mother, Jane Seymour, whom the late king had considered his 'true' first wife and queen. If his marriages to Catherine of Aragon and Anne Boleyn had both been declared null and void, then surely Northumberland (and Edward) could succeed at striking both Mary and Elizabeth from the line of succession. After all, they were bastards – regardless of their inclusion in Henry's own will – of which over sixty per cent had been devoted to the painstaking detail of naming heirs.[2] Although he had included them after Edward, Northumberland reasoned now, surely the option he had chosen designated Elizabeth as the most appropriate choice – she had been born legitimate and had been lawfully conceived. She also happened to be young, malleable and Protestant, which was a happy coincidence.

As it had been written in Henry's will, 'the heirs of the body of Lady Frances, our niece, eldest daughter to our late sister the French Queen,' were to inherit the throne in the extremely unlikely event that Edward, Mary, and Elizabeth all died childless.[3] Seventeen-year-old Lady Jane Grey was the eldest of Frances's daughters by Henry Grey, and therefore next in line for the throne, should that unlikely event prevail. In Northumberland's eyes, Lady Jane was the perfect candidate. She held the same fervent Protestant views as the king – having been educated by some of the same tutors who had instructed Edward and Elizabeth. She was young, impressionable, and would certainly require a knowledgeable guide if she were to find herself sitting upon the throne – a seat she would surely never have envisioned herself occupying. Perhaps most attractive of all her qualities was that she was yet unmarried, and this gave Northumberland the perfect means to tie his family to hers. Doing so would ensure that their good and powerful fortunes were legally entwined.

Northumberland would have known that Lady Jane Grey would be the preferable choice of successor in Edward's eyes, too. Close as he had been to his eldest sister very early in his life, there could be no questioning that his cousin would make for a better fit to carry on the reform that had been so passionately pursued during his reign. Of course, if the line of succession diverted back to 'the heirs of the body of Lady Frances' – which really meant Jane – there was also the chance that Jane might produce a male heir before too long, being young and in her peak childbearing years. This scenario would, to Northumberland's mind, accomplish two vital tasks that would undoubtedly please King Edward. First, if Jane married Guildford and then became queen, it would remove the possibility of one of Edward's fears – that of 'subject[ing] the realm to foreign domination' through marriage to a foreigner.[4] Then, if Jane soon bore a son, female rule over England would be blessedly brief, with a legitimate male heir promising to hold the Tudor throne secure. As it had been of the utmost importance to Henry VIII, Northumberland knew that an all-male succession was also

Edward's aim.⁵ With Mary having already reached the age of 37, and likely to look to Spain for her future husband, the teenaged Jane Grey was by far the better bet – even when taking the subject of religion out of the equation.

In April Scheyfve reported that 'during the last few days', Northumberland 'has found means to ally and bind his son, my Lord Guildford, to the Duke of Suffolk's eldest daughter'.⁶ It was also around this time (probably) that Edward was beginning to write his will – boldly titled 'My Devise for the Succession of the Crown', and the young king did exactly what Northumberland wanted – he excised both his half-sisters from his will. This decision was reportedly supported and encouraged by his tutor, Cheke, as well as his Chief Gentleman of the Privy Chamber, John Gates, and his confessor, Thomas Goodrich, Bishop of Ely.⁷ All these men knew full well the real danger Mary would pose to their Reformation, and Edward likely needed very little convincing to reach that particular decision. One can imagine that it was not so easy for him to disinherit his favourite sister, who had always been as much a friend and companion as a royal relation – and yet, her mother had died a traitor and an adulteress – 'more inclined to couple with a number of courtiers rather than reverencing her husband', Elizabeth was, therefore, the illegitimate offspring of tainted, unholy blood.⁸ So, what choice did he have, when faced with the godly alternative of Jane Grey? He now wrote that the line of succession would continue 'to the Lady Frances's heirs males'. This was a bit of wishful thinking, considering Frances was reaching the end of her childbearing years and was unlikely to produce a son at such short notice. Certainly, at this point in time, the crown would fall to Jane.

All was going according to the plans laid by Northumberland and his wife, but first Henry and Frances Grey would have to agree to the proposed marriage of their daughter. They had been burned once before when Thomas Seymour had dangled Edward himself under their noses as a prospective groom for Jane – only to be disappointed by the king's apparent disinterest in a betrothal. Were they now to trust yet another nobleman with their daughter's marriage prospects – and to the *fourth* son of a duke, no less? Guildford was the best Northumberland could offer, as his three elder sons were already wed, but he promised the Greys 'proverbial mountains of gold', should they choose to throw their lot in with him.[9] They conceded, of course. Henry Grey was also an ambitious man and could clearly see the prize to be won if Jane succeeded the current king. With only a bit of convincing, Northumberland had won his support and permission – though Duchess Frances reportedly was bitterly against the betrothal plans. To be fair, Jane wasn't pleased with the arrangement, either.[10]

Guildford and Jane were betrothed by 28 April with the king and council's consent, and they were married less than a month later on 25 May at Durham Place. The wedding ceremony jointly celebrated their union alongside that of Jane's twelve-year-old sister, Katherine, and Henry Herbert, as well as Katherine Dudley (Northumberland's daughter) and Henry Hastings.[11] All these marriages bound the Dudleys tightly to the Greys and promised either shared success and prosperity, or shared tragedy and destruction. All that Northumberland could see at this time was the former. Edward's 'Devise for the Succession' was neatly setting in place all that Northumberland needed in order to retain control. Edward's health continued to decline and he was not present at the wedding of his cousin (though he did send 'rich ornaments and jewels' to Jane), and it seems that soon afterwards he realized how unlikely it was to expect Duchess Frances to give birth to a son and heir before his own death.[12] He hastily edited his will, adding to the existing clause, 'to the Lady Frances's heirs males' the following words: 'if she have any such issue before my death to the Lady Jane and her heirs males'.[13] Edward was realizing the need to face facts – death was looming ever-closer, and his successor would very likely be a woman.

Indeed, by the end of May, he was in horrible shape. Physicians who cared for him at Greenwich Palace were made to swear oaths of secrecy before members of the council, as they were forbidden to disclose any details of the king's rapidly declining health to anyone.[14] Our best contemporary account of Edward's condition comes from a young medical student named John Banister, who attended Edward in his final months. On 28 May he wrote:

> He does not sleep except when he be stuffed with drugs, which doctors call opiates ... first one thing then another

are given him, but the doctors do not exceed twelve grains at a time, for these drugs are never given by doctors (so they say) unless the patient is in great pain, or tormented by constant sleeplessness, or racked by violent coughing ... The sputum which he brings up is livid, black, fetid and full of carbon; it smells beyond measure; if it is put in a basin full of water it sinks to the bottom. His feet are swollen all over. To the doctors all these things portend death, and that within three months, except God of his great mercy spare him.[15]

Sheyfve also reported to the Emperor what he had heard regarding Edward's health – that, 'He is beginning to break out in ulcers; he is vexed by a harsh, continuous cough, his body is dry and burning, his belly is swollen, he has a slow fever upon him that never leaves him.'[16] Things were evidently appearing ominous to his subjects as well, as rumours began circling about Edward's death – despite the council's best efforts to keep things hush-hush. In one instance of uncontrolled rumour-spreading, a man was whipped by two men in Cheapside while bound to a wooden post by an iron collar and chains, for the crime of 'pretend[ing] visions and for opprobrious and seditious words' about the king's condition.[17] In answer to this, the council began their own rumour that the king had suffered a brief illness but was well on his way back to restored health. According to Scheyfve, no one was particularly convinced. 'The people do not believe the said rumours,' he wrote in June, 'as the King does not show himself, but no one dares to voice any comments, at least not openly.'[18] Regardless of what the council was saying to quell people's anxieties, murmurings continued throughout London that the king had serious afflictions, such as stomach and lung tumours, and some were saying that he was already dead.

On 12 June, Edward's 'Devise for the Succession' was brought before the council and the judges of the King's Bench, and he commanded that they legalize the document as his last will and testament. Many of them, as expected, were astonished to see Edward's dramatic revision to the line of succession that Henry VIII had laid out more than six years earlier. How could Edward cast aside his sisters and place an unknown teenager on the throne? How had any of the advisors around him supported the decision? And could the complete undoing of Henry VIII's decreed succession cost the councillors and judges their very souls in the eyes of the Almighty? They insisted on requiring more time to mull the matter over, and when pressed by a heated Northumberland, they attempted to strike a compromise. What if they left the succession plans alone – keeping Mary as heir – but stipulated to her that she could not make any religious changes upon her accession to roll back the reformist changes effected by Edward? This attempt at negotiation was flatly denied.

The following day, Edward himself questioned the judges about their hesitancy to legalize his will. He confronted them – frail, yet angry – and asserted that Mary would prove a real danger if allowed to succeed him. She would 'provoke great disturbances' and leave 'no stone unturned' to undo the work that he and his religious men had worked so hard to accomplish. 'It would be all over for the religion whose fair foundation we have laid,' Edward argued.[19] But while certain councillors would have agreed with Edward's reasoning, the fact remained that overturning the previous king's Act of Succession was illegal. Those who stood before the king feared both retribution from God and prosecution for treason. But their hands were tied, forced to appease their sovereign who was unwavering in his determination to have his will signed according to his wishes. On 21 June, the Devise was signed by over a hundred men – council members, nobility, judges, and other officials – many of whom required bribes before putting pen to parchment.[20] Once signed, it was now as legal and official as it could possibly be, without the ratification of Parliament – which would not take place until September.[21] In addition to the change in the order of succession, Edward's will stipulated that his executors were to uphold the religious progress already made over the last several years, and also, 'To diligently travail to cause godly ecclesiastical laws to be made and set forth, such as may be agreeable with the reformation of religion now received within our realm, and that done shall also cause the canon laws to be abolished.'[22] This declaration in particular is what made Cranmer agree to 'uphold the new succession unto death' – at which he had previously balked, given the fact that doing so would nullify the same promise he had made to the last king.²³ In the end, the promise of the ultimate culmination of Cranmer's reformation efforts won out, and he signed his wholehearted agreement and promise to see Jane Grey succeed to the throne.²⁴

Following this victory which legalized his will, Edward once again returned to his chambers, where another violent bout of fever took hold and plunged him into such misery that he reportedly whispered to Cheke, 'I am glad to die.'²⁵ While no information was reaching the ears of his subjects, rumours and whisperings continued around court, causing Scheyfve to write:

> His doctors dare reveal nothing ... Only two of them are in attendance on his person; the other three, when they go to visit the King, examine his urine and excrements, but are not allowed to approach him. The King's ordinary attendants are unable to stir abroad, so that it is exceedingly difficult to obtain any information as to his state ... Up to the present there seems to be no sign of improvement, so the general conviction is that he cannot escape, and has been poisoned.²⁶

Rumours swirled around the European courts as well, with some even wondering if the young king was already dead by the end of June. Perhaps having heard of the fear and anxiety swarming both England and abroad, Edward dragged himself out of bed on 1 July to make an appearance at his Greenwich Palace window. Crowds below, which had gathered in order to glimpse their king and to be assured that he was indeed alive, were in fact deeply shocked at his appearance. He had wasted away to skin and bone – his pale, drawn face peered out of the window for only a few moments before retreating to bed. Far from reassured, his waiting subjects were disturbed at the sight of him and whispered among each other that he was surely doomed.²⁷ Still, they were told that the king would appear for them again in the coming days. In fact, this would not come to pass. This one brief encounter at the window would be Edward's final 'public' appearance. Just three days later, Scheyfve wrote to Charles V:

> Sire, the King is very ill today and cannot last long. He will die suddenly, and no one can foretell whether he will live an hour longer, notwithstanding his having been shown to the people, for that was done against the physicians' advice.[28]

On the same day, Northumberland summoned both Mary and Elizabeth to Greenwich, writing that their presence would greatly comfort their dying brother. Of course, in all actuality, Northumberland simply needed to keep the two women close, in order to control their every movement in case the king did die suddenly. Mary was no longer Edward's legal heir, after all, but she did not yet know that, and having her and Elizabeth under his guard would provide less of an opportunity for his plans to go awry when the time came. Elizabeth regretfully declined the summons, claiming that illness prevented her from travelling. Mary, however, chose to make the trip to Greenwich with extreme caution – putting her loyalty and care for Edward above her fear and mistrust of Northumberland – and departed Hunsdon on 4 July. Hearing of this, Scheyfve feared the worst for her, writing to the emperor that, 'It is to be feared that, as soon as the King is dead, they will attempt to seize the Princess.'[29]

Another rumour that ran rampant in these final days of the young king's life was the notion that Northumberland was attempting to prolong Edward's life by having a wise woman drug him with antidotes, such as arsenic. One of Scheyfve's reports claimed that 'the Duke is utterly loathed and suspected of having poisoned the King, and is only able to command obedience by terrorising the people'.[30] The wise woman was dismissed from the king's service within the first days of July, with some suspecting that she may have been murdered on behalf of Northumberland (though there is no contemporary evidence to support this).[31] Henry Machyn and Robert Parkyn also wholly believed that Northumberland was responsible for the king's ultimate fate – blaming him for having poisoned Edward. Machyn wrote in his diary on 6 July that 'the noble King Edward the VI … was poisoned, as everybody says, where now, thank be to God, there be many of the false traitors brought to their end.'[32]

Regardless, Edward's body was failing fast and the end was obviously near. Though he had become skeletal in appearance, his body swelled unnaturally, and the skin of his extremities grew mottled and discoloured. His hair and nails had begun to fall out, and his pulse was severely weakened. Each breath became more laborious and painful, even as he vomited and coughed up the putrid matter that had been filling his lungs for months. On Thursday, 6 July, the fifteen-year-old king lay in agony while a storm raged outside. Through the afternoon hours, he began to pray and murmur to his attendants as he drifted in and out of sleep.[33] Those who surrounded him included two Chief Gentlemen of the Privy Chamber, his groom, Christopher Salmon, and two of his doctors.[34] That evening, as he drearily woke once more, he uttered a final desperate prayer:

> Lord God, deliver me out of this miserable and wretched life, and take me among thy chosen: howbeit not my will, but thy will be done. Lord I commit my spirit to thee. O Lord! Thou knowest how happy it were for me to be with thee: yet, for thy chosen's sake, send me life and health, that I may truly serve thee. O my Lord God, bless thy people, and save thine inheritance! O Lord God save thy chosen people of England! O my Lord God, defend this realm from papistry, and maintain thy true religion; that I and my people may praise thy holy name, for thy Son Jesus Christ's sake![35]

Hearing these words his attendants drew nearer to him. This startled Edward, who looked at them in confusion and asked, 'Are you so nigh? I thought ye had been further off.' In an effort to comfort the puzzled king, Henry Sidney slid onto the bed and pulled Edward into his arms. Held in the embrace of his childhood friend, Edward murmured his final words: 'I am faint; Lord have mercy upon me, and take my spirit.'[36]

Three months shy of his sixteenth birthday, Edward VI died from what is assumed to have been consumption – likely compounded by suppressed immunity from his April 1552 bout of measles. Modern-day medical research has proven measles to have a negative effect on subsequent diagnoses of tuberculosis by 'reactivating the bacteria that can survive intracellularly within healthy lung tissue'. Indeed, when

Edward's surgeons performed a post-mortem examination they noted the diseased appearance of his lungs, with 'two great ulcers' – which stacks up to modern reasoning and description as to what the combination of these two diseases might have looked like.[37] Of course, it is impossible to be certain of the true nature of his death, but given the contemporary reports and our twenty-first century research, this stands as quite a convincing theory.

The storm continued to batter the city outside. As reported in the *Grey Friars Chronicle* – 'great trees were uprooted, the streets turned into rivers, and the hail lay in the city's gardens as red as blood'.[38] Later, people would claim that the tempest was a sign from Henry VIII in protest of the disregard for his will. Regardless, as the storm raged on, the king's lifeless body was kept carefully under wraps for a full day, as Northumberland now needed time to set the newly revised succession plans into motion. Lady Jane Grey had been informed of the king's Devise for the Succession some days earlier by her new father-in-law, and she had recorded:

> After having been openly stated that there was no hope of saving the life of the King, as the Duchess of Northumberland had promised me that I could remain with my mother, after she heard that news from her husband the Duke, who was also the first person to tell me about it, she did not allow me any more to leave my house saying that when God would be pleased to call the King to his mercy, not remaining any hope of saving his life, I had immediately to proceed to the Tower, as I had been made by his Majesty heir to the crown.[39]

The news had horrified her. Having already been aware that she was third in line to the throne, she had never expected to be bumped up in the order of succession – and she had surely never considered the real possibility of being crowned. In her own words, the news 'caught me quite unaware' and 'very deeply upset me'.[40] Possibly overcome by the stress of this news, Jane had fallen ill in the following days and had relocated from Durham Place to Chelsea – eager to distance herself from both her new husband and her in-laws. She was still recovering there when messengers reached her on the evening of 6 July, stating that King Edward had died, and she must now make haste to London.

While Elizabeth remained at Hatfield, having informed the council of her illness, Mary had never quite made it to Greenwich, despite her initial willingness to come to court. In fact, she had been warned on the very day of the king's death that she was likely entering a trap if she continued on her way. These sympathisers who were 'most loyal to her' advised her to avoid London, and so she secretly diverted east towards her home of Kenninghall in Norfolk,[41] in East Anglia. She had many supporters there and knew she would be able to rally followers against Northumberland if need be. Soon after her arrival at Kenninghall she received confirmation that Edward was already dead, and, sure enough, that Northumberland and his cronies on the council had ousted her from her rightful place as her brother's heir. She had been passed over for her Protestant cousin, Jane, and she was irate at the news.

Mary faced two options – evade Northumberland's grasp, as he would surely be coming for her the moment he caught wind of her decision to avoid his summons to court, or stand and fight for her place on the throne. She would surely find sanctuary abroad if she fled to Charles V's court, where she would be free to practice her Catholic faith and, no doubt, find a suitable marriage prospect. But Mary was the daughter of King Henry VIII and Catherine of Aragon. She was descended from the warrior Queen Isabel of Castile, as well as the conquering, dynasty-founding King Henry VII. She had been heiress to the English throne from the moment of her birth thirty-seven years prior, and despite being deemed illegitimate for a spell, she had been rightfully reinstated to the line of succession before her father's death. Her brother – likely guided by Northumberland, as Mary suspected – had no right to remove her now and strip away everything for which she had suffered. In fact, Edward's untimely death surely was a sign from God that she was needed to rule over England and return the country to Catholicism. So, while she may have been reminded briefly of her option to flee for the Holy Roman Empire, her mind was firmly decided. She would stay and fight.

At the time Robert Wingfield reported:

> With her usual wisdom the lady now perfectly judged the peril of her situation, but nothing daunted by her limited resources, she placed her hopes in God alone, committing, as they say, the whole ship of her safety, bows, stem, sails and all, to the winds of fortune, and firstly decided to claim the kingdom of her father and her ancestors, which was owed to her as much by hereditary right as by her father's will.[42]

She informed her household and attendants of the king's death, and how 'the right to the Crown of England had therefore descended to her by divine and by human law'. She asked for 'the aid of her most faithful servants, as partners in her fortunes'.[43] Those who heard her were inspired to fight for her and her crown, and she immediately set to work gathering more supporters who would join her in standing against Northumberland and Jane Grey. That same day, she made her intentions clear to the very people who had turned on her, when she penned a letter to the council. 'My lords,' she started:

> We greet you well and have received sure advertisement that our deceased brother the king, our late sovereign lord, is departed to God's mercy ... It seemeth strange that the dying of our said brother upon Thursday at night last past, we hitherto had no knowledge from you thereof ... We require you, and every of you, that every of you, of your allegiance which you owe to God and us, and to none other, for our honour and the surety of our person, only employ yourselves, and forthwith upon receipt hereof, cause our right and title to the Crown and government of this Realm to be proclaimed in our City of London, and other places as to your wisdoms shall seem good.[44]

The council's swift reply was not what Mary wanted to read, but it couldn't have taken her much by surprise. They responded in no uncertain terms that Jane Grey was to be formally proclaimed queen, 'For as much as our sovereign Lady Queen Jane is after the death of our sovereign Lord Edward the sixth ... not only by good order of old ancient laws of this Realm, but also by our late sovereign Lord's letters patent signed with his own hand.'[45] Lord Robert Dudley had already found Mary's Hunsdon home vacant when he had travelled from court to collect her, and his father, Northumberland, had grown anxious at the thought of where Mary might have escaped, having so clearly avoided Greenwich. Now, her words to the council only increased anxieties that she might engage a foreign ally such as her cousin Charles V against them. The sooner they could see Jane crowned, the better. Their letter was returned to Mary, signed by all twenty-three of them, including Archbishop Cranmer. There would be no meek bowing to Mary's demands – Jane was queen, as decided by Edward, and that was that.

As the news of the young king's death was still largely under wraps, it seemed battle lines were being drawn. While the reluctant new queen was being thrust towards her coronation, the disregarded heiress assembled her retinue of followers to take back what was rightfully hers. It would soon be proved true that Edward VI's 'Devise for the Succession', and his hastily ratified will and testament, would not have quite the final say that he had intended, after all.

Chapter 13

The Immediate Aftermath

On the day following Edward's death, Northumberland held a banquet in honour of the new, still secret, Queen Jane. It was not yet public knowledge that the king was dead, and Mary remained at large – frustratingly beyond the council's grasp. Still, Northumberland chose to celebrate his victory early, and the reluctant Jane acquiesced as he had primed her to do. As rumours swirled around London that King Edward was no more – and likely due to the evil machinations of Northumberland – the council set its plans into motion. Mary would be taken care of in due time, no matter how they eventually got their hands on her. Of course, she'd likely not make it easy, but what could she do once Jane had been crowned queen?

On that note, Jane would have to be introduced to her people. It was time to unveil the true Tudor heir – the one set forth and signed into the succession by none other than Edward VI himself. And so, on 8 July, the Lord Mayor and other London officials were formally notified of Edward's passing and shown the ratified will signifying Jane's rightful succession. Jane's coronation was planned for two days later, and every Tower of London guard swore to protect her as their rightful monarch.[1] Rowland Lea, author of *The Chronicle of Queen Jane*, wrote that on 10 July, 'Lady Jane was conveyed by water to the Tower of London, and there received as queen.'[2] She rode by royal barge from Syon along with her family, husband, and in-laws, as well as a retinue of ladies – and though she was indeed 'received as queen', she was not given a warm reception by London onlookers. According to three additional Ambassadors to the Holy Roman Empire (sent by Charles V to support Sheyfve in his advocation of Mary), 'No one present showed any sign of rejoicing, and no one cried: "Long live the Queen!" except the herald who made the proclamation and a few archers who followed him.'[3]

Although the three new ambassadors – Jehan de Montmorency, Jacques de Marnix, and Simon Renard – were pleased at Jane's apparent unpopularity, they were not at all optimistic about Mary's chances of claiming her throne.[4] Around the same time, they had written to Charles V from Scheyfve's house, complaining, 'All the forces of the country are in the Duke's hands, and my Lady has no hope of raising enough men to face him, nor means of assisting those who may espouse her cause.'[5] At this time, as Jane was being crowned, Mary's letter to the council was on its way – to be delivered to them that very same day. She would not give up her birth right without a fight.

Jane's coronation was in sharp contrast to the pomp and circumstance of Edward's, six years earlier. While Jane's mother, Frances, carried her long train, she was accompanied only by her own attendants, her family, and the necessary council members and city authorities. The only indication that anything of importance had occurred in London was the peal of cannon fire from Tower Wharf following her crowning, and when heralds announced Edward's death thereafter, scores of Londoners stared, puzzled by the heralds' words, their faces 'sorrowful and averted'.[6]

Not only were they in shock at the death of their young king – but many of the anti-Catholics also mistrusted and disliked Northumberland, and now Jane was associated with him. They did not necessarily need to support the idea of Mary's accession in order to oppose any alternative that stank of Northumberland's plotting, and the fact that Jane was virtually unknown did not help things either. Sure, she was a noblewoman, and there were plenty who would have known of her parents and her association with the royal family – but she was decidedly not in the direct line of Tudor succession. Aside from only a few court appearances during Edward's short reign, hardly any Londoner had ever seen Jane in any formal capacity. How could anyone have expected them to warm to her so quickly?

Jane was mortified, though not everyone was disappointed to see her. The council was largely supportive, and her husband, Guildford, doted on her with 'much attention'.[7] Once again, the enormity of the situation frightened Jane; she evidently felt in her core that it was not right for her to be in this position. She balked when the Marquess of Winchester came forward to place the crown on her head, and he attempted to reassure her by saying, 'Your Grace may take it without fear.'[8] Winchester then commented that her husband should also be crowned, which set Jane's back up even more. She was certainly not ignorant of her father-in-law's ploy to gain power for his family, and now the notion that Guildford should be crowned king alongside her put her on her guard. Such would be the topic of the newlyweds' first argument later that evening.

Along with the official proclamation announcing that Jane was England's new queen, Rowland Lea reported:

> [c]riers at the street-corners published an order given under the Great Seal of England, which, by the new Queen's authority, declared the Lady Mary unfitted for the Crown, as also the Lady Elizabeth. Both ladies were declared to be bastards; and it was stated that the Lady Mary might marry a foreigner and thus stir up trouble in the kingdom and introduce a foreign government, and also that as she was of the old religion she might seek to introduce popery.[9]

It was around this time that the council received Mary's letter, indicating her shock and disappointment that she had not been informed of her brother's death sooner, and asserting herself as the rightful queen. By all accounts, Northumberland and the other council members were perplexed to read such a strongly worded letter, but they were not deterred in the slightest. Scoffing, Northumberland addressed Mary's messenger, Thomas Hungate, saying, 'I am truly sorry that it was your lot to be so immature and thus rashly to throw yourself away in this embassy.'[10] Hungate was then led away to his prison cell in the Tower of London while Northumberland began seriously to plot his next moves against Mary. After the council's written reply (much to Mary's annoyance and chagrin), Northumberland decided that some of his followers should ride to Hunsdon to apprehend Mary themselves.

Meanwhile, Jane and Guildford were arguing in the royal apartments. Not having forgotten Winchester's remarks about her husband needing a crown of his own, Jane made it known in no uncertain terms that she had no intention of ever allowing Guildford to be king. She might acquiesce to having him formally styled 'consort', if Parliament was to petition her – and she even agreed to name him Duke of Clarence – but he would certainly not be crowned in his own right, as he had no royal blood in his veins. Guildford was flabbergasted, but being newly married to the Queen of England, he kept his mouth shut and gave the initial impression that he would respect her wishes. Quietly, he turned to his mother for support against Jane's cruel denial, and the Duchess of Northumberland was quick to jump to her son's defence. Her answer to her daughter-in-law's unfairness was to insist that Guildford keep away from her bed for a time, so as to deny her the immediate opportunity to conceive England's heir. The punishment did nothing to chastise or hurt Jane, as she cared so little for Guildford anyway. She had more pressing matters to attend to, rather than her already unhappy marriage bed.[11]

Shocked and disappointed by his daughter-in-law's show of defiance, Northumberland met with his council at Durham Place the following morning. There he made plans to apprehend Mary, whom he and his supporters now knew to be wholly against his cause. He gathered around him weapons and artillery in case he needed them, and he addressed the men of the council as they dined. He reminded them of 'God's cause' for which they were prepared to fight – their collective mission to stay true to their beloved King Edward VI's Devise for the Succession, which they had all signed just weeks prior. Their stance against Mary was to prevent 'papistry's re-entrance,' he reminded them, and followed this with a warning: 'If ye mean deceit,' he said, 'though not forthwith yet hereafter, God will revenge the same. I can say no more; but in this troublesome time wish you to use constant hearts, abandoning all malice, envy, and private affections.' One of his councillors chastised him for his disbelief in them, saying, 'If ye mistrust any of us in this matter, your grace is far deceived.'[12]

The next morning, Northumberland departed London for Mary's residence, along with 'a force which amounted to some 2,000 horse and 3,000 foot at least', and their mission was no secret to those around them.[13] Scheyfve reported to the emperor that he feared Mary would be in custody within four days, and, according to Northumberland himself, 'The people press to see us, but not one sayeth God speed us.'[14] Indeed, throughout England discontent and confusion spread as towns were made aware by official proclamation of the new queen. Hatred of

Northumberland increased the displeasure of citizens at the news, and of course the Catholics who had been disappointed by Edward's reign and the religious changes he had enacted were unwavering in their support of Mary. It was suggested by one Richard Troughton of Lincolnshire that 'over a hundred thousand men would rise' in Mary's defence and reclaim what was rightfully hers.[15]

Unsurprisingly, Northumberland was not deterred by the lack of public support. Though it was clear enough that plenty of people rallied behind Mary's cause and openly questioned the validity of Jane's accession, he made his way with his armed retinue towards Cambridge, where he believed he would be hot on her heels. Mary, however, was receiving plenty of notice about the duke's whereabouts from her many supporters. On 12 July, she departed Kenninghall for Framlingham, deeming it a more suitable stronghold in case she should need to defend herself against an army. Her distrust of Northumberland was growing and she could not put such an idea past him.

When she reached Framlingham the following evening, Mary knew that a handful of towns had already proclaimed her queen and refused to acknowledge Jane, despite the council's edicts. Some towns, such as Norwich and Gloucester, went a step further by sending weapons and men of their own to use against her enemies, and she continued to rally further support by sending letters and messengers from town to town.[16] Her efforts worked, and although Scheyfve's report of '15,000 men' in her force is likely an exaggeration, there could be no denying that the number of her supporters grew by the day and that she was infinitely more popular than was Queen Jane.[17] Men flocked to Framlingham with the noble intention of aiding her in any way possible and setting her upon the throne. Reports of this flurry of pro-Marian activity flourished through the countryside, but Northumberland nevertheless pressed ahead in his mission.

Back in London, however, the threat of Mary's success was growing more frightening – not to mention more realistic – by the day. The council wrote on 16 July that 'the bastard daughter of Henry VIII' was rallying support 'by all ways and means she can'. They feared what would happen if she succeeded in casting Jane from the throne and reclaiming her place in the succession. Would she marry a foreign prince, as many suspected?

If so, the result for England would be 'bondage … to the old servitude of the Antichrist of Rome, the subversion of the true preaching of God's word, and of ancient laws, usages, and liberties of this Realm.'[18] Their aim was to convince justices across the country of Mary's evil intentions and to sway them all to stand against her, should she come seeking their support. But just days later, it appeared that their cause was all but lost. Northumberland – though still in pursuit of Mary and now moving from Cambridge to Bury – learned of the Earl of Oxford's defection to Mary's cause. Sir Richard Rich followed suit, riding towards Framlingham that same day, in order to proclaim for Mary. Following these betrayals to Northumberland and Queen Jane, other noble elites dropped like flies. It was clear to all, except perhaps Northumberland, that he had been beaten, and that Mary's popularity with the majority would outweigh his clever scheming.

Arundel was torn in his loyalties but ultimately spoke to the members of council at Baynard's Castle and urged them to abandon Northumberland once and for all. He spoke passionately about the deep divide that had scoured the country over the past weeks, threatening the following:

> Consider that now the factions are divided, some biding with Mary, others with the Duke, which be the utter overthrow of this Land; for you shall see brother against brother, uncle against nephew, father in law against son in law, cousin against cousin, and so from one unto another, you shall see those enemies that be of the same blood. Thus will they weaken the strength of this kingdom by such a dangerous division, which at last will be an occasion to draw foreign forces into this Land, so as, in short time, we can expect no other than to have ourselves, our substance, our children and wives, a prey to the soldiers, with the utter ruin of our nobility.

So moving and convincing were Arundel's words, that Pembroke stood, ardently gripped his sword, and addressing the men and saying: 'If my Lord of Arundel's persuasions cannot prevail with you, either this sword shall make Mary Queen, or I will lose my life.'[19]

It was the end of Northumberland's grand plan, and Mary's name was proclaimed across towns as celebratory bonfires were lit in the streets. The letter 'M' was hastily emblazoned on livery and *Te Deums* were sung in thanksgiving of her triumph. When news finally reached Northumberland on 20 July, his hands were tied and he had no choice but to follow suit in proclaiming Mary the rightful Queen of England. All his work over the past months had come to naught and his daughter-in-law and son were likely unaware of what had transpired from their royal apartments in the Tower of London. As he held up his staff of office in Cambridge, he 'so laughed that the tears ran down his cheeks for grief'.[20] Now all that he could hope for was the new queen's mercy, of which there would prove to be little. In fact, upon meeting Arundel and Paget and learning of the council's obeisance and support of her royal right, her first order was to have Northumberland arrested and hauled to the Tower. Meanwhile, the Imperial ambassadors were ecstatic at this news and reported to the emperor that 'the Lady Mary was proclaimed Queen of England amid the greatest rejoicing it is possible to imagine'.[21]

Arundel arrested Northumberland on 21 July, and days later they were riding through the streets of London towards the Tower, amidst hostile crowds of onlookers who were only too glad to see the duke in such a state. That same evening, Jane's father interrupted her supper with Guildford in the Tower. He grabbed the canopy of state above her and ripped it down, tearing the silk as it fell to the floor. Apparently stunned and unnerved, he then proclaimed that 'this place did no longer belong to her, having to submit to Fortune as changeable and envious of its own gifts'.[22] He then said to Jane, 'You must put off your royal robes and be content with a private life.' This solemn order was not nearly so painful to Jane as he might have imagined.[23] She replied calmly:

> I much more willingly put them off than I put them on. Out of obedience to you and my mother, I have grievously sinned and offered violence to myself. Now I do willingly and obeying the motions of my own soul relinquish the crown and endeavour to solve those faults committed by

others if, at least, so great faults can be solved, by a willing and ingenuous acknowledgement of them.[24]

Queen for only nine short days, Jane's reign had ended almost before it had begun, but she was not sad to see the brief moment pass by. Now, however – much like Northumberland – she found herself awaiting the hopeful mercy of the rightful Queen Mary. Any who had previously supported her accession to the throne now visibly distanced themselves from her and threw themselves into full support of Mary. Jane learned that she could not simply go home; instead, she would have to await her fate in the Tower – and she found herself very much alone.

Mary made her grand entrance into London on 3 August, dressed in purple velvet – the colour of royalty. She was flanked by around 12,000 supporters, including her sister Elizabeth and nearly two hundred ladies-in-waiting. She was greeted warmly by the mayor, amid the display of hanging tapestries of the Virgin Mary and saintly statues that had already been pulled out from hiding, in celebration of a restored Catholic era in England.[25] Just days earlier, Henry Grey, Jane's father, had been arrested and taken back to the Tower after attempting to escape with his wife, and Mary found that one of the first of her subjects to seek an audience with her was none other than Frances Grey, on behalf of her fallen family.

According to the Imperial ambassadors, Frances claimed that '[h]er husband had been the victim of an attempt to poison him, and that the Duke of Northumberland had done it. She then prayed for her husband's release from the Tower.'[26] Despite the awkward situation, Mary was evidently moved by Frances's words, and felt convinced that the Greys had played no active part in Northumberland's plots. Also, this was not the first time that he had been accused of poison, and Mary knew all too well how ambitious and self-serving the duke had been in her years of knowing him. In answer, Mary released Henry Grey from the Tower but insisted that he remain under house arrest – not quite free, but certainly not a prisoner to the same degree as Northumberland. Interestingly, despite Frances's swift endeavour to fight for her husband's life and freedom, Dr Nicola Tallis (Lady Jane Grey's biographer) points out that, 'No contemporary source makes any reference to Frances's interceding with Queen Mary on behalf of her eldest daughter during her audience at Beaulieu.'[27] Consequently, much to Jane's dismay, she remained at the Tower while her parents were escorted to the Charterhouse at Mary's pleasure.

Rather predictably, the Duchess of Northumberland was not as fortunate as Frances. Just after Mary had released Henry Grey, the duchess made haste towards Beaulieu 'to move [Mary] to compassion towards her children' (and presumably her husband). But five miles from her destination, she was turned away by the queen's messenger and informed that she would not be given an audience. Mary had no sympathy for Northumberland or any of his family, and she would make certain that they would pay dearly for their many grievous insults to her.[28]

Jane was at a loss for what to do. Knowing that Mary was now resident within the very same royal residence, she was also aware that she would likely not be afforded the chance to plead her innocence to the queen in person. On the night of Mary's arrival at the Tower, Jane set to writing at her desk – likely hoping that a passionate explanation of the events that had transpired, events beyond her control, would win her some forgiveness in Mary's eyes. While the original letter has not survived the centuries, Commendone and Pollini reported Jane's words a few months after the fact, so we can be reasonably confident that her letter was much the same as the words that follow:

> Although my fault be such that, but for the goodness and clemency of the queen, I can have no hope of finding pardon, nor in craving forgiveness, having given ear to those who at that time appeared, not only to myself, but also to a great part of this realm, to be wise, and now have manifested themselves the contrary, not only to my and their great detriment, but with the common disgrace and blame of all, they having with such shameful boldness made so blameable and dishonourable an attempt to give others that which was not theirs, neither did it become me to accept (wherefore rightful and justly am I ashamed to ask pardon for such a crime), nevertheless, I trust in God that as now I know and confess my want of prudence, for which I deserve heavy punishment, except for the very great mercy of your

majesty, I can still on many grounds conceive hope of your infinite clemency, it being known that the error imputed to me has not been altogether caused by myself. Because, although my fault may be great, and I confess it to be so, nevertheless I am charged and esteemed guilty more than I have deserved.[29]

In addition to these words, Jane also claimed to have been poisoned twice, 'First in the house of the duchess of Northumberland, and afterwards here in the Tower.'[30] Her reasoning for suspecting such a thing? Apparently, her hair had begun to fall out. While never verified by contemporary evidence or description of her appearance, this may well have been due to the extreme stress that she had endured for weeks. Nevertheless, the repeated mention of poison, as it related to Northumberland, caught Mary's attention. Though she did not see her young cousin in person during her entire stay at the Tower, she did, in fact, have some pity on her. The blame for the entire treasonous arrangement lay squarely on Northumberland's shoulders, she believed, though the Imperial ambassadors noted that within Mary's first few weeks in London, she had not yet pardoned anyone. They reported to the emperor that there were those who whispered in the queen's ear that 'Jane of Suffolk deserved death according to English law', but evidently Mary felt enough sympathy for the poor girl – who was, of course, related to her by blood – to refuse to order her execution.[31]

A week or so after Mary's entry into the capital, her deceased brother, the late King Edward VI, was finally laid to rest. On the evening of 7 August 1553 his embalmed body, which had already been transported from Greenwich to Whitehall, was transported to Westminster Abbey, with 'a great company of children in their surplus', while Londoners flanked the streets to pay their respects, 'weeping and lamenting'. His coffin was carried on a horse-drawn chariot draped in cloth of gold, and atop the coffin, covered in blue velvet, rested a life-like effigy of the fifteen-year-old king, complete with crown and sceptre, with his garter ribbon around his leg.[32] According to Henry Machyn, as his coffin passed by his sorrowful subjects, there was 'the greatest moan made for him of his death as ever was heard or seen.'[33]

Inside the Abbey, the walls were draped in black cloth and lit tapers led the way to the altar, where Archbishop Cranmer presided over the solemn ceremony under the rites of the 1552 Book of Common Prayer. As one can imagine, this would have been a contentious point for the new Queen Mary, who despised the Book and all that it represented, including Cranmer, for that matter. In fact, negotiations regarding the specifics of the funeral were likely part of the reason that Edward was not buried for more than a month after his death.[34] But Mary was apparently prepared to allow her deceased brother this one final victory in death – to be sent off to his eternal rest in the way he would have wanted. She acquiesced to the Protestant ceremony but did not attend herself. Instead, as reported by the Imperial ambassadors, she ordered 'a plain office [to be] sung at the castle [i.e. the Tower], beginning to-day at vespers,' and for requiem masses for Edward's soul to be said there for three days – an irony that would have made Edward's blood boil, as he had done away with masses for the dead during his brief reign as England's Protestant king.[35] Another nail in the proverbial Protestant coffin: Mary had appointed a Catholic preacher for the funeral – George Day, Bishop of Chichester, whose sermon 'prepared the way for papistry', according to one attendant.[36]

In the presence of Edward's former attendants, council members (minus Northumberland), friends, advisors, and tutors, his lead coffin was lowered into the vault at the centre of the Lady Chapel, beneath the tomb of Henry VII and Elizabeth of York. Much like his father's burial, Edward's resting place would go unmarked for the next four hundred and thirteen years. Again, like his predecessor, a plan had indeed been made for the design of an elaborate monument (which can still be viewed in the Bodleian Library, Oxford), but neither Mary nor Elizabeth would order its construction. In the years and dynasties to come, there would be precious little thought given to the teenaged king who sat upon England's throne for only six years, and thus the memorial would never come to be. Finally, in 1966, a simple plaque would be set into the marble floor of the chapel by Christ's Hospital school in West Sussex, reading, 'In Memory of King Edward VI Buried In This Chapel This Stone Was Placed Here By Christ's Hospital In Thanksgiving For Their Founder 7 October 1966.'[37]

Once Mary departed the Tower for Richmond Palace, she wasted no time in bringing the treasonous Duke of Northumberland to justice. His trial was set for 18 August at Westminster, alongside his son, John, and the Marquis of Northampton, William Parr. They were tried and judged by a panel of their peers. Northumberland first attempted to excuse his actions by referencing the king's wishes, the council's agreement, and the power of the Great Seal. Scoffing, his former colleagues, who now sat in judgment on him, retorted that he had used the Great Seal as 'the seal of a usurper'.[38] Making his final point, Northumberland wondered 'whether any such persons as were equally culpable of that crime … might be his judges now.'[39] Afterwards, he appeared to have accepted his likely fate. He requested an execution befitting a nobleman, rather than a traitor's death, and he begged for the lives of his sons.[40] He also asked for the right to confess his sins 'for the settling of his conscience' – something which Edward and Cranmer would not have approved, having dismissed the need for confession and penance.[41]

Northumberland's sentence was swift and decisive. He was found guilty of treason and his execution was scheduled for 21 August, though it would be rescheduled due to his sudden desire to hear the Catholic mass. In the Chapel of St Peter ad Vincula, he received the holy sacrament, renounced his Protestant faith and bemoaned all that he had done in the previous years to destroy the mass. His confession was heard, and Mary may have been pleased that at the end of the duke's life he had returned to the 'true' faith – if she believed him at all. It is, of course, very difficult to say whether this sudden conversion was genuine or a last-ditch effort to win over the new Catholic queen. There is little doubt that he would have embraced the Catholic faith and rejected any and all traces of Protestantism – if she had chosen to pardon him – given his words to Arundel: 'Oh, that it would please her good Grace to give me life, yea the life of a dog, that I might but live and kiss her feet.'[42]

Alas, this would not come to pass. The following morning – 22 August 1553 – Northumberland was led from his cell in the Tower to the grounds of Tower Hill, where he was the first of those accused to mount the scaffold. Once again, he openly confessed his evildoings against the queen and asked the crowds for their forgiveness. He would not go down alone, however. He acknowledged that he had not been alone in his treason, and that the real sinners were those false preachers who had caused him to turn from 'the Catholic faith and true doctrine of Christ'. He hurled some of the blame at Edward VI, too, saying:

> For I pray you, see, since the death of King Henry the Eighth, into what misery we have been brought; what open rebellion, what sedition, what great division hath been brought throughout the whole realm; for God hath delivered [us] up to [our] own sensualities, and every day [we] wax worse and worse.[43]

Harsh words directed at a king under whose reign Northumberland had profited and prospered, but then he had everything to lose and his aim was to earn the sympathy and prayers of those in attendance at his end. It seemed to work, too, as many who heard his final words were evidently convinced that he might indeed have been led astray against his better judgment. Those who had personally known him during the past six years, however, were likely not so persuaded by his pretty words. He died by one stroke of the executioner's axe (likely grateful that Mary had complied with this request), and was swiftly followed by Sir John Gates and Thomas Palmer. Simon Renard, one of the Imperial ambassadors who would become particularly close to Mary, reported to her that Northumberland's 'head was cut off in the presence of over fifty thousand people', much to the relief and pleasure of the new queen.[44] His body was then interred in the Chapel of St Peter Ad Vincula to join those of other convicted and executed traitors, including Anne Boleyn, Katherine Howard, and – in an ironic twist of fate – his one-time sworn enemy during Edward's reign, the Duke of Somerset.

Chapter 14

The Tudor Dynasty Continues

From her rooms in the Tower, Lady Jane Grey was likely able to hear – and even, perhaps, to see – part of the execution of the Duke of Northumberland on 22 August 1553. While we cannot know with any certainty what might have been running through her mind at this time, we do know that at the news of her father-in-law's death, her chief concern was that he had damned his soul to Hell – not purely due to his treason against Queen Mary – but because he had abandoned the Protestant faith with his final breaths. This, to Jane's mind, was the single most evil deed he could have committed – to recant the holy work of God's reformed church and crawl back to Rome in order to appease a Catholic queen. That Northumberland had publicly lamented and regretted the changes made under Edward VI's regime, and the works written by Archbishop Cranmer dispelled any sympathy Jane might otherwise have felt at the duke's demise – and took with it any fear she might have harboured for her own soul. For she, Jane, would never turn up her nose at Protestantism – not even to save her own life. And this, as time would prove in just six months, would be her very undoing.

While Mary had intended to spare Jane's life upon claiming her throne, her unfortunate cousin – queen in name alone for less than two weeks – would, in fact, lay her head on the executioner's block on 12 February 1554. The trial of Lady Jane Grey and her husband, Guildford, had taken place on 13 November, but this was likely only a formality, as the new queen needed to prove to her subjects that she was not to be trifled with. Innocent of evil plotting or not, Jane had nevertheless signed documents as 'Jane the Quene' and 'there falsely and treacherously assumed and took up for herself the title and power of the Queen of this kingdom of England'.[1] Though she may not have expected to find herself standing in such circumstances at Guildhall, Jane pled guilty to the charges laid before her. She and Guildford were both sentenced to die, together with two of Guildford's brothers and Archbishop Cranmer. It would be a traitor's death for the men, while Jane would be 'led to Tower Hill and there burned, or the head cut off, as it will then please the Queen'.[2] While this must have been an unspeakably terrifying verdict for Jane to hear, her fate was far from sealed on that November day. According to a letter from the Imperial ambassador to Charles V, Mary did not have any real intention of seeing Jane executed. He wrote to the Emperor on 17 November, 'I am told that her life is safe.'[3]

Unfortunately for Jane, an attempted Protestant plot known as Wyatt's Rebellion, which took place in January 1554, marked the true beginning of her end. This uprising, led by Sir Thomas Wyatt the Younger in opposition to the queen's proposed marriage to King Philip II of Spain, served to complicate things for Mary, in regard to Jane's religion. Protestantism was still a more attractive denomination to many in England, and the notion of Mary's upcoming alliance with Spain infuriated many reformers. They feared the effects of the Spanish Inquisition reaching England's shores and tormenting its people.[4] While returning Protestant Jane to the throne was never made the explicit goal of Wyatt's Rebellion, the implication of Protestantism versus Catholicism was clear enough to Mary. And when Jane's own father and uncles joined forces with the rebellion, the new queen's mind was set. Jane would have to die – if for no reason other than to prove another, stronger, point.

Jane was given one final chance at redemption, however, but the opportunity would have made her lips curl in distaste as she recalled the Duke of Northumberland. Mary sent her chaplain, John Feckenham, to Jane's cell in the Tower of London in an effort to 'free her from the superstition in which she had grown up' and submit to Catholicism, but Jane remained rigid in her reformist beliefs.[5] This stubborn piety and devotion to Protestantism proved in these final days of Jane's life that she would indeed have been Edward VI's ideal successor, (and one can assume that he would have applauded her steadfastness for his reformed church), had she been afforded the chance to reign. But these same traits were also her undoing in the eyes of her disappointed royal Catholic cousin, who finally – and unhappily – signed Jane's death warrant. Jane and Guildford were beheaded on 12 February 1554, their bodies joining the Duke of Northumberland's in the Chapel of St Peter ad Vincula. Almost immediately upon her death Jane was hailed as a Protestant martyr and a heroine of her faith – a notion that would have pleased her and gratified her predecessor, Edward.

The tragedy of Lady Jane Grey is one of the most striking misfortunes to have taken place in the aftermath of Edward VI's death (after all, the poor girl would likely have lived a long life, had the teenaged king not signed her into his will). However, this short blip in the original order of Tudor succession was only one of many outcomes of Edward's six-year reign, in which much religious change had been enacted. When Mary entered London in August 1553, she had no doubt passed several parish churches dotting the villages through which she had travelled, and she would likely have taken notice of many stark changes to their appearance: the lack of grand altars, gold plate, statuary, and stained glass. She had been aware of – and made distraught by – Edward's grand reform over the previous years. Now, as England's rightful queen, she possessed the ability to undo much of what had been done to these houses of worship – which, in her mind, had been desecrated and violated.

Prior to Jane's execution Mary had ordered the release of imprisoned Catholic noblemen – the Duke of Norfolk, Stephen Gardiner, and Edward Courtenay.[6] Almost immediately following her arrival in London, Charles V had suggested the marriage alliance with Philip II, which would serve to strengthen Mary's Catholic stronghold and grant her the support necessary to reverse the changes made by her younger brother. This was, of course, exactly what the rebels of Wyatt's Rebellion feared when they attempted to rise against her the following January, but Mary remained unconcerned. 'Let the prince come and all will be well,' she is reported to have said when she was told that the rebels were gathering.[7] And she was right. The rebellion was ultimately squashed, King Philip arrived in England on 20 July, and married the Queen of England five days later in a grand ceremony at Winchester Cathedral.[8] With strong, Catholic Philip now at her side, Mary's confidence grew tenfold, and she knew that the two of them together would right the religious wrongs of the past – like a modern-day King Ferdinand and Queen Isabella – her formidable maternal grandparents.

While Mary I would certainly have been a staunch Catholic – and perhaps, punishing – English queen, regardless of whom she succeeded, the hallmarks of her (also brief) reign are all the more striking when compared with those of her brother. In 1553, she inherited an England vastly different from the one she had envisioned and longed for. Henry VIII's England in 1547 had already been a far cry from the traditionally Catholic realm that Mary would have wished to inherit – but his 'cautious political Reformation permitted a more determined popular Reformation' under Edward, and so by 1553 there had been so much religious transformation that Mary may have struggled to know just where to start.[9] One of her first decrees was to 'order the return of plate to the parishes' that had been stripped by Edward's regime, but this was only a small step in the direction of returning the churches to their former glory.[10] Music – especially traditional Latin verse 'had been swept aside as redundant' and barred from worship, and of course paintings, saintly statues and icons, vestments, and elaborate stained glass had been, at best, hidden from sight, and, at worst, utterly destroyed.[11] Efforts by Northumberland's men to seize parish property and valuables in the last two years of Edward's reign had been 'the largest government confiscation of local property in English history'.[12] Mary's task to replenish the parishes with what they lacked in 1553 was a gargantuan, intimidating task – and certainly not one which immediately garnered the approval of all of her subjects.

While Edward's speedy Reformation may not have been especially popular at first, it had grown in acceptance over time and by 1553 had become the religious norm for the majority of Englishmen. Public opinion about many of the old Catholic sacraments – most notably that of the real presence in the bread and wine of holy communion – had changed drastically in those six years, and parishioners had adopted and adapted to the revised Book of Common Prayer. Now anyone and everyone could read an English-printed bible, clergy could freely marry, and the outdated superstitions – of prayers to transport souls to heaven, and striving to attain salvation by charitable and financial contributions – were notions of the past. The country was peopled, by and large, by English Protestants who worshipped simply and in their native tongue, and who achieved closeness to God through their faithful acts and their own understanding of scripture. While this does not mean that everyone agreed that the Protestant Reformation was the correct course of action for England, the truth remained that the average Englishman was not nearly so enthusiastic about the idea of Mary's intended Catholic restoration as she likely assumed.[13] Her expectation that England as a whole had been evilly misled, and was, at heart, still fervently Catholic, was simply not true. There was a great mixture of religious opinion throughout the country, and while there were many who rejoiced at Mary's succession, there were many others who dreaded what it might mean for England's religious future.

After five years of adjusting to such a new religious landscape, Mary's accession and swift Spanish marriage struck fear into the hearts of many. The Spanish Inquisition – which saw to the prosecution and execution of many religious dissidents across Europe – had been established less than one hundred years prior by none other than her own maternal grandparents. Encouraging the arrival of a Spanish prince on English soil which would strengthen Catholic control over a newly Protestant realm was perhaps the least popular decision that Mary could make. But somewhat surprisingly – and likely in an effort to buy herself time and to quell the unease felt by her new subjects – Mary issued a proclamation soon after arriving in London. The declaration indicated that while she wholeheartedly intended to restore papal supremacy in England, she would not immediately force anything upon her subjects. The proclamation stated:

> Her Majesty being presently by the only goodness of God settled in the just possession of the imperial crown of this realm and other dominions thereunto belonging, cannot now hide that religion which God and the world knoweth she hath ever professed [to] observe and maintain for herself by God's grace during her time, so doth her highness much desire and would be glad the same were all of her subjects quietly and charitably [to] embrace. And yet she doth signify unto all her Majesty's said loving subjects that of her most gracious disposition and clemency her highness mindeth not to compel any [of] her said subjects thereunto

unto such time as further order by common assent may be taken therein.[14]

Some Englishmen, however, were not so lucky as to be 'quietly and charitably embraced'. Thomas Becon, Archbishop Cranmer, John Hooper, John Rogers, Hugh Latimer, and Nicholas Ridley were all arrested and imprisoned within her first few weeks as queen.[15] All but Becon would be executed by burning in the next two years, as in Mary's view they were some of the most egregious heretics in the country.[16] This method of persecution would come to define Mary's reign throughout the coming centuries. Despite her initial proclamation she would send more than 280 Protestants to be burnt at the stake within a time span of under four years.[17] This is widely believed to be, 'The most intense religious persecution of its kind anywhere in sixteenth-century Europe.'[18] It would also earn Queen Mary the well-known moniker, 'Bloody Mary' (coined by John Foxe).[19]

But despite Mary's quest to rid England of its infectious Protestantism, the burnings between 1555 and 1558 served only to more closely consolidate and define reformers as a 'dissident group'.[20] Those who were able to avoid arrest and execution (and who could afford it) fled England as Protestant refugees and turned to cities such as Strasburg and Frankfurt. Those who either chose or were forced to remain in England and continued outwardly to practice their Protestant faith were led into city streets and burned alive in public, much to the horror and distaste of those who watched – including even Mary's own supporter and friend, Ambassador Renard, who warned Philip: 'I do not think it well that your Majesty should allow further executions to take place unless the reasons are overwhelmingly strong and the offences committed have been so scandalous as to render the course justifiable in the eyes of the people.'[21] The Venetian ambassador, Michieli, felt similarly some months later, when he reported:

> two days ago, to the displeasure as usual of the population here, two Londoners were burnt alive, one of them having been a public lecturer in Scripture, a person sixty years of age, who was held in great esteem. In a few days the like

will be done to four or five more; and thus from time to time to many others who are in prison for this cause and will not recant, although such severity is odious to many people.[22]

But discontinuing the burnings in order to appease her unhappy subjects was simply not something that Mary's conscience would allow her to do. The soul's cleansing by burning had long been considered necessary to give heretics any hope of salvation – so while the executions were brutal and unspeakably painful, to Mary's mind they served a deeper, more theological purpose. The irony of her own dissident behaviour under her brother's reign was inconsequential to her as well, as she had commented to Edward only a few years prior that she herself would gladly face death for her own faith, if he so desired it. Devotion to one's religion was, as Mary believed, worth dying for. And while her own husband came to mildly resent the hasty and violent strategy, she used to reintroduce Catholicism into the hearts and minds of their subjects, men and women continued to be burnt at the stake until 15 November 1558, halting only with the queen's own death two days later.

During Mary's short five-year reign, the brief resurgence of Catholicism was 'part of the posthumous history of medieval Christendom', but far from a complete and total resurrection of the faith in England.[23] While she succeeded, in part, in restoring many of the Grand altars in parish churches, gold plate and valuables, as well as Latin liturgical music, elements leftover from Edward's reign nevertheless endured. Among her reign's shortcomings, she had not been able to persuade members of the gentry to return their newfound wealth to the parishes and monasteries from which they had come, and 'her own attempts to re-found religious houses were limited'.[24] The 1552 Book of Common Prayer had, of course, been removed from churches during Mary's reign, but it survived nonetheless, along with other reformist texts written by Cranmer and his associates. By the end of Mary's life – cut short possibly by a uterine or ovarian tumour – England was in a strange and uncomfortable religious limbo.[25] It is altogether possible that her grand ambition of fully restoring the pope's supremacy in England may have come to fruition, had she lived long enough to see it through. Indeed, the frequency of the burnings had reduced somewhat in the final months of her reign, which may have indicated that the initial 'conversion by fire' phase of the Marian regime was ending. Of course, to consider what might have happened beyond the initial conversion phase if Mary had lived beyond the age of forty-two, is to speculate, and nothing more. The fact remains that, among some of Mary's other failures as queen – including the disastrous loss of Calais in January 1558 – she was unable to provide a Catholic heir to inherit her throne. This may be due largely to Philip's constant absence from England, and despite at least two believed-to-be pregnancies, the first in late 1553, and another in late 1557, Queen Mary never produced a baby, and.it is likely that neither of these were true pregnancies at all.[26]

Unfortunately for Mary – but much to the jubilation of the 800 or so Protestant refugees who had fled from England to the Continent in previous years – there was no possible heir to England's throne aside from Mary's younger, Protestant sister, Princess Elizabeth.[27] Mary had failed in her goal and duty to provide a fully-Catholic, half-Spanish heir, to inherit her throne. She was well aware, upon her death on 17 November 1558, that she had no reasonable successor other than her younger sister. This awareness had crystallised throughout the summer, as she became increasingly ill. During this time Mary had added the following supplement to her will: 'Forasmuch as God hath hitherto sent me no fruit nor heir of my body, it is only in his most divine providence whether I shall have any or no.' If she could have no heirs of her own, she conceded to be 'succeeded by my next heir and successor by the Laws and Statutes of this realm'.[28] Of course, the gravity of the religious situation would have been obvious to her: Elizabeth was no Catholic, and instead closely followed the belief system of their younger, deceased brother, Edward. For this reason, Mary stipulated in her will that her beloved husband, King Philip, would guide and protect England 'as a father in his care, as a brother in his love and favour... and a most assured and undoubted friend to her country and subjects.'[29] She may have known that there was every possibility of a halt to her attempted Catholic revival in England, when she died, but she could not have guessed its full extent.

Within six hours of Mary's death at St James's Palace, the twenty-five-year-old, spirited Elizabeth was proclaimed queen at Whitehall.[30] So began the forty-five-year-long reign that would re-ignite the flame of the Protestant Reformation, welcome home to England the refugees who had fled during Mary's reign, and fully reverse the work that her elder sister had painstakingly undertaken over the previous five years. Upon hearing the news of Mary's death from Nicholas Throckmorton, who had set out for Hatfield in the early hours of the morning on 18 November 1558, Elizabeth dropped to her knees and exclaimed, 'This is the doing of the Lord, and it is marvellous in our eyes!'[31] She was not alone in this sentiment. Protestants throughout England – many of whom had done their best to hide their true beliefs during the fiery reign of Queen Mary – knew that Princess Elizabeth shared the religion of the late King Edward. Refugees on the Continent would shortly have received word that the young Protestant queen had unexpectedly risen to the throne, and they would have looked towards England with bated breath, wondering just how soon it might be safe to return home.

They would not need to wait long. Elizabeth demonstrated no qualms and immediately following her sister's death she did decidedly the opposite of what Mary had stipulated in her will. For one, she ignored the request to move Catherine of Aragon's body from Peterborough Cathedral to rest beside Mary's body in Westminster Abbey. She also openly criticized Mary's religious policies, gave little impression that she was in mourning, and most crucially, put an immediate end to the persecution of Protestants.[32] Elizabeth learned quickly that inheriting the English throne in 1558 was a complicated business. While the last five years of strict and violent action by Mary was clearly not sanctioned by Elizabeth, neither did she wish immediately to turn back the clock to the days of Edward VI. As a young woman who likely had never seriously considered the likelihood of her own inheritance, Elizabeth possessed the commendable sense to reason that 'The issue of religion needed to be resolved in a way that would unite her people behind her while allowing them freedom of conscience.' This approach indicated that she would not divide and destroy at the whim of her own personal religious views.[33] Still, despite the necessity for some constraint and moderation in her religious policy, Elizabeth would go on to be, without question, a Protestant queen.

Following Mary's death, Philip approached Elizabeth about a possible remarriage, which she politely refused.[34] This would have been another clue to English subjects that she would decidedly not continue the Catholic reign of her sister, though no one would reasonably have expected that she would. People would have known that Elizabeth had enjoyed a warm and friendly relationship with her younger brother, Edward, and they might have recalled her frequent visits to court during his reign. Those especially close to her would surely have remembered the fond letters shared between the two from their earliest days of penmanship – their relationship only somewhat marred by Elizabeth's indiscretion with Thomas Seymour in the first years of Edward's reign.[35] They would also have known of the threat to her freedom and life during her sister's reign – during which time Elizabeth had been confined to the Tower of London following Wyatt's Rebellion in 1554.[36] After suffering several declarations of illegitimacy by her father and siblings (only to be re-declared a princess in some of these instances), Elizabeth had come a long way since her first brush with misfortune in 1536, when her ill-fated mother, Queen Anne Boleyn, had been executed by order of Henry VIII. Now, as England's rightful queen, Elizabeth would make her mark on the country once and for all – and in terms of religion, she would side much more closely with her brother than her sister.

Following Elizabeth's refusal to marry Philip of Spain, his position and influence in England waned dramatically – much to the relief of many Englishmen. As he retreated to Spain in search of a new bride, Elizabeth took matters into her own hands in England, making a swift and clear signal to her people on Christmas Day, when she 'ordered Archbishop Oglethorpe not to elevate the host at mass in accordance with the Catholic rite'. When he refused to comply, she stormed out of the church. Following this incident, she proclaimed that certain portions of the mass should be spoken in English once again, just as they had been under her brother.[37] So began her quest to re-establish Protestant order to England, and as Elizabeth believed, she had the people behind her in doing so. The outpouring of support and enthusiasm at her coronation ceremony on 15 January 1559 endorsed Elizabeth's impression that many of her subjects 'saw her as the Protestant saviour providing the nation with new hope, prosperity, and independence from the foreign influence that rankled so during her sister Mary's reign'.[38] Although this impression clearly was also the perception held by her people, they would be surprised in the years to come to find that this was not quite so true as they had imagined.

While Elizabeth may not have been so adamantly opposed to every facet of the Catholic faith as her brother had been (she did, after all, retain some Catholic trinkets throughout her life – such as her own personal crucifix), she was more sympathetic to and accommodating of the majority of Protestant beliefs. The Count of Feria wrote to Philip II in November 1558 that he was 'very much afraid that [Elizabeth] will not be well disposed in matters of religion, for I see her inclined to govern through men who are believed to be heretics'.[39] Elizabeth's beliefs differed in some ways from her late brother's religious preferences. She did not condone lengthy reformist sermons, for example, and she preferred the old, traditional vestments to the dour Protestant robes. She disliked clerical marriage, and she even re-instituted candles and a crucifix in the Chapel Royal within a year of her reign.[40] That same year, she reportedly told the Spanish ambassador that she 'differed very little' from Catholics, 'as she believed that God was in the sacrament of the eucharist, and only dissented from three or four things in the mass'.[41] But while she favoured certain aspects of Catholicism (and had made a show of conforming to the faith under her sister's reign), Elizabeth hated extremism on either side of the religious aisle. She did not, therefore, appear at the time of her coronation, to be a monarch who would strive to further the Protestant Reformation in England, but neither did it seem likely that she would attempt to mend relations with the pope. In truth, her subjects had every reason to question exactly what the religious future of England might hold, with Elizabeth as their queen.

Elizabeth's religious policy would ultimately prove to be the most successful when compared with those of any of her Tudor predecessors. Beginning in 1559, Elizabeth's Parliament would establish the English church as based largely on the Protestant ideals of Edward VI (taking into account much of what his reign had accomplished), while also maintaining the elements of Catholicism with which Elizabeth agreed – such as vestments. The Act of Supremacy of 1559 named Elizabeth Supreme Governor of the Church of England, and she subsequently repealed the heresy laws that Mary I had used in order to persecute practicing Protestants. She also passed her own Act of Uniformity, which re-established the 1552 Book of Common Prayer as compulsory reading in churches.[42] Much of this early action in her reign nullified the Catholic progress made under Mary and returned England to a much more Edwardian flavour (with a decidedly Elizabethan twist), the aim of which was to satisfy both Protestant and Catholic subjects. Differing from Edward's beliefs, Elizabeth 'held that a certain amount of ceremony helped enhance the faith of simple believers,' and felt that 'a retention of some ancient usages was essential if those who had felt affection for the Catholic rites were to become acclimatized to her Church.'[43]

This viewpoint would never have satisfied her brother, but it demonstrated a remarkably wise approach to ruling a spiritually divided country. In her own words, she had no desire to 'see into men's souls', and she required only outward conformity to the laws her government set forth. She maintained that there was only 'one Jesus Christ ... and all the rest was a dispute over trifles'.[44] While many have argued that her religious policies pleased 'very few' during her forty-five-year reign, ultimately she accomplished the impressive task of avoiding civil war – a very serious reality that plagued much of Europe during her years on the throne.[45] If she had wavered at all in either direction and given more credence to either group, she could have risked her supremacy. In this, she held fast to her personal motto, *'Semper Eadem'* ('Always one and the same').[46] And although she was ultimately excommunicated by Pope Pius V in 1570, she would never go down in history as having been a reformist hero in the narrative of England's Protestant history.[47] In fact, she would be associated much more closely with the legacy of Henry VIII – having established a half-Catholic, half-Protestant church that looked, in the end, only somewhat different from that of its predecessor, a Catholic church. She 'gloried in Henry VIII and rebuilt most of his achievement,' though in certain facets of the Church of England (such as the Book of Common Prayer), she relied considerably on the work done during Edward's reign.[48]

The reign of Elizabeth I came to an end in 1603, and with it, the end of the Tudor dynasty. Like her siblings, she left no heirs of her body to inherit the throne. Having never married and instead proudly maintaining the moniker of the 'virgin queen', Elizabeth left England in the hands of her Catholic cousin's son, King James VI of Scotland – who become

James I of England. Luckily for her (and her Protestant subjects), he would prove to have an agenda opposite that of his mother, Mary, Queen of Scots. In fact, James I continued the religious policy determined by Elizabeth. This was continued by a long line of Protestant English monarchs, and eventually culminated in the Church of England that Britons know today. The formation and structure of the modern-day English church was, of course, revised and adapted over centuries, by a number of different monarchs and parliaments. However, as is evidenced by the progression of religious policy throughout the latter-half of the Tudor period, Edward VI – through the publications and laws written during his reign – certainly made his own distinct and palpable mark.

Conclusion

The Legacy of King Edward VI

At the time of this book's writing, there exists only a handful of cultural representations of Edward VI in the form of television, movies, and novels. Most often, Edward is featured only as one of many supporting players in the tragic and dramatic stories of other Tudor figures – most commonly that of Lady Jane Grey. His most popular representation is in Mark Twain's *The Prince and the Pauper*, published in 1881, and still one of the only novels centred on Edward and his court (albeit being a rather far-fetched depiction of his real-life personality). Edward VI's reign does not garner the same interest as those of his predecessor or his three Tudor successors – and this cannot be owed to his reign's short length, as his reign lasted more than a year longer than his eldest, most notorious sister, Mary I. It seems that his nearly six-and-a-half-year rule has been largely glossed over by Tudor enthusiasts for centuries, primarily because of his youth and the mistaken impression that nothing dramatic or long-lasting occurred during this brief period.

It is true that Edward never reached the age of majority (though he died only a few frustrating months short of that coveted milestone), and thus he relied on many older advisors and councillors to oversee the important business of government. But Edward was not one to be easily passed over or ignored because of his age, and especially as he matured, he made it well-known that he expected to be heard and obeyed – much like his late father. One needs only to look back at his impassioned and unmoving stance against his sister Mary's religion, in order to see that he was unwilling to be swayed by councillors if he disagreed with them.[1] His uncle, Thomas Seymour, learned this lesson too, when Edward soundly refused to sign a bill which would have made him Governor of the King's Person in 1547.[2] And while the most noteworthy features of his reign – including the Book of Common Prayer, the Forty-Two

Articles, and the near-complete overhaul of the Catholic mass and traditional Roman liturgy in England – were largely orchestrated by men other than Edward himself, it must be acknowledged that these features and products of his reign simply would not have existed if not for his own full agreement and blessing.

Edward VI was a champion of Protestant reform in England, and his reign in large part allowed the Reformation to continue under Elizabeth I. The changes made under his rule were undeniably *not* the total and complete proselytism that he and his reformers had dreamed of and attempted; the whole of England was not converted to Protestantism by the time of his death. But Archbishop Cranmer's Forty-Two Articles, published in 1553, formed the basis for Elizabeth's Thirty-Nine Articles of 1563 – scaled back only slightly in order to appease her more traditional subjects.[3]

The fact that Mary I lived only a few short years following her Catholic accession in 1553 meant that the Reformation's hiatus was brief and easily reinvigorated upon Elizabeth's coronation, thanks largely to the number of influential Protestant refugees who had fled under Mary's reign and swiftly returned to England after 1558. This reformist work would prove not to have been in vain. An examination of today's Church of England shows that its modern-day doctrine still relies on the Thirty-Nine Articles and the Book of Common Prayer as foundational pillars of its faith. The martyred Archbishop Thomas Cranmer and Richard Hooker stand to this day as sources of theological authority for the Church – the two men having been undeniably influential and favoured under King Edward VI. Thus, it is evident that – despite its brief pause with the accession of Mary I – the Reformation that had grown so significantly in its fervour between 1547 and 1553 has had long-lasting impacts on religion in England (and for Protestantism across the globe), continuing into the twenty-first century. To assume that Edward VI's reign was insignificant or less worthy of note in relation to his fellow Tudor monarchs is to ignore this fact.

Of course, a close study of Edward's reign cannot (nor should it) avoid a close study of the *de facto* rulers of his government, as well as the religious leaders of the time.[4] An evaluation of this period of Tudor history is as much a study of King Edward VI as it is a study of the Dukes of Somerset and Northumberland, as well as Archbishop Cranmer, at the very least. But to write off the work accomplished during these six years as having been purely the machinations of such men and having nothing at all to do with Edward's own personal feelings, desires, and goals for his reign, is to discredit and ignore the contemporary evaluations of those who knew him best. His tutors, John Cheke and Roger Ascham, as well as Cranmer himself, all viewed Edward as having been a true divine scholar – capable of and accomplishing more in the name of Protestant reform than men decades older than he.[5] A fair amount of over-flattery to the monarch can naturally be assumed with their words, but the fact remains: the young king's contemporaries viewed him as being an active participant in the religious changes that would become the hallmarks of his reign.

Had Mary I lived longer and succeeded in her mission to revitalize Catholicism across the country, Edward's reign might truly have proven to be little more than a blip on the radar of England's religious history. As it happened, the opposite might instead be true. Mary's influence on religion in England lasted only a brief five years (quickly to be largely overturned), and her reign arguably is remembered only for its dramatic bloodshed. Lady Jane Grey, who rose so swiftly from obscurity, only to wear England's crown for less than two weeks, is remembered in much the same way – the hallmarks of her reign being tragedy and shock. Compared with these two, it is little wonder why Edward himself is so often overlooked. His reign was not known for its bloody executions (though they did exist). He himself was not executed, nor did he have a romantic life to speak of. In contrast with the other Tudor monarchs, Edward as a person has proven (whether rightly or wrongly) to appear rather less interesting – and that, it cannot be denied, is due to his tender age. He did not have the time to make the same personal impact on England's history as did the other Tudor monarchs.

But we can be sure of one thing regarding Edward's posthumous reputation: his immediate biographers got him all wrong. He was not the weak, sickly child destined from birth to die young, as many went on to say in the coming centuries. In fact, he was a perfectly healthy, active boy who enjoyed many of the same pursuits as his father. He hunted, fenced, gambled, danced, and fraternized with his peers – all the while proving to be an apt and bright student. In short, he 'was a typical aristocratic youth of the sixteenth century.'[6] Raised to emulate his father, his health and physical appearance were carefully noted and documented, and astrologers foresaw a long, prosperous life ahead of him.[7] Until the final months of his life, there was no reason to paint Edward as anything other than a perfectly healthy teenaged boy.

Far from deserving the title 'overshadowed son' of Henry VIII, Edward VI and his reign should be celebrated and remembered for the significant religious advances made in England in such a brief period of time. His rule should be lauded for the part it played in paving the way for Elizabeth's England to become one of relative religious peace – allowing the aftershocks of the Reformation to reverberate through the centuries, resulting in the Church of England as we know it today. We should remember the state of government for what it was between 1547 and 1553 – the time of the last 'boy king' in England's history, and the last attempt at a Lord Protector's rule. For better or worse, we should view Edward's reign as a time of great upheaval and change in England, both politically and religiously.[8]

And we should acknowledge that Edward was, after all, the only Tudor-born person destined to sit on the throne at all – no matter how short a time that might have been. Hopefully, as the true impacts of his reign begin to overshadow the bleak, inaccurate portrayals of his life that have persisted for so long, perhaps Edward can finally step out of the shadows, and the footnotes of Tudor history, and be recognized as the 'reformer king' that he strove to be. After all, in the words of Mark Twain, 'Yes, King Edward VI lived only a few years, poor boy, but he lived them worthily.'[9]

Notes

Introduction: A Footnote in Tudor History?

1. Dan Jones, *The Wars of the Roses* (2014), pp. 6–7.
2. Eamon Duffy, *Fires of Faith* (2009), p. ix.
3. Charles Beem (ed.) *The Royal Minorities of Medieval and Early Modern England* (2008), p. 2.
4. Stephen Alford, *Edward VI* (2015), p. 6.
5. Thomas Penn, *Winter King* (2011), pp. 2–3.
6. Ibid, pp. 9–10.
7. David Loades, *Henry VIII: Court, Church, and Conflict* (2007), pp. 15.
8. Ibid, pp. 15–6.
9. Peter Ackroyd, *Tudors* (2012), p. 2.
10. Suzannah Lipscomb, *The King is Dead* (2016), p. 68.
11. *L&P,* II i, p. 438.
12. Alison Weir, *Children of England* (1996), pp. 2, 7, 18.
13. Lipscomb, *The King is Dead,* p. 68.
14. Ibid, p. 69.
15. Lipscomb, *The King is Dead*, p. 122.
16. G.F. Commendone, *The Accession, Coronation and Marriage of Mary Tudor* (ed. C.V. Malfatti) (1965), p. 7 (cited in Nicola Tallis, *Crown of Blood* (2016), p. 152).
17. Chris Skidmore, *Edward VI* (2007), p. 14.
18. Ibid, pp. 48–9; Weir, *Children of England*, p. 27.
19. Lipscomb, *The King is Dead,* pp. 74–5.
20. Tallis, *Crown of Blood*, p. 130.
21. Ackroyd, *Tudors,* p. 237; Lipscomb, *The King is Dead*, p. 100.
22. Tallis, *Crown of Blood,* pp. 185–6.

23. John Stow, *Two London Chronicles,* ed. Charles Lethbridge Kingsford (1910), p. 27.
24. Duffy, *The Stripping of the Altars*, p. 2, 7.
25. Ackroyd, *Tudors*, p. 252.
26. Ibid., p. 83.
27. Loades, *Henry VIII*, p. 191; Christopher Haigh, *English Reformations* (1993), pp. 168, 180.

Chapter 1: Long-Awaited Heir

1. Jennifer Loach, *Edward VI* (1999), p. 5.
2. *L&P* XII ii, p. 317.
3. Lauren Johnson, *So Great a Prince* (2017), p. 49.
4. Canon law forbade a man from taking his brother's widow: "Thou shalt not uncover the nakedness of thy brother's wife: it is thy brother's nakedness." (Leviticus 18:16)
5. Johnson, *So Great a Prince*, pp. 19–20; Ackroyd, *Tudors*, p 2.
6. J. Dewhurst, 'The alleged miscarriages of Catherine of Aragon and Anne Boleyn,' *Medical History,* Vol. 28,1 (1984), pp. 50–2.
7. Ackroyd, *Tudors,* p. 18.
8. Dewhurst, "The alleged miscarriages"*,* p. 53.
9. *CSP Venice*, Vol. 11, item 1123, p. 480 (cited in Dewhurst, 'The alleged miscarriages,' p. 53).
10. Elizabeth Norton, *Bessie Blount* (2011), p. 129. '
11. Ibid, p. 137.
12. Ibid, p. 181.
13. Kelly Hart, *The Mistresses of Henry VIII* (2011), pp. 21–8, 49–53.
14. Ackroyd, *Tudors,* pp. 34–6.
15. Ibid, p. 42.
16. Ibid, p. 45.
17. Skidmore, *Edward VI*, pp. 2, 12; Alison Weir, *The Lady in the Tower* (2009), p. 16.
18. Dewhurst, 'The alleged miscarriages,' p. 54.
19. Ibid, p. 55; Dewhurst explains in his article that this case of abdominal swelling can occur in women who are not pregnant, but are either desperate to conceive or anxiously fearing it.

20. Ibid, p. 56.
21. Weir, *The Lady in the Tower*, p. 13.
22. Elizabeth Norton, *Jane Seymour* (2009), pp. 17, 46–7, 57.
23. Ibid, p. 16.
24. *The Lisle Letters*, ed. Muriel St. Clare Byrne (1981), p. 166.
25. Ibid, p. 276; *L&P* X, p. 411.
26. Norton, *Jane Seymour*, pp. 89–90.
27. The *Te Deum* is an ancient hymn of thanksgiving to God, sung for special blessings such as coronations, royal weddings, births, canonizations of saints, and more.
28. *Wriothesley's Chronicle* I, p. 64.
29. David Starkey, *The Reign of Henry VIII* (1985), p. 94.
30. Norton, *Jane Seymour*, p. 142.
31. *Chronicle of Henry VIII*, p. 72 (cited in Norton, *Jane Seymour*, p. 142.) In *Edward VI*, Chris Skidmore further specifies that this rumor circulated by November 1538 – a year after Edward's birth.
32. Skidmore, *Edward VI*, pp. 19–20; Loach, *Edward VI*, p. 4; Norton, *Jane Seymour*, p. 142.
33. Loach, *Edward VI*, p. 4.
34. Norton, *Jane Seymour*, p. 144. Nicola Tallis points out that the name could also have derived from the prince's great-grandfather, Edward IV (*Crown of Blood*, p. 34).
35. Edward Hall, *Hall's Chronicle* (1809), p. 825.
36. Norton, *Jane Seymour*, p. 142.
37. Alford, *Edward VI*, p. 7.
38. Ackroyd, *Tudors*, p. 136.
39. Ibid.
40. Chris Skidmore points out in *Edward VI* that this almost impacted Gertrude Courtenay, Marchioness of Exeter, who had been selected to carry Prince Edward at his christening. She reportedly successfully pled with the king to remain a part of the ceremony.
41. Skidmore, *Edward VI*, pp. 16–7.
42. College of Arms MS M6, fo. 82v. (cited in Loach, *Edward VI*, p. 6).
43. *Wriothesley's Chronicle*, p. 68.
44. Norton, *Jane Seymour*, p. 145.
45. *Gairdner 1891*, p. 339 (cited in Norton, *Jane Seymour*, p. 147).

46. Skidmore, *Edward VI*, p. 19.
47. Hall, *Hall's Chronicle*, p. 825.
48. John Foxe, *The Acts and Monuments of John Foxe*, Vol. V (1843–9), p. 148.
49. Ackroyd, *Tudors*, p. 136; Skidmore, *Edward VI*, p. 23.
50. Skidmore, *Edward VI*, p. 23.

Chapter 2: His Father's Son

1. *Edward VI's Chronicle*, p. 8; Loach, *Edward VI*, p. 9.
2. *Lady Bryan to Cromwell*, March 1539, SP 1/156, fol. 118 (*Literary Remains,* I, pp. xxxvii–xxxviii) (cited in Alford, *Edward VI*, p. 9).
3. Skidmore, *Edward VI,* p. 22.
4. Borman, *The Private Lives of the Tudors*, p. 212.
5. *L&P* XII ii, p. 348.
6. Skidmore, *Edward VI*, p. 24.
7. *State Papers of Henry VIII, Vol. 1*, p. 586 (cited in Skidmore, *Edward VI*, p. 25).
8. John Oliver Hand and Sally Mansfield, *German Paintings* (1993), pp. 84–6.
9. Ackroyd, *Edward VI*, p. 12.
10. *L&P* XVI, p. 380.
11. This form of malaria, also transferred via the bites of infected female mosquitos, displays an onset of fever after three-to-four days post-infection, giving it the name 'quartan.'
12. *L&P* XVIII i, p. 904.
13. Skidmore, *Edward VI,* p. 28.
14. *L&P* XVII, p. 1221.
15. John Guy, *Queen of Scots* (2004), p. 23.
16. Ibid.
17. Marcus Merriman, *The Rough Wooings: Mary Queen of Scots 1542–1551* (2000), p. 166.
18. Guy, *Queen of Scots,* p. 31.
19. J. Wormald, *Mary, Queen of Scots* (1988), pp. 58–9 (cited in Skidmore, *Edward VI*, p. 30).

20. Tracey Borman, *The Private Lives of the Tudors* (2016), p. 209.
21. Ibid.
22. Around this time, a new style of handwriting, known as 'italic' was on the rise in Italy, which was now being taught among the elite class, replacing the more commonly-used 'secretary hand'.
23. Weir, *Children of England*, p. 14.
24. Borman points out that William Sidney was the brother-in-law of Edward's dry nurse, Sybil Penn, and a member of the king's privy chamber (*The Private Lives of the Tudors*, p. 175).
25. Weir, *Children of England*, pp. 14–5.
26. Nicola Tallis argues against the long-held theory that Jane was born within days of Edward, pointing out that Jane's mother attended the prince's christening – something that she surely would not have done, had she just given birth (*Crown of Blood*, p. 2).
27. Borman, *The Private Lives of the Tudors*, p. 239.
28. Among others, Alison Weir (*Children of* England) and Nicola Tallis (*Crown of Blood*) both mention Barnaby Fitzpatrick in this way.
29. Skidmore, *Edward VI*, p. 32.
30. Borman, *The Private Lives of the Tudors,* p. 211; Alison Weir describes the incident further in *Children of England*, suggesting that Edward 'likened himself to the falcon, whom everybody plucked, but that he would pluck them too hereafter, and tear them in four parts.' (p. 16).
31. Borman, *The Private Lives of the Tudors*, p. 237.
32. Weir, *Children of England*, p. 15.
33. Borman, *The Private Lives of the Tudors,* p. 210.
34. BL Harleian MS 5087, fo. 7, printed RL, p. 14 (cited in Skidmore, *Edward VI*, p. 34).
35. Borman, *The Private Lives of the Tudors*, p. 225.
36. Skidmore, *Edward VI*, p. 164.
37. Ackroyd, *Edward VI*, p. 5.
38. *Edward VI's Chronicle*, p. 72.
39. Ibid, p. 4.
40. Skidmore, *Edward VI,* p. 34; Borman, *The Private Lives of the Tudors*, p. 225.

41. *Calendar of State Papers, Venetian, 1534–1554*, pp. 535–6 (cited in Borman, *The Private Lives of the Tudors*, p. 239).
42. Borman, *The Private Lives of the Tudors,* pp. 210–11.
43. Loach, *Edward VI*, p. 13.
44. Leanda de Lisle, *The Sisters Who Would Be Queen* (2008), p. 33.
45. Birrell, *English Monarchs*, p. 16 (cited in Loach, *Edward VI*, p. 13); Ibid.
46. *L&P* XIX ii, p. 110.
47. Skidmore, *Edward VI*, p. 35.
48. Ibid.

Chapter 3: Royal Relations and Marriage Proposals

1. Ackroyd, *Tudors,* p. 146.
2. Skidmore, *Edward VI*, p. 29.
3. Linda Porter, *Katherine the Queen* (2010), p. 174.
4. Ibid, pp. 176, 179.
5. *L&P* XXI i, p. 136.
6. Ibid.
7. Porter, *Katherine the Queen*, p. 180.
8. Halliwell, James O., *Letters of the Kings of England* (1848) p. 4 (cited in Porter, *Katherine the Queen*, p. 180).
9. BL Cotton MS Nero, C.x. f. 8. (cited in Porter, *Katherine the Queen*, p. 181).
10. Porter, *Katherine the Queen*, p. 181.
11. Ibid, p. 182.
12. Lansdowne Rolls I, p. 9 (cited in Skidmore, *Edward VI*, p. 38).
13. Ibid.
14. Ackroyd, *Tudors*, p. 169.
15. Weir, *Children of England*, p. 17.
16. BL Harleian MS 5087, fo. 11 (cited in Skidmore, *Edward VI*, pp. 37–8).
17. Skidmore, *Edward VI*, p. 26; Borman, *The Private Lives of the Tudors*, p. 175.
18. Ibid, pp. 24–5.
19. Ibid, p. 37.

20. Weir, *Children of England*, p. 17.
21. Skidmore, *Edward VI*, p. 26; Borman, *The Private Lives of the Tudors*, p. 175.
22. Ibid, p. 39; Weir, *Children of England*, p. 17.
23. Tracy Borman argues that it is more likely for Jane to have joined the young Elizabeth's lessons, rather than Edward's (*The Private Lives of the Tudors*, p. 228).
24. Tallis, *Crown of Blood*, p. 88. It is possible that Edward had previously met Jane during her time at Seymour Place between 1547–8, when she was under the wardship of Thomas Seymour and his then-wife, Katherine Parr.
25. Ibid, pp. 46–9.
26. Ibid, p. 42.
27. Ibid, p. 60.
28. Skidmore, *Edward VI*, p. 76–7.
29. Tallis, *Crown of Blood*, pp. 62–7. Jane would return home to Bradgate Park briefly in 1548, when the Lord Admiral became entangled in scandal involving the young Elizabeth, who was also a temporary ward of his and Katherine Parr's.
30. de Lisle, *The Sisters Who Would Be Queen*, p. 32.
31. Merriman, *The Rough Wooings*, p. 163.
32. de Lisle, *The Sisters Who Would Be Queen*, p. 26. Jane Dormer, a childhood friend of Edward's, later recalled that it was possible to spend 'many happy hours with him', engaging in activities such as these.
33. Porter, *Katherine the Queen*, p. 172.
34. de Lisle, *The Sisters Who Would Be Queen*, p. 33.

Chapter 4: The King is Dead

1. Ackroyd, *Tudors*, p. 176.
2. Hayward and Ward (eds), *The Inventory of King Henry VIII*, Vol. II, p. 105 (cited in Borman, *The Private Lives of the Tudors*, p. 215).
3. Ackroyd, *Tudors*, p. 176.
4. Borman, *The Private Lives of the Tudors*, pp. 215–6.

5. Ibid, p. 215. David Starkey points out in *The Reign of Henry VIII* that earlier assumptions of Henry's ailment pointed to syphilis, but the lack of mercury prescribed by the king's physicians proves this to be unlikely. Starkey instead argues that the ulceration in Henry's legs were caused either by varicose veins or fragments of bone broken off from a riding accident (p. 121).
6. Starkey, *The Reign of Henry VIII*, p. 120.
7. Borman, *The Private Lives of the Tudors*, p. 217. Borman notes here that Henry generally preferred clothes of black, crimson, and white up until this point, so the change in color preference is striking.
8. Lipscomb, *The King is Dead*, p. 36.
9. *Calendar of State Papers, Spanish, 1546*, p. 534.
10. Lipscomb, *The King is Dead*, p. 41.
11. Ibid, p. 46; Eric Ives, 'Henry VIII's Will', pp. 780-1 (cited in Skidmore, *Edward VI*, p. 45).
12. Lipscomb, *The King is Dead*, pp. 48–9.
13. Skidmore, *Edward VI*, p. 45.
14. Lipscomb, *The King is Dead*, p. 50.
15. *The Statutes of the Realm, Vol. III, 28 Hen. VIII* c.7, p. 661 (cited in Lipscomb, *The King is Dead*, p. 73).
16. Albert Frederick Pollard, 'Rich, Richard,' *Dictionary of National Biography, 1885–1900, Vol. 48* (1896), p. 125; S.T. Bindoff (ed.) *The House of Commons, 1509–1558,* vol I (1982), pp. 634–7.
17. Hugh Chisholm, ed., 'Arundel, Earls of', *Encyclopaedia Brittanica, Vol 2* (1911), p. 707.
18. E 23/4/I, fo. 18 (cited in Skidmore, *Edward VI*, p. 45); Lipscomb, *The King is Dead*, p. 127.
19. Skidmore, *Edward VI*, p. 46.
20. Lipscomb, *The King is Dead*, p. 54.
21. Ibid. Lipscomb is pointedly arguing against David Starkey's assertion that the ten witnesses must have signed a blank sheet where the 'unfulfilled gifts' clause would be added.
22. Ibid, p. 53.
23. Borman, *The Private Lives of the Tudors*, p. 216.
24. Skidmore, *Edward VI*, p. 46; Lipscomb, *The King is Dead*, p. 55.
25. Lipscomb, *The King is Dead*, p. 73.

26. Charles Beem, *The Royal Minorities of Medieval and Early Modern England* (2008), pp. 17–8; Desmond Seward, *The Demon's Brood*, pp. 67–8.
27. Seward, *The Demon's Brood*, pp. 148–50.
28. Beem, *Royal Minorities*, p. 104.
29. Ibid.
30. Seward, *The Demon's Brood*, p. 234.
31. Beem, *Royal Minorities*, p. 195.
32. Ibid.
33. Ibid, p. 250.
34. Lipscomb, *The King is Dead*, pp. 74–5.
35. Weir, *Henry VIII*, p. 502 (cited in Borman, *The Private Lives of the Tudors*, p. 219).
36. Ibid.
37. Borman, *The Private Lives of the Tudors*, p. 219.
38. Lipscomb, *The King is Dead*, p. 76.
39. Johnson, *So Great a Prince*, pp. 49–50.
40. BL Cotton Titus F III, in John Strype, *Ecclesiastical Memorials* (1822), Vol. 2, Part II, Appendix HH, p. 430 (109) (cited in Lipscomb, *The King is Dead*, p. 77).
41. Lipscomb, *The King is Dead*, p. 77.
42. Ibid, p. 78.
43. Borman, *The Private Lives of the Tudors*, p. 220.
44. Tytler, P.F. (ed.), *England under the Reigns of Edward VI and Mary.* Vol. I, pp. 15–16 (cited in Skidmore, *Edward VI*, p. 49).
45. Letter from William Wightman, former servant of Sir Anthony Browne to Mr Cecill, 10 May 1549 (Tytler, *England under the Reigns of Edward VI and Mary.* (1839), Vol. I, p. 169 (cited in Lipscomb, *The King is Dead*, p. 80).

Chapter 5: King Edward VI and the Rise of Somerset

1. *Edward VI's Chronicle*, p. 8.
2. *Acts of the Privy Council of England, 1547–49,* eds. J.R. Dasent et al. (1890–1964), p. 5 (cited in Skidmore, *Edward VI*, p 50).

3. *Edward's Chronicle*, p. 8.
4. Weir, *Children of England*, p. 28.
5. Skidmore, *Edward VI*, p. 51.
6. BL Harleian MS 5087, no. 34; printed LR I, pp. 38–9, RL II, p. 25 (cited in Skidmore, *Edward VI*, p. 51).
7. BL Harleian MS 5087, no. 35; printed LR I, pp 39–40, RL II, p. 26 (cited in Skidmore, *Edward VI*, p. 51).
8. Porter, *Katherine the Queen*, p. 276.
9. *L&P* XXI, ii, p. 634.
10. Porter, *Katherine the Queen*, p. 276.
11. National Archives MS E101/426/3, ff. 6 and 23 (cited in Porter, *Katherine the Queen*, p. 281).
12. Elias Gruffyd, *Calais Chronicle*, p. 54 (cited in Skidmore, *Edward VI*, p. 51).
13. Skidmore, *Edward VI*, p. 51.
14. Ibid, pp. 51–2; Borman, *The Private Lives of the Tudors*, p. 220.
15. Porter, *Katherine the Queen*, p. 275.
16. Hume, M. A. S. (trans. and ed.), *Chronicle of King Henry VIII of England. Being a contemporary record of some of the principal events of the reigns of Henry VIII and Edward VI* (1889), p. 154 (cited in Skidmore, *Edward VI*, p. 55).
17. Weir, *Children of England*, p. 29.
18. Skidmore, *Edward VI*, p. 55.
19. *Edward VI's Chronicle*, p. 8.
20. Ibid.
21. Weir, *Children of England*, p. 29.
22. Skidmore, *Edward VI*, p. 56; Weir, *Children of England*, p. 29.
23. Skidmore, *Edward VI*, p. 56.
24. Borman, *The Private Lives of the Tudors*, pp. 220–1.
25. Loach, *Edward VI*, p. 31.
26. Ibid.
27. Weir, *Children of England*, p. 31.
28. Skidmore, *Edward VI*, pp. 57–8.
29. Ibid, p. 58.
30. Ibid, p. 57.
31. Weir, *Children of England*, p. 31.

32. *Calendar of State Papers, Spanish, 1547–49*, p. 47.
33. Loach, *Edward VI*, p. 33.
34. *Edward VI's Chronicle*, p. 8.
35. Weir, *Children of England*, p. 31.
36. Loach, *Edward VI*, p. 34; Skidmore, *Edward VI*, p. 60.
37. Skidmore, *Edward VI*, p. 60.
38. Loach, *Edward VI*, p. 34.
39. Ibid.
40. J.E. Cox (ed.), *Miscellaneous Writings and Letters of Thomas Cranmer...*, Vol. II, pp. 126–7.
41. Loach, *Edward VI*, p. 35.
42. Weir, *Children of England*, p. 28.
43. *Calendar of State Papers, Spanish, 1547–49*, pp. 19–20.
44. Ibid.
45. G.R. Elton, *Reform and Reformation* (1977), pp. 333–4.
46. John Roche Dasent (ed.) *Acts of the Privy Council of England*, Vol. II, 1547–50 (1890), p. 56.
47. Skidmore, *Edward VI*, p. 65.
48. Ibid, p. 65–6.
49. *Calendar of State Papers, Spanish, 1547–49*, p. 19.
50. Skidmore, *Edward VI*, p. 66. This pretentiousness reportedly earned Somerset a rebuke from the French king, and a warning to remember his place.

Chapter 6: England's Josiah

1. Mark Chapman, *Anglicanism* (2006), p. 20.
2. Ibid, pp. 15–7.
3. Ibid, p. 19.
4. Ibid, p. 21.
5. Diarmaid MacCulloch, *All Things Made New* (2016), p. 112.
6. Ibid, p. 113.
7. Lipscomb, *The King is Dead*, pp. 14–5.
8. Ibid, p. 15.
9. MacCulloch, *All Things Made New*, p. 109.

10. Lipscomb, *The King is Dead*, p. 15.
11. Chapman, *Anglicanism*, p. 22.
12. *Statutes of the Realm 1/180,* f. 69 (cited in Lipscomb, *The King is Dead*, pp. 19–21).
13. MacCulloch, *All Things Made New*, p. 114.
14. Ibid; Chapman, *Anglicanism,* p. 23.
15. *Henry VIII's Last Will and Testament,* f. I (cited in Lipscomb, *The King is Dead*, p. 61).
16. Lipscomb, *The King is Dead*, pp. 64–5.
17. Weir, *Children of England*, pp. 32–3.
18. Maurice Elliott, 'Cranmer's Attitude to the Monarchy: Royal Absolutism and the Godly Prince', *The Churchman*, Vol. 109/3 (1993), p. 3.
19. Skidmore, *Edward VI*, p. 69.
20. Ibid, p. 66.
21. John Strype, *Ecclesiastical Memorials,* Vol. II:II, App. B (1822), p. 311.
22. Duffy, *The Stripping of the Altars*, p. 448.
23. Cranmer, *Remains,* p. 127 (cited in Duffy, *Stripping of the Altars*, p. 448).
24. Skidmore, *Edward VI,* p. 68.
25. Chapman, *Anglicanism*, p. 24; Skidmore, *Edward VI*, p. 68.
26. *Calendar of State Papers, Spanish, 1547–49,* pp. 49–50.
27. British Library Royal Manuscript D III, fo. 3r (cited in Skidmore, *Edward VI*, p. 69); According to Greek mythology, Theseus was the hero who founded the kingdom of Athens.
28. Samuel Haynes, *A Collection of State Papers* (1740), p. 90.
29. Porter, *Katherine the Queen,* p. 285.
30. Skidmore, *Edward VI*, p. 71.
31. Weir, *Children of England*, p. 36.
32. Ibid, p. 37.
33. Though most historians refer to Katherine as 35 years old at this time, Linda Porter argues for her birth dating to August 1512 (*Katherine the Queen*, p. 21).
34. Susan James, *Kateryn Parr* (1999), p. 404 (cited in Porter, *Katherine the Queen*, p. 288).

35. Skidmore, *Edward VI,* p. 74.
36. *Edward VI's Chronicle,* p. 9.

Chapter 7: Brotherly Rivalry

1. SP 10/6/10; BL Hatfield MS M485/39, Vol. 150, fo. 51 (cited in Skidmore, *Edward VI,* p. 84).
2. Haynes, Samuel (ed.) *A Collection of State Papers,* p. 75.
3. Skidmore, *Edward VI,* p. 85.
4. William Patten, 'The Expedicion into Scotlande' in *Fragments of Scottish History* (1798), pp. 67–8.
5. BL Lansdowne MS 1236, fo. 16 (cited in Skidmore, *Edward VI,* p. 78).
6. Haigh, *English Reformations,* pp. 171–2.
7. Chapman, Mark, *Anglicanism,* p. 24; H. Gee and W.J. Hardy, *Documents Illustrative of English church History* (1896), p. 328 (cited in Duffy, *Stripping of the Altars,* p. 454).
8. Haigh, *English Reformations,* p. 171.
9. Skidmore, *Edward VI,* pp. 81–2; Haigh, *English Reformations,* p. 171.
10. Ackroyd, *Tudors,* p. 196.
11. Skidmore, *Edward VI,* p. 85.
12. *Calendar of State Papers, Domestic,* Vol. VI, p. 182.
13. Haynes, Samuel (ed.) *A Collection of State Papers,* p. 83; *Calendar of State Papers, Domestic,* Vol. VI, p. 182.
14. Weir, *Children of England,* pp. 47–9.
15. Haynes, Samuel (ed.) *A Collection of State Papers,* p. 105.
16. Skidmore, *Edward VI,* p. 87.
17. Weir, *Children of England,* p. 49.
18. According to Katherine Ashley, Seymour's flirtation had begun 'incontinent [immediately] after he was married to the queen.' (Porter, *Katherine the Queen,* p. 308.)
19. Porter, *Katherine the Queen,* p. 309.
20. Haynes, Samuel (ed.) *A Collection of State Papers,* p. 99.
21. Ibid, p. 96.

22. Skidmore, *Edward VI,* p. 88.
23. Porter, *Katherine the Queen*, pp. 323–4.
24. Haynes, Samuel (ed.) *A Collection of State Papers,* p. 77.
25. Skidmore, *Edward VI*, p. 100.
26. *State Papers* 10/6/22, fos. 57r–58v (cited in Skidmore, *Edward VI,* p. 100).
27. *Calendar of State Papers, Spanish, 1547–49*, p. 332 (cited in Skidmore, *Edward VI*, p. 103).
28. Skidmore, *Edward VI*, p. 103.
29. Haynes, Samuel (ed.) *A Collection of State Papers,* p. 84.
30. Porter, *Katherine the Queen*, p. 332–3.
31. Ibid, p. 334–5.
32. Lansdowne Rolls I ccxxi (cited in Skidmore, *Edward VI,* p. 105).
33. Skidmore, *Edward VI*, p. 105.
34. BL Lansdowne MS 94, fos. 15–15v. (cited in Skidmore, *Edward VI*, p. 105).
35. *Edward VI's Chronicle*, p. 12.
36. Weir, *Children of England*, p. 78.

Chapter 8: How Far the Mighty Fall

1. MacCulloch, *All Things Made New*, p. 139.
2. Interestingly, 'no Catholic was executed solely for his or her belief by Edward's governments'. (Ibid, p. 130).
3. Diarmaid MacCulloch, *The Reformation: A History* (2003), pp. 248–9.
4. P.R. Coleman-Norton, 'The Correspondence of S. John Chrysostom.' (1929), pp. 279–80. This letter in which Chrysostom supposedly questioned the corporeal real presence is now considered a forgery, but it was convincing to Cranmer at the time.
5. Haigh, *English Reformations,* p. 174.
6. Ackroyd, *Tudors*, pp. 209–10.
7. 'Robert Parkyn's Narrative' in A.G. Dickens, *Reformation Studies* (1982), pp. 295–6 (cited in Duffy, *Stripping of the Altars*, pp. 462–3).
8. Haigh, *English Reformations*, p. 174.

9. Ibid; Robinson (ed.) *Original Letters*, ii. p. 543 (cited in Haigh, *English Reformations*, p. 181).
10. Duffy, *Stripping of the Altars*, p. 462.
11. Ibid, p. 197.
12. Ibid, p. 211.
13. Morgan Dix (ed.), *The Book of Common Prayer, 1549* (1881), p. i.
14. F. Rose-Troup, *The Western Rebellion of 1549* (1913), p. 127 (cited in Haigh, *English Reformations*, p. 174).
15. J. Vowell (alias Hooker), *The Description of the City of Excester* (1919), ii, p. 57 (cited in Haigh, *English Reformations*, p. 174).
16. Skidmore, *Edward VI*, pp. 115–17.
17. Susan Brigden, *New Worlds, Lost Worlds* (2000), p. 183.
18. Haigh, *English Reformations*, p. 175.
19. Skidmore, *Edward VI*, p. 123.
20. Ibid, pp. 126–7.
21. Ibid, pp. 131–33.
22. Loach, *Edward VI*, p. 87.
23. Weir, *Children of England*, p. 91.
24. Ibid.
25. Haigh, *English Reformations*, p. 175.
26. Skidmore, *Edward VI*, p. 136.
27. *Acts of the Privy Council of England*, eds. J.R. Dasent *et al*, vol. II (1890–1964), pp. 328–9 (cited in Skidmore, *Edward VI*, p. 136).
28. *Edward VI's Chronicle*, p. 16.
29. *Calendar of State Papers, Spanish, 1547–9*, p. 45.
30. Patrick Fraser Tytler (ed.) *England under the Reigns of Edward VI and Mary*. Vol. II (1839), p. 242.
31. *Edward VI's Chronicle*, p. 16.
32. Skidmore, *Edward VI*, p. 142.
33. Patrick Fraser Tytler (ed.) *England Under the Reigns of Edward VI and Mary* Vol. I (1839), p. 215.
34. Skidmore, *Edward VI*, p. 145.
35. A.F. Pollard, *England Under Protector Somerset: An Essay* (1900), pp. 251.
36. John Stow, *The Annales of England* (1615), p. 598.

37. Patrick Fraser Tytler (ed.) *England Under the Reigns of Edward VI and Mary.* Vol. I, pp. 221–2.
38. Skidmore, *Edward VI*, p. 148.
39. M.A.S. Hume (ed.) *Chronicle of King Henry VIII of England…* (1889), pp. 190–2.
40. Ibid, pp. 192–3.

Chapter 9: Changing Tides

1. Elton, *Reform & Reformation*, pp. 353–4.
2. Weir, *Children of England*, p. 96.
3. Ackroyd, *Tudors*, p. 222.
4. Skidmore, *Edward VI*, p. 152.
5. Ibid, p. 151; Weir, *Children of England*, p. 96.
6. Weir, *Children of England*, p. 96.
7. Ibid; MacCulloch, *All Things Made New*, pp. 118–21.
8. Skidmore, *Edward VI*, pp. 151–2.
9. Ibid, p. 153.
10. Ibid, p. 154.
11. Weir, *Children of England*, p. 97.
12. Ibid, p. 98; Borman, *The Private Lives of the Tudors*, pp. 235–6.
13. Christopher Falkus, 'The Private Lives of the Tudor Monarchs' (1974), p. 97 (cited in Borman, *The Private Lives of the Tudors*, pp. 235–6).
14. Weir, *Children of England*, p. 99.
15. G.B. Harrison (ed.) *The Letters of Queen Elizabeth I* (1968), p. 15.
16. Skidmore, *Edward VI*, p. 157.
17. Ibid, p. 158.
18. *Calendar of State Papers, Spanish, 1550–52,* p. 62.
19. Ibid, p. 159.
20. *Edward VI's Chronicle*, p. 18. The editor notes that the original manuscript containing Edward's writing is torn and frayed at this section, leaving the exact wording somewhat unclear.
21. *Calendar of State Papers, Spanish, 1550,* pp. 32–46.
22. Weir, *Children of England*, p. 103.

23. Ibid, pp. 103–4.
24. *Edward VI's Chronicle*, p. 20.
25. Skidmore, *Edward VI*, p. 160.
26. *Calendar of State Papers, Venetian, 1534–54*, p. 535.
27. Skidmore, *Edward VI*, pp. 160–1.
28. J.A. Giles (ed.) *The whole works of Roger Ascham now first collected and revised, with a life of the author.* Vol. I (1864), p. 226.
29. Loach, *Edward VI*, p. 53.
30. Skidmore, *Edward VI*, p. 164.
31. *Edward VI's Chronicle*, p. 24.
32. Weir, *Children of England*, pp. 107–113.
33. *Calendar of State Papers Spanish, 1550*, pp. 167–81.
34. Ibid, pp. 184–192.
35. Weir, *Children of England*, p. 117.
36. *Calendar of State Papers Spanish, 1550–52*, pp. 209–10.
37. Ibid, p. 213.
38. *Edward VI's Chronicle*, p. 38.
39. Ibid, p. 35.
40. *Edward VI's Chronicle*, p. 38.
41. Foxe, *The Acts and Monuments of John Foxe*, Vol. V, p. 701.

Chapter 10: A King Rises; A Duke Falls

1. *Calendar of State Papers, Spanish, 1551,* pp. 286–99.
2. Ibid, pp. 251–71.
3. *Edward VI's Chronicle*, p. 40.
4. Ibid.
5. *Calendar of State Papers, Venetian, 1551,* pp. 338–62.
6. British Library Royal MS VIII B VII (cited in Skidmore, *Edward VI*, pp. 195–6).
7. *Edward VI's Chronicle*, pp. 39–40.
8. *Calendar of State Papers, Spanish, 1551,* pp. 299–317.
9. Weir, *Children of England*, p. 123.
10. Ibid.

Notes

11. *Edward VI's Chronicle*, p. 48.
12. Machyn, *The Diary of Henry Machyn*, pp. 7–8.
13. Borman, *The Private Lives of the Tudors*, p. 239.
14. Skidmore, *Edward VI*, p. 200.
15. Ibid, p. 202. The proposition of marriage between Edward and Elizabeth had first been broached sometime in 1550 (Frederick Baumgartner, *Henry II, King of France, 1547–1559* (1988), p. 123).
16. Baumgartner, *Henry II*, p. 123.
17. Scepeaux, *Memoires,* I, p. 381 (cited in Skidmore, *Edward VI*, pp. 202–3).
18. Weir, *Children of England*, pp. 124–5.
19. Ibid, p. 126.
20. *Report to the Privy Council of the delivery of their message to Princess Mary, 29 August 1551* (SP10/13/35, f.71r–71v).
21. Weir, *Children of England*, pp. 130–1.
22. Loach, *Edward VI*, p. 102. As Loach points out, this story may not be at all trustworthy, as Palmer cannot be considered a very reliable source, being an associate of Warwick's.
23. *Edward VI's Chronicle,* pp. 57–8.
24. Skidmore, *Edward VI*, p. 208.
25. *Edward VI's Chronicle*, p. 57.
26. *Calendar of State Papers, Spanish, 1551*, pp. 376–91.
27. *Edward VI's Chronicle*, p. 58.
28. Weir, *Children of England*, pp. 131–2.
29. *Calendar of State Papers, Spanish, 1551,* pp. 376–91.
30. Skidmore, *Edward VI*, pp. 211–12.
31. Ibid, p. 212.
32. *Calendar of State Papers, Spanish, 1551,* pp. 376–91.
33. *Edward VI's Chronicle,* p. 61.
34. Ibid, p. 66.
35. Skidmore, *Edward VI*, p. 217.
36. *Acts of the Privy Council III*, p. 462 (cited in Skidmore, *Edward VI*, p. 217).
37. *Edward VI's Chronicle*, p. 66.
38. Skidmore, *Edward VI*, pp. 217–18.
39. Ibid, p. 220.

40. BL Cotton Charter iv, p. 17 (cited in Skidmore, *Edward VI*, pp. 221–3).
41. Skidmore, *Edward VI*, p. 223.

Chapter 11: The Second Prayer Book

1. Haigh, *English Reformations*, p. 178–9.
2. Ibid, p. 175.
3. MacCulloch, *All Things Made New*, p. 143.
4. Haigh, *English Reformations*, p. 179.
5. Ibid.
6. Chapman, *Anglicanism*, p. 26.
7. Haigh, *English Reformations*, p. 180; Chapman, *Anglicanism*, p. 27.
8. Chapman, *Anglicanism*, p. 27.
9. Skidmore, *Edward VI*, p. 231.
10. Ibid, p. 230.
11. *Calendar of State Papers, Spanish, 1552,* pp. 572–3.
12. Weir, *Children of England*, pp. 134–5.
13. Penry Williams, *The Later Tudors: England 1547–1603*, p. 76 (cited in Skidmore, *Edward VI*, p. 232).
14. Dickens (ed.), *Parkyn's Narrative*, pp. 74–6 (cited in Haigh, *English Reformations*, p. 180).
15. MacCulloch, *All Things Made New*, p. 143.
16. Haigh, *English Reformations*, pp. 179–80. 'Extreme unction' is the traditional name for the Catholic rite of anointing the sick upon their deathbed, and thus preparing their soul for the journey to Heaven.
17. Ibid, p. 179.
18. Loades, *Henry VIII,* p. 191.
19. Ibid; Haigh, *English Reformations*, pp. 180–1.
20. *Edward VI's Chronicle,* p. 77; Weir, *Children of England*, p. 135.
21. *Calendar of State Papers, Spanish, 1552*, p. 508.
22. Weir, *Children of England*, p. 135.
23. Haigh, *English Reformations*, p. 180.
24. Weir, *Children of England*, p. 135.
25. Skidmore, *Edward VI*, p. 234.
26. *Edward VI's Chronicle*, p. 91.

27. Ibid, pp. 90–4.
28. Skidmore, *Edward VI, p. 235.*
29. Haynes, *State Papers,* p. 137.
30. Public Record Office State Papers: Edward VI 10/15/11; 10/15/71 (cited in Skidmore, *Edward VI*, pp. 238–9).
31. Haigh, *English Reformations*, p. 181.
32. Ibid.
33. Ibid, p. 182.
34. Skidmore, *Edward VI*, p. 241.
35. Ibid.
36. Ibid, pp. 240–1.
37. Peter Levens, *The Pathway to Health* (1632), fo. 12, printed LR I, ccxv (cited in Skidmore, *Edward VI*, p. 241).
38. Skidmore, *Edward VI*, p. 242.
39. Weir, *Children of England*, p. 137.
40. *Edward VI's Chronicle*, p. 103.
41. Haigh, *English Reformations*, p. 180.
42. Skidmore, *Edward VI*, p. 243.
43. John Stow, *Annals to England to 1603,* (1603), p. 1028.
44. Sir Henry Ellis (ed.), *Original Letters Illustrative of English History* (1825), p. 141 (cited in Tallis, *Crown of Blood*, p. 127).
45. *Calendar of State Papers, Spanish, 1553,* p. 9.
46. Ibid.
47. Ibid.
48. Commendone, *Accession,* p. 4 (cited in Tallis, *Crown of Blood*, p. 128).

Chapter 12: Devise for the Succession

1. de Lisle, *The Sisters Who Would be Queen*, p. 87.
2. Lipscomb, *The King is Dead*, pp. 66–9.
3. Ibid, p. 69.
4. Anna Whitelock, *Mary Tudor: Princess, Bastard, Queen* (2009), p. 171.
5. Eric Ives, *Lady Jane Grey: A Tudor Mystery* (2009), p. 145.

6. *Calendar of State Papers, Spanish, 1553*, p. 35.
7. de Lisle, *The Sisters Who Would be Queen*, p. 89; Skidmore, *Edward VI*, p. 248.
8. Diarmaid MacCulloch (ed.), 'The Vita Mariae Angliae Reginae of Robert Wingfield of Brantham', *Camden Miscellany, 28* (1984), pp. 247–8 (cited in Skidmore, *Edward VI*, p. 251).
9. Robert Wingfield, 'Vita Mariae Reginae', p. 245 (cited in Tallis, *Crown of Blood*, p. 130).
10. Tallis, *Crown of Blood*, pp. 132–3.
11. de Lisle, *The Sisters Who Would be Queen*, p. 93; Tallis, *Crown of Blood*, p. 136.
12. Tallis, *Crown of Blood*, p. 137.
13. Skidmore, *Edward VI*, p. 249.
14. Tallis, *Crown of Blood*, p. 142.
15. S.T. Bindoff, 'A Kingdom at Stake, 1553', *History Today* (1953), p. 647.
16. *Calendar of State Papers, Spanish, 1553*, p. 40.
17. Henry Machyn, *The Diary of Henry Machyn, citizen and merchant-taylor of London, from A.D. 1550 to A.D. 1563* (1848), p. 34.
18. *Calendar of State Papers, Spanish, 1553*, p. 48.
19. Skidmore, *Edward VI*, p. 251.
20. Tallis, *Crown of Blood*, p. 146; Skidmore, *Edward VI*, p. 252.
21. Skidmore, *Edward VI*, p. 255.
22. MacCulloch, *Thomas Cranmer*, p. 541.
23. Skidmore, *Edward VI*, p. 252.
24. MacCulloch, *Thomas Cranmer*, pp. 540–1.
25. Skidmore, *Edward VI*, p. 254.
26. *Calendar of State Papers, Spanish, 1553*, p. 53.
27. Ibid, p. 70.
28. Ibid.
29. Weir, *Children of England*, pp. 150–2; Tallis, *Crown of Blood*, p. 149; *Calendar of State Papers, Spanish, 1553*, p. 69.
30. *Calendar of State Papers, Spanish, 1553*, p. 53.
31. Weir, *Children of England*, p. 150.
32. Machyn, *The Diary of Henry Machyn*, p. 35.
33. Weir, *Children of England*, pp. 152–3.

34. Skidmore, *Edward VI*, p. 257.
35. Foxe, *The Acts and Monuments of John Foxe*, Vol. VI, p. 352.
36. Skidmore, *Edward VI*, p. 258.
37. Ibid, p. 260.
38. Ackroyd, *Tudors*, p. 240.
39. Commendone, *Accession*, p. 45 (cited in Tallis, *Crown of Blood*, p. 147).
40. Ibid.
41. Tallis, *Crown of Blood*, p. 162.
42. Wingfield, *Vita Mariae*, p. 251 (cited in Tallis, *Crown of Blood*, p. 163).
43. Ibid.
44. Foxe, *The Acts and Monuments of John Foxe*, Vol. VI, p. 385.
45. Ibid.

Chapter 13: The Immediate Aftermath

1. Skidmore, *Edward VI*, p. 265.
2. J.G. Nichols (ed.), *The Chronicle of Queen Jane and Two Years of Queen Mary* (1850), p. 3.
3. *Calendar of State Papers, Spanish, 1553*, p. 80.
4. Tallis, *Crown of Blood*, p. 333.
5. *Calendar of State Papers, Spanish, 1553*, pp. 73–5.
6. Skidmore, *Edward VI*, p. 265.
7. Ibid.
8. Tallis, *Crown of Blood*, p. 160–1.
9. Ibid.
10. Wingfield, *Vita Mariae*, p. 253 (cited in Tallis, *Crown of Blood*, p. 162).
11. Tallis, *Crown of Blood*, pp. 166–7.
12. Nichols (ed.), *The Chronicle of Queen Jane*, p. 7.
13. *Calendar of State Papers, Spanish, 1553*, p. 107.
14. Skidmore, *Edward VI*, p. 269.
15. Ibid.
16. Ibid, pp. 269–70.
17. *Calendar of State Papers, Spanish, 1553*, p. 86.

18. Skidmore, *Edward VI*, p. 274.
19. J.G. Nichols, 'Life of the last FitzAlan, Earl of Arundel', *Gentleman's Magazine,* 1st ser., 103, ii (1833), pp. 118–20 (cited in Skidmore, *Edward VI*, p. 276).
20. Eric Ives, *Lady Jane Grey: A Tudor Mystery* (2009), p. 242.
21. *Calendar of State Papers, Spanish, 1553,* p. 96.
22. Commendone, *Accession*, p. 20 (cited in Tallis, *Crown of Blood*, p. 187).
23. Hester Chapman, *Lady Jane Grey*, p. 146 (cited in Tallis, *Crown of Blood*, p. 187).
24. Ibid.
25. Tallis, *Crown of Blood*, pp. 202–3; Skidmore, *Edward VI*, p. 282.
26. *Calendar of State Papers, Spanish, 1553,* p. 133.
27. Tallis, *Crown of Blood*, p. 201.
28. Ibid, pp. 202–3.
29. Pollini, *L'Historia,* p. 355 (cited in Tallis, *Crown of Blood*, p. 205).
30. Ibid.
31. *Calendar of State Papers, Spanish, 1553,* p. 168.
32. Skidmore, *Edward VI*, p. 283.
33. Machyn, *The Diary of Henry Machyn*, p. 39.
34. Edward VI | Westminster Abbey (westminster-abbey.org), accessed 6 November 2021.
35. *Calendar of State Papers, Spanish, 1553, pp. 155–7*
36. MacCulloch, *Cranmer*, p. 547 (cited in Skidmore, *Edward VI*, p. 284).
37. Edward VI | Westminster Abbey (westminster-abbey.org), accessed 6 November 2021.
38. Skidmore, *Edward VI*, p. 285.
39. Ives, *Lady Jane Grey*, pp. 96–7.
40. In the sixteenth century, a nobleman would often be afforded the less painful and much more dignified execution method of beheading, rather than the Traitor's Death of hanging, drawing, and quartering.
41. Skidmore, *Edward VI*, p. 285.
42. Ibid, p. 287.
43. Ibid, pp. 287–8.
44. *Calendar of State Papers, Spanish, 1553,* p. 210.

Chapter 14: The Tudor Dynasty Continues

1. Tallis, *Crown of Blood*, pp. 224–5.
2. Ibid, pp. 227–8. Mary would later commute Jane and Guildford's sentences to beheading.
3. *Calendar of State Papers, Spanish, 1553*, pp. 363–74.
4. Borman, *The Private Lives of the Tudors*, p. 252.
5. Ives, *Lady Jane Grey*, pp. 268–9.
6. Anna Whitelock, *Mary Tudor: Princess, Bastard, Queen* (2009), p. 192. For a brief time, Courtenay and Mary were close and it was suspected that the two might marry. However, his involvement in Wyatt's Rebellion resulted in his fall from grace and banishment from England.
7. Borman, *The Private Lives of the Tudors*, p. 253.
8. Ibid, pp. 258–9.
9. Haigh, *English Reformations*, p. 168.
10. Ibid, p. 183.
11. Duffy, *Fires of Faith*, p. 3.
12. Ibid, p. 4.
13. Robert Tittler, *The Reign of Mary I* (1983), p. 24.
14. Whitelock, *Mary Tudor*, pp. 199–200.
15. Tittler, *The Reign of Mary I*, pp. 24–5.
16. Upon Becon's release from the Tower the following spring, he would flee England as a Protestant refugee, returning later under Elizabeth I's reign.
17. Duffy, *Fires of Faith*, p. 7.
18. Ibid.
19. Una McIlvena, 'What Inspired Queen 'Bloody' Mary's Gruesome Nickname?' *HISTORY* (25 October 2018) Retrieved from https://www.history.com/news/queen-mary-i-bloody-mary-reformation.
20. Whitelock, *Mary Tudor*, p. 286.
21. *Calendar of State Papers, Spanish, 1555*, pp. 138–9.
22. *Calendar of State Papers, Venetian, 1555*, p. 94.
23. John Blossy, *The English Catholic Community* (1975), p. 4 (cited in Duffy, *Fires of Faith*, p. 189).

24. John Cannon and Anne Hargreaves, *The Kings and Queens of Britain* (2001), p. 269.
25. Maureen Waller, *Sovereign Ladies: Sex Sacrifice and Power: The Six Reigning Queens of England* (2006), p. 108.
26. Whitelock, *Mary Tudor*, pp. 273, 326.
27. Waller, *Sovereign Ladies*, p. 113.
28. Whitelock, *Mary Tudor*, p. 327.
29. Ibid.
30. Ibid, p. 329.
31. Anne Somerset, *Elizabeth I* (2003), p. 57.
32. Weir, *Children of England*, p. 365.
33. Susan Ronald, *Heretic Queen: Queen Elizabeth I and the Wars of Religion* (2012), p. 26.
34. Cannon and Hargreaves, *The Kings and Queens of Britain*, p. 271.
35. Ibid, p. 270.
36. Ibid.
37. Ronald, *Heretic Queen*, p. 31.
38. Ibid, p. 35.
39. Loades, *Henry VIII*, p. 214.
40. Cannon and Hargreaves, *The Kings and Queens of Britain*, p. 271; Waller, *Sovereign Ladies*, p. 173.
41. Somerset, *Elizabeth I*, p. 75.
42. Ibid, pp. 79–80.
43. Ibid, p. 81.
44. Waller, *Sovereign Ladies*, pp. 173–4.
45. Ronald, *Heretic Queen*, p. xii.
46. Waller, *Sovereign Ladies,* p. 173.
47. Cannon and Hargreaves, *The Kings and Queens of Britain*, p. 271.
48. Loades, *Henry VIII*, p. 213.

Conclusion: The Legacy of King Edward VI

1. *Edward VI's Chronicle*, p. 38.
2. Skidmore, *Edward VI,* p. 85.

3. Ackroyd, *Tudors*, p. 232.
4. Loach, *Edward VI*, p. 181.
5. Foxe, *The Acts and Monuments of John Foxe*, Vol. V, p. 701; J.A. Giles (ed.) *The whole works of Roger Ascham now first collected and revised, with a life of the author.* Vol. I (1864), p. 226; Ellis (ed.), *Original Letters Illustrative of English History*, p. 141 (cited in Tallis, *Crown of Blood*, p. 127).
6. Loach, *Edward VI*, p. 180.
7. Skidmore, *Edward VI*, p. 242.
8. Loach, *Edward VI*, p. 183.
9. Mark Twain, *The Prince and the Pauper* (1881), p. 207.

Bibliography

Primary Sources

Acts of the Privy Council of England Volume 2, 1547–1550, ed. John Roche Dasent (London, 1890).

Byrne, Muriel St. Clare (ed.) *The Lisle Letters* (Chicago, 1981).

Calendar of State Papers, Domestic, 1547–1580, eds. Mary Anne Everett Greene *et al.* (179 vols.; London, 1856).

Calendar of State Papers, Spanish, 1547–1558, eds. Martin A.S. Hume and Royall Tyler (5 vols.; London, 1912).

Calendar of State Papers Relating to English Affairs in the Archives of Venice, Vol. 5, 1534–1554 (London, 1873).

Cox, J.E. *Miscellaneous Writings and Letters of Thomas Cranmer, Archbishop of Canterbury, Martyr 1556*, Vol. II (London, 1846).

Dix, Morgan (ed.) *The Book of Common Prayer, 1549* (New York, 1881).

Eggington, Ben (ed.), *Edward VI's Chronicle* (2021). Kindle.

Foxe, John, *The Acts and Monuments of John Foxe* (8 vols.; London, 1837–41).

Giles, J.A. (ed.) *The whole works of Roger Ascham, now first collected and revised, with a life of the author* (3 vols.; London, 1864).

Hall, Edward and Ellis, Henry (ed.) *Hall's Chronicle: containing the history of England, during the reign of Henry the Fourth, and the succeeding monarchs, to the end of the reign of Henry the Eighth, in which are particularly described the manners and customs of those periods* (London, 1809).

Hamilton, W.D. (ed.) 'A Chronicle of England during the reigns of the Tudors from 1485 to 1559, by Charles Wriothesley', *Windsor Herald*, vol. 2 (Camden Society, n.s., 11, London, 1875–7).

Harrison, G.B. (ed.) *The Letters of Queen Elizabeth I* (New York, 1968).

Haynes, Samuel (ed.) *A Collection of State Papers: relating to Affairs in the Reigns of King Henry VIII, King Edward VI, Queen Mary and Queen Elizabeth: From the year 1542 to 1570* (London, 1740).

Hayward, Sir John and Beer, Barrett L. (ed.) *The life and Raigne of King Edward the Sixth* (Kent, 1993).

Hume, Martin A.S. (ed.) *Chronicle of King Henry VIII of England* (London, 1889).

Kingsford, Charles Lethbridge (ed.) 'Two London Chronicles From the Collections of John Stow,' *Camden Miscellany,* vol. 4 (Camden Society, 3rd ser., 18; London, 1910).

Nichols, J.G. (ed.) *The Diary of Henry Machyn, Citizen and Merchant-Taylor of London, 1550–1563* (Camden Society, London, 1848).

Nichols, J.G. (ed.) *The Chronicle of Queen Jane and Two Years of Queen Mary* (Camden Society, London, 1850).

Patten, William, 'The Expedicion into Scotlande' in *Fragments of Scottish History* (ed. J.G. Dalyell) (Edinburgh, 1798).

Pollard, A.F., *England Under Protector Somerset: An Essay* (London, 1900).

Stow, John, *The Annales of England* (London, 1615).

Strype, John, *Ecclesiastical memorials relating chiefly to religion and the reformation of it, and the emergencies of the Church of England, under King Henry VIII, King Edward VI and Queen Mary the First.* (London, 1721).

Tytler, Patrick Fraser (ed.) *England Under the Reigns of Edward VI and Mary: with the contemporary history of Europe, illustrated in a series of original letters never before printed,* 2 vols. (London, 1839).

Secondary Sources

Ackroyd, Peter, *Tudors: The History of England from Henry VIII to Elizabeth I* (New York, 2012).

Alford, Stephen, *Edward VI: The Last Boy King (Penguin Monarchs)* (London, 2014). Kindle.

Baumgartner, Frederic J, *Henry II, King of France, 1547–1559* (Durham, 1988).

Beem, Charles, *The Royal Minorities of Medieval and Early Modern England* (New York, 2008).

Bindoff, S.T. (ed.) *The House of Commons, 1509–1558,* vol. I (London, 1982).

Borman, Tracy, *The Private Lives of the Tudors* (New York, 2016).

Brigden, Susan, *New Worlds, Lost Worlds* (New York, 2000).

Cannon, John and Hargreaves, Anne, *The Kings and Queens of Britain* (Oxford, 2001).

Chapman, Mark, *Anglicanism: A Very Short Introduction* (Oxford, 2006).

Chisholm, Hugh, ed. 'Arundel, Earls of', *Encyclopaedia Britannica* (11th ed.). (Cambridge, 1911).

Coleman-Norton, P. R., 'The Correspondence of S. John Chrysostom (With Special Reference to His Epistles to Pope S. Innocent I).' *Classical Philology*, Vol. 24, 3 (1929).

de Lisle, Leanda, *The Sisters Who Would Be Queen* (New York, 2008).

Dewhurst, J., 'The alleged miscarriages of Catherine of Aragon and Anne Boleyn.' *Medical History* vol. 28,1 (1984).

Duffy, Eamon, *Fires of Faith: Catholic England under Mary Tudor* (London, 2009).

Duffy, Eamon, *The Stripping of the Altars* (Yale, 1992).

Elliott, Maurice, 'Cranmer's Attitude to the Monarchy: Royal Absolutism and the Godly Prince', *The Churchman*, Vol. 109/3 (Watford, 1995).

Elton, G.R. *Reform & Reformation: England, 1509–1558* (Harvard, 1977).

Guy, John, *Queen of Scots: The True Life of Mary Stuart* (New York, 2004).

Haigh, Christopher, *English Reformations* (Oxford, 1993).

Hand, John Oliver and Mansfield, Sally, 'German paintings of the fifteenth through seventeenth centuries.' *National Gallery of Art Systematic Catalogue* (Washington, D.C., 1993).

Hart, Kelly, *The Mistresses of Henry VIII* (Gloucestershire, 2011).

Ives, Eric, *Lady Jane Grey: A Tudor Mystery* (West Sussex, 2009).

Johnson, Lauren, *So Great a Prince: The Accession of Henry VIII: 1509* (New York, 2017).

Jones, Dan, *The Wars of the Roses: The Fall of the Plantagenets and the Rise of the Tudors* (New York, 2014).

Lipscomb, Suzannah, *The King is Dead: The Last Will and Testament of Henry VII* (New York, 2016).

Loach, Jennifer, *Edward VI*, ed. G. Bernard and P. Williams. (London, 1999). Kindle.

Loades, David, *Henry VIII: Court, Church, and Conflict* (Kew, 2007).

MacCulloch, Diarmaid, *All Things Made New: The Reformation and its Legacy* (New York, 2016).

MacCulloch, Diarmaid, *The Reformation: A History* (New York, 2003).

MacCulloch, Diarmaid, *Thomas Cranmer* (Glasgow, 1996).

McIlvena, 'What Inspired Queen 'Bloody' Mary's Gruesome Nickname?' *HISTORY* (25 October 2018).

Merriman, Marcus, *The Rough Wooings: Mary Queen of Scots 1542–1551* (East Linton, 2000).

Norton, Elizabeth, *Jane Seymour: Henry VIII's True Love* (Gloucestershire, 2009).

Norton, Elizabeth, *Bessie Blount: Mistress to Henry VIII* (Gloucestershire, 2011).

Penn, Thomas, *Winter King: Henry VII and the Dawn of Tudor England* (New York, 2011).

Porter, Linda, *Katherine the Queen: The Remarkable Life of Katherine Parr, the Last Wife of Henry VIII* (New York, 2010).

Ronald, Susan, *Heretic Queen: Queen Elizabeth I and the Wars of Religion* (New York, 2012).

Seward, Desmond, *The Demon's Brood* (London, 2014).

Skidmore, Chris, *Edward VI: The Lost King of England* (New York, 2007).

Somerset, Anne, *Elizabeth I* (New York, 2003).

Starkey, David, *The Reign of Henry VIII: Personalities and Politics* (London, 1985).

Tallis, Nicola, *Crown of Blood: The Deadly Inheritance of Lady Jane Grey* (New York, 2016).

Tittler, Robert, *The Reign of Mary I* (London, 1983).

Twain, Mark, *The Prince and the Pauper* (Boston, 1881).

Waller, Maureen, *Sovereign Ladies: Sex, Sacrifice, and Power – The Six Reigning Queens of England* (New York, 2006).

Weir, Alison, *Children of England: The Heirs of King Henry VIII* (London, 1996).

Weir, Alison, *The Lady in the Tower: The Fall of Anne Boleyn* (London, 2009).

Whitelock, Anna, *Mary Tudor: Princess, Bastard, Queen* (London, 2009).

Index

Act for the Advancement of True Religion (1543), 63
Act of Six Articles (1539), 75, 86, 130, 135
Act of Succession (1536), 38
Act of Supremacy (1559), 61, 173
Act of Uniformity (1549), 85, 86, 87
Act of Uniformity (1552), 129, 132
Anne of Cleves, 27, 28, 67, 68
Arthur, Prince, xi, 1–2
Arundell, Sir Thomas, 100
Ascham, Roger, 101, 105, 178
Ashley, Katherine, 76, 77, 78, 80
Ashridge, 28, 31
Askew, Anne, 65
Audley, Thomas, 15, 16

Banister, John, 140
Barbaro, Daniel (Venetian Ambassador), 113
Beaufort, John of, xi
Beaufort, Lady Margaret, xi, 9
Belmayne, John, 19
Berwick, 71
Blount, Elizabeth, 3
Bodmin, Parish of, 86

Boleyn, Anne, 4–6, 31, 137, 162, 172
Boleyn, Mary, 4
Book of Common Prayer (1549), 83, 126, 127
   conception and writing, 83–84
   changing doctrine, 85–86
   public reception, 85–87, 127
   protests and rebellion, 85–86
   punishment for non-conformity, 86
Book of Common Prayer (1552), 129
   Bishop Hooper's involvement, 126–127
   changing opinions on the eucharist, 127–129
   reactions to the rewriting, 129
Bosworth, Battle of, ix, xi
Boulogne, 89, 90
Brandon, Charles, 1st Duke of Suffolk, 9, 20, 32
Brandon, Charles (son of the 1st Duke of Suffolk), 20, 115
Brandon, Henry (son of the 1st Duke of Suffolk), 20, 115
Bristol, 75
Bromley, Sir Thomas, 38

Brooke, Elizabeth, 138
Browne, Sir Anthony, 37, 45, 51
Bryan, Lady Margaret, 8, 14, 16, 17, 21
Bryan, Sir Francis, 51
Bucer, Martin, 84, 86, 87, 105, 126
Buckinghamshire, 86
Butts, William, 17

Cambridge, 19, 89, 154, 155, 156
Camp, Treaty of, 33
Calvinism, xv
Cardano, Hieronymus (Astrologer), 133–134
Catherine of Aragon, xii, 1–2, 4, 31
Catholicism, x, 5, 24, 127, 164, 165
  under Henry VIII, 66
  under Edward VI, 83–84, 91, 99, 126
  under Mary I, 147, 169, 178
  under Elizabeth I, 173
Chantries Act (1547), 72
Chapuys, Eustace (Imperial Ambassador), 5, 44
Charles V, Emperor, 5, 58, 112, 117, 143–144, 147, 149–151, 164–165
  correspondence with Princess Mary, 87, 101
  and Princess Mary's attempted escape from England, 106–107
  threatens war with England over Princess Mary's religion, 110
Cheke, John, 19, 22, 24, 28, 73–75, 105, 110, 134, 139, 143, 178
Chelsea, 67, 71, 74, 76, 101, 146
Cheney, Sir Thomas, 38–39
Chertsey Abbey, 83
Church of England (Anglicanism), xv, 5, 24, 60–62, 64, 83–84, 173–175, 177–179
Chrysostom, John, 84
Clement VII, Pope, 4
Coin debasement, 77, 82, 87, 132
Courtenay, Gertrude, Marchioness of Exeter, 182
Cox, Richard, Bishop of Ely, 19–21, 24
Crane, William, 120
Cranmer, Thomas, Archbishop of Canterbury, 9, 24, 37, 66, 94–95, 96, 125, 160, 161, 163, 177–178
  service under Henry VIII, 5, 43
  role in Edward VI's coronation, 54, 60, 64–65
  writing the Book of Common Prayer (1549), 83, 86
  changing theological views, 83–85
  transubstantiation, 84–85
  English versus Latin language, 83

Index

relationships with European reformers, 84
establishing England as a refuge for Protestant exiles, 84
hesitancy about the speed of reform, 99, 112, 126–127
opinion of Edward VI, 110
revising the Book of Common Prayer (1552), 127, 129–130
role in Edward's Devise for the Succession, 142–143, 149
under Queen Mary I, 164, 168, 169
Cromwell, Thomas, 5, 10, 11, 16, 63
correspondence about Prince Edward's infancy, 14, 21
involvement in reformation, 62

Denny, Sir Anthony, 37, 40, 43, 77
Devon, 87
Dispensations Act (1534), 61
Doncaster, 85
Dormer, Jane, Duchess of Feria, 20, 30, 186
Dubois, Jean, 106–107
Dudley, Guildford, 138
marriage to Lady Jane Grey, 138–139, 140, 151
strained relationship with Jane, 152–153
downfall, 156, 163–165
Dudley, John, Earl of Warwick and Duke of Northumberland, xiii, 20, 37, 102, 104–105, 108, 118, 132, 134, 165, 166, 178
relationship with Edward Seymour, 50–51, 56, 79, 91, 103, 110, 111, 112, 118–119, 120
crushing Kett's Rebellion, 89
rising popularity with the council, 90–91
planned coup against Somerset, 79, 92–94,
increasing influence over the council, 96–100, 103, 104
allowing Edward VI more control, 98, 106, 113–114, 117, 119–120, 128, 130–131
religious beliefs, 99–101, 161, 163–164
reaction to Somerset's release from the Tower, 100
and Princess Mary, 101, 104, 107, 112, 135–136, 147–149, 152–156, 158
threats by Somerset, 120–122
involvement in Somerset's downfall, 121–123, 124
health, 131, 134
marriage proposal with the Greys, 138–140
involvement in the changing of succession, 136–139, 142, 146
and Edward VI's death, 144, 157
and Queen Jane, 150–151, 155–156

arrest and trial, 156, 157, 161
execution, 161–162, 163
Dudley, Katherine, 140
Dudley, Robert, Earl of
Leicester, 149
Dudley, Sir Andrew, 100
Durham Place, 140, 146, 153

Edinburgh, 18–19
Edinburgh Castle, 19
Edward III, King *see* Minority
rule, 41–42
Edward V, King *see* Minority rule, 42, 66
Edward VI, King, x–xi
birth, xiii, 1, 7–8
infancy, 8–9, 12, 14–17
christening, 9–10
childhood prophecy, 12
household, 14, 19
relationship with Henry VIII, 14–16, 22, 24–26, 27
appearance 15–6, 133, 25–26
childhood illness, 17
marriage negotiations
  with Mary, Queen of Scots, 17–18, 33, 77, 115–116
  with Lady Jane Grey, 33
  with Elizabeth of Valois, 116
education, 19–20, 21–22, 24, 105
  accolades by his tutors, 24, 105
Chronicle, 22–23
character and temperament, 21, 102
interests
  sports, 23, 105–106, 114
  friendships, 20, 115
  clothing, 13, 106
religious beliefs, xv–xvi, 24, 64–65
reaction to Henry VIII's death, 45, 48
coronation, 51
  procession, 51–53
  ceremony, 53–55
early feelings about being king, 70
influence of Thomas Seymour, 70–71, 73–75
reaction to Thomas Seymour's downfall, 81–82
changing opinion of Somerset
  reaction to being taken to Windsor, 92–93
  letter to the council, 95
  confusion about his arrest, 96
  reaction to his ultimate execution, 125
increased presence on the council, 98–99, 106, 108, 113
increased security, 104
illness (1550), 107–108
fraying relationship with Princess Mary, 108–110, 117
illness (1552), 130, 132, 134–135, 140–141, 143–145
royal progress (1552), 131
crisis over the succession, 137–139, 141–143

214

Index

death, 146
funeral, 159–160
Edward the Confessor, 8, 55
Elizabeth, Princess (later
    Elizabeth I), ix–xi, xii, xiv, xv,
    7, 39, 43, 67, 74, 137, 139
  birth, 5
  relationship with Edward VI,
    9, 20, 21, 30–32, 34, 45,
    102, 108–109, 130
  education, 8, 138
  religious beliefs, 101, 170, 171
  scandal with Thomas Seymour,
    76–77, 82
  reaction to Thomas Seymour's
    downfall, 80
  Christmas appearance at court
    (1549), 101
  proclaimed queen, 170–171
  as queen, 171–174
  death, 174
Elizabeth of Valois, 116
Elizabeth of York, 1, 160
Ely Place, 36, 92
Enclosures, 82, 87
Enfield, 45
Erasmus, 24
Essex, 14, 112, 117
Eyre, Giles, 24

The Family of Henry VIII
    (painting), 13–14
Fayery, Robert, 12
Ferdinand, King of
    Aragon, 2, 165
Fisher, John, 61

FitzAlan, Henry, Earl of Arundel,
    38–39, 100
Fitzpatrick, Barnaby, 106, 131
  possible use as Edward's
    whipping boy, 20–21
Flanders, 106
Forest, William, 66
Forster, Bridget, 8
Forty-Two Articles (1552), xv,
    130, 177
Fowler, John, 68, 71, 75, 79
Foxe, John, 32, 168
Framlingham, 154–155
Francis, Dauphin of France, 33,
    77, 116
Francis I, King of France, 11, 58

Gardiner, Stephen, 35–37, 49, 57,
    61, 165
Gates, John, 119, 139, 162
Gaunt, John of, xi
Goodrich, Thomas, Bishop of Ely,
    99, 139
Greenwich Palace, 3, 103, 134,
    140, 143–144, 147, 149, 159
Greenwich, Treaty of, 18
Grey, Henry, Marquess of Dorset,
    51, 53, 74–75, 99, 118,
    138–140, 157–158
Grey, Katherine, 140
Grey, Lady Frances, xii, 33–34,
    138–140, 151, 157–158
Grey, Lady Jane, ix–x, xii–xiv, 39,
    176, 178
  relationship with Edward VI,
    20, 32

education and upbringing, 32
proposed marriage to Edward, 32–34, 74–75, 139
wardship under Thomas Seymour, 33–34, 74, 78
chosen as Edward VI's successor, 138–140, 143, 147
marriage to Guildford Dudley, 138, 140, 152–153
reaction to Edward VI's death, 146–147
accession, 149–152
coronation 151–152
informed of Queen Mary's victory, 156–157
imprisonment, 157–159, 163–164
execution, 164–165

Hall, Edward, 8
Hamilton, James, Earl of Arran, 18
Hampshire, 86, 91
Hampton Court Palace, 1, 8, 9–11, 13, 15–16, 19, 28, 30, 79, 91–92, 96, 115, 118, 132
Hanworth, 67, 76
Harington, John, 32, 74
Hastings, Henry, 140
Havering, 14, 28
Henri II, King of France, 88, 116
Henry, Prince (son of Henry VIII), 2
Henry Fitzroy, Duke of Richmond and Somerset, 3, 7, 9

Henry III, King see Minority rule, 41
Henry VI, King see Minority rule, 42
Henry VII, King, ix, xi, 1–2, 147
Henry VIII, King, ix–x, xi, xv
struggles for an heir, 1–7
relationship with Edward VI, 8, 13–14, 25, 27
reformation efforts, xv, 60–64
illness and death, 35–37, 43
last will and testament, 36–41
formation of the regency council, 37–38, 41
funeral, 49–50
Herbert, Henry, 140
Herbert, William, 118, 155
Hertford, 28, 45
Hertfordshire, 16, 45
Herbert, Sir William, 37, 91, 118
Hoby, Sir Philip, 94
Holbein, Hans the Younger, 15–16, 25, 114
Holinshed, Raphael, 3
Holt Castle, 79
Hooker, Richard, 177
Hooper, John (Bishop), 114–115, 126–127, 129, 168
Howard, Henry, Earl of Surrey, 36
Howard, Katherine, 27, 28, 63, 162
Howard, Thomas, Duke of Norfolk, 9, 10, 36, 165
Hunsdon, 28, 144, 149, 152

Isabella, Queen of Castile, 1–2, 165
Isabella, Queen of England, 42

James V, King of Scotland, 17, 119
James VI, King of Scotland (James I, King of England), 174–175,
Josiah, King of Judah, 54–55, 60, 64, 66
Julius III, Pope, 116

Kenninghall, 147, 154
Kent, 85
Kett, Robert, 88–89
Kett's Rebellion, 88–90
Knox, John, 65, 127

Lambert, John, 63
Latimer, Hugh, 65, 87, 106, 168
Leland, John, 16
Lever, Thomas, 106
Luis of Portugal, Duke of Beja, 104
Luther, Martin, 62
Lutheranism, 18, 24, 62

Machyn, Henry, 115, 144, 159
Maldon (harbor), 107
Manners, Henry, Earl of Rutland, 75
Martyr, Peter, 84
Mary, Princess (daughter of Henry VII), xii, 32,
Mary, Princess (later Mary I), ix–xiv, 3, 5, 8, 24, 39, 67, 81, 135, 137–139, 158–164, 176
  relationship with Henry VIII, 31, 43
  relationship with Edward VI in childhood, 9, 29–31, 34, 48, 65, 75
  dividing over religion, 97, 107–110, 117, 130
  interactions with Edward Seymour, 76, 87, 104
  reaction to the Book of Common Prayer, 87–89
  correspondence with Charles V, 101, 107
  supposed involvement in Kett's Rebellion, 89
  interactions with John Dudley, 91, 99–100, 104, 111
  plans to leave England, 101, 106–107
  plot to escape (1550), 107
  and Edward VI's death, 143–44
  fleeing London (1553), 147–49
  rallying support, 150–55
  proclaimed queen, 156
  entrance into London, 157
  marriage to Philip II of Spain, 164–165, 167, 170
  attempted Catholic restoration, 166–167, 169, 174, 177–178
  burning of Protestants, 168
  death, 169–170
Mary, Queen of Scots, 17, 33, 39–40, 71, 77, 116, 175
Mary of Guise, 18, 33, 116
Matilda, Empress, xii
Montagu, Sir Edward, 38
Morison, Richard, 15
Mortimer, Roger, 42

Netherlands, the, 107
Norfolk, 85, 88, 90, 147
North, Sir Edward, 38, 39

Oatlands Palace, 71
Ochino, Bernardino, 84
Oglethorpe, Archbishop, 172
Otway, Anthony, 24
Oxfordshire, 86

Paget, Sir William, 36, 37, 40, 44–45, 56, 59, 89, 91, 94–95, 99, 102, 134, 154
Palmer, Sir Thomas, 118, 162, 197
Parkyn, Robert, 85, 129, 144
Parliament, 18, 63, 72, 73, 137, 138, 142, 152, 173, 175
   following Henry VIII's death, 40, 43, 47
   publication of the Book of Common Prayer, 85
Parry, Thomas, 77, 78, 80
Parr, Katherine, 28, 33, 38, 69
   marriage to Henry VIII, 28
   relationship with Edward VI, 28–29, 34
   religious beliefs, 64
   following Henry VIII's death, 38, 48–50
   marriage to Thomas Seymour, 33, 67, 74, 77, 186
   illness and death, 78
   funeral and burial, 78
Parr, William, Earl of Essex and Marquess of Northampton, 38, 161

Paulet, William, 37, 100, 118
Penne, Sybil, 8, 16
Peterborough Cathedral, 171
Petre, Sir William, 38, 39, 117
Philip II, King of Spain, 164, 168, 173
   marriage to Queen Mary I, 165, 170
   public reception in England, 167
   proposes marriage to Queen Elizabeth, 171–172
Pikington, John, 24
Pilgrimage of Grace, 62
Pinkie Cleugh, Battle of, 33, 71
Pius V, Pope, 174
Pole, Reginald, 21
Plague, 9, 123

Radcliffe, Robert, Earl of Sussex, 7
Randolph, Master, 19
Reformation, ix, xv, 54–55,
   under Henry VIII, xv, 32, 60–64
   dissolution of monasteries, 60–62, 169
   removal of statues and icons, xv, 72, 157, 166
   English language replacing Latin, 75, 83, 85, 166
   penance, 62, 79, 84, 161
   communion, 72, 84–85, 127–129, 166
   transubstantiation, 84, 129, 130
   baptism, 62, 129
   purgatory, 62, 64, 72, 84, 130

chantries, 72, 99
Edward VI schools, 72–73
Renard, Simon (Imperial Ambassador), 151, 162, 168
Rich, Sir Richard, 38, 39, 99, 117, 155
Richard, Duke of York *see* Minority rule, 42
Richard II, King *see* Minority rule, 42
Richard III, King, ix, xi, 42, 66
Richmond Palace, 30, 161
Rochester, Sir Robert, 107
Rogers, John, 168
Rogers, Sir Edward, 100
Rough Wooing, the, 19, 33, 77, 88, 115, 132
Royal Injunctions (1536), 62
Russell, Jane, 8
Russell, Lord John, 37, 79, 88, 91
Ryan, John, 12

Sampford Courtenay, 87
Scheyfve, Jehan (Imperial Ambassador)
  replacement of Van der Delft, 106–107
  attempts to help Mary, 107
  writing of Somerset and Warwick, 108, 111
  reporting on Somerset, 112, 118–119, 122
  reporting on Edward VI, 128, 130, 141
  on Mary's reception at court, 135
  reporting on Northumberland, 139
  on Edward VI's death, 143–144
  fearing Mary's custody, 144, 153
Scrots, William, 116
Seymour, Edward, Earl of Hertford and Duke of Somerset, 9, 37, 87
  and Henry VIII's will, 36–37, 40
  becoming Lord Protector, 44–47, 50, 57–59
  role in Edward VI's coronation, 51–53, 55
  relationship with Edward VI, 56, 70–71, 103, 119
  conflict with John Dudley, 56
  friction with members of council, 57
  and reform, 66, 72, 75–77, 86, 99
  conflict with Thomas Seymour over his marriage plans, 67, 69
  military pursuits in Scotland, 19, 33–34, 71–73, 88, 90, 132
  losing the council's favour, 75, 77, 88, 90–91
  increasing public unpopularity, 73, 77, 87
  religious convictions, 64–65, 112
  suspecting a coup against him, 79–81, 90–93
  and Kett's Rebellion, 89

taking the king to Windsor,
    92–93
first arrest, 94–96
pardon and release from the
    Tower, 100, 102–103
continuing conflict with John
    Dudley, 108, 110–112,
    118–119
second arrest, 119–122
execution, 122–125
Seymour, Jane, xiii, 9, 13
    marriage to Henry VIII, 6–7
    birth of Prince Edward, 1
    illness and death,
        10–12, 27
    funeral, 11
Seymour Place, 33, 74
Seymour, Margery, 78
Seymour, Mary (daughter of
    Thomas Seymour), 78
Seymour, Thomas, 1st Baron
    Seymour of Sudeley, 32–34,
    38, 50, 176
    friction with Edward Seymour,
        50, 67
    role in Edward VI's coronation,
        53–55
    relationship with Edward VI,
        70, 73–74
    marriage ambitions, 67, 78
    marriage to Katherine Parr,
        67–69
    plotting against Edward
        Seymour, 75–76, 79
    scandal with Princess
        Elizabeth, 76–77, 172
    attempt to kidnap Edward,
        79–80
    arrest and imprisonment,
        80–82
    execution, 82–83
Sharington, Sir William, 75, 79
Sidney, Henry, 145
Sidney, Sir William, 20
Smith, Sir Thomas, 96
Spanish Armada, x, xv
Southwell, Sir Richard, 38–39,
    100
St James Palace, 170
Stafford, Anne, 4
Stanhope, Anne, Duchess of
    Somerset, 65, 69, 91, 96
Stanhope, Sir Michael, 58
Stow, John, 3
Sudeley Castle, 78
Suffolk, 88, 101
Surrey, 83
Sweating Sickness, xi, 20,
    114–116, 118

Ten Articles (1536), xv, 62, 84
Thirlby, Thomas, Bishop of
    Westminster, 37
Thirty-Nine Articles (1571),
    xv, 177
Throckmorton, Nicholas, 171
Tong, Roger, 24
Tower of London, 1, 47, 51, 80,
    81, 95, 97, 100, 102, 112, 117,
    119, 120, 121, 123, 124, 146,
    150, 152, 156–159, 160, 161,
    163, 164, 172

Troughton, Richard, 154
Tunstall, Cuthbert, Bishop of Durham, 37
Twain, Mark, 176, 179

Van der Delft, Francois (Imperial Ambassador), 107
   reporting on Edward VI's council, 36, 66, 90
   reporting on Somerset, 51, 58, 96
   on Edward VI's coronation, 55
   on friction between Somerset and Warwick, 56
   on military action in Scotland, 71
   attempts to help Princess Mary, 101, 106
   on Princess Elizabeth, 101
   on Warwick, 103–104
   death, 106
van Wilder, Philip, 22

Wales, 62, 101
Wars of the Roses, ix
West Country, 44, 86
Westminster Abbey, 53, 55, 159–160, 171
Westminster Hall, 53
Westminster Palace, 52, 100, 109–110, 119

Whitehall Palace, 6, 35, 43, 49, 53, 55, 159, 170
Wightman, William, 45
Winchester Cathedral, 165
Windsor Castle, 11, 25, 49, 83, 92–95, 131, 132
Wingfield, Sir Anthony, 94, 117, 148
Wolsey, Thomas (Cardinal), 3–5
Wotton, Dr Nicholas, 37
Wotton, Sir Edward, 38
Wriothesley, Thomas, Earl of Southampton, 35, 36, 37, 47, 75, 79
   relationship with Edward Seymour, 50, 56
   removal from the regency council, 56–57
   following Somerset's arrest, 96
   attempts to take down Somerset and Warwick, 100
   house arrest, 100
Wyatt's Rebellion (1554), 164–165, 172, 203
Wyatt, Sir Thomas (the Younger), 164
Wymondham, 88

Yorkshire, 102